INTEREST
AND PROFIT

Christopher Dougherty

INTEREST
AND PROFIT

NEW YORK

COLUMBIA UNIVERSITY PRESS

1980

Printed in the United States of America

Library of Congress Cataloging in Publication Data
Dougherty, Christopher.
Interest and profit.
Bibliography: p.
Includes index.
1. Capital. 2. Interest and usury. 3. Profit.
I. Title.
HB501. D67   332'.041   80-17033
ISBN 0-231-05012-7

Contents

Contents

Acknowledgements

I wish to thank Mervyn King, John Sutton and Adrian Wood for comments on earlier drafts of this book. They are of course absolved of any responsibility for its contents.

1
Introduction

1.1 The neoclassical and Cambridge schools

The rate of profit is determined by the average reproductive capacity of nature. Or so thought Henry George, one of the most influential economists of his time, writing in 1879 (1879, Book III, Chapter 3). It was a bold if ingenuous attempt to resolve what has always been the most controversial issue in economics, an issue that has been overtaken so often and so easily by its obvious moral and political implications that its discussion has become at times more holy war than scientific enquiry.

One might have expected that by the late nineteenth century, when George was writing, some sort of progress towards establishing common ground might have been achieved. But, if anything, the reverse was the case. The marginalists were mounting their challenge to the classical laws of distribution, and it was at about that time that Marx's doctrine of the exploitation of the worker was beginning to make an impact. The century that has followed has witnessed a debate as vigorous and as ill-tempered as any that preceded it.

Even now there is no consensus in sight, but for most purposes the participants have formed two camps. The dominant one, in the sense that it has attracted the largest following, is usually described as neoclassical and is based on the general equilibrium analysis whose origins are associated with Walras and Pareto. Loosely speaking, it holds that the behaviour of the economy is determined by the efforts of individuals and firms to maximize satisfaction, on the one hand, and profits, on the other, subject to certain constraints.

The other camp, which makes up in intensity what it lacks in numbers, is much harder to label on account of its diversity. Sometimes it is called neo-Ricardian or neo-Marxist, but these descriptions cover relatively few individuals. Sometimes the terms neo-Keynesian or post-Keynesian are used, but these have the disadvantage of suggesting that adherents of the approach are somehow truer inheritors of Keynes than the neoclassicals, a contention which many of the latter would dispute. Indeed any search for a name with theoretical connotations must be in vain, for its members are united, not by a matrix of common principles, but by their rejection of the neoclassical approach. It will, however, be convenient to pick out the influential subgroup that has formed around Robinson, Kaldor and Pasinetti and has often been the standard-bearer for the non-neoclassicals in the struggle with the mutual adversary. Following tradition, it will be designated the Cambridge school, after its bastion (Cambridge, England, of course, not Cambridge, Massachusetts).

The turbulence of the exchanges between the two camps may seem surprising for a discipline that has pretensions to be employing the scientific method. There are those who insist that it should be possible for the economist to be objective, his role being that of providing a dispassionate analysis of the data for the use of the politician who is responsible for the subjective element required in policy formation. But this view is naive. Economic analysis must abstract from reality to some extent if it is to be manageable. It must focus on the more important factors at the expense of the lesser ones. It necessarily follows that the results of the simplified model cannot be applied directly to the real world. The effects of the excluded factors must be considered and in the transition to the final interpretation of his analysis the economist cannot avoid introducing his subjective judgement.

The choice of the simplifying assumptions themselves is a second and sometimes more subtle source of subjectivity. They will be determined by his view of the world (what Schumpeter (1954) describes as his vision), the same view of the world that underlies his personal political beliefs. It is thus impossible for him to keep his analysis free of value judgements, and it follows that there is no neat way of separating the functions of the economist and the politician.

On the surface at least the neoclassical/non-neoclassical division does not look politically highly charged. Certainly the neoclassical school takes an optimizing framework as its starting point, but it does not automatically ensue that its adherents necessarily prefer a market to a command economy. And even when they do, social equity may be served by the redistribution of income through taxation and transfer payments. But this is not enough to satisfy the more radical members of the Cambridge school, who perhaps rightly pay scant attention to the first point and regard the existence of private property, especially the private ownership of the means of production, as a fundamental determinant of the law in general and the rules of government in particular.

Thus one has a chronic source of mistrust and friction. The neoclassical tends to regard his analysis as essentially apolitical and wishes that those subscribing to other theories could exercise enough self-restraint to maintain the same detachment. Those of the Cambridge school believe that politics are inextricably interwoven with economics and that the neoclassical is an apologist for their capitalist opponents.[1]

A second source of friction has been the failure of some members of the Cambridge school to understand the neoclassical position. Historically the neoclassical approach has evolved in two versions, the general equilibrium model which is built up from the microeconomic foundations of the individual and the firm, and the aggregate neoclassical model in which aggregate capital, labour and output are treated as economic variables in their own right. The latter was first given formal expression by Clark (1891, 1899) who had almost a Gestalt theory of the nature of capital which encouraged the formulation of such 'laws' as the existence of an inverse relationship between the rate of interest and the capital-intensity of efficient production techniques. Partly because such laws seemed plausible, partly because it fitted easily with short-run macroeconomic analysis and models of the trade cycle, and no doubt partly because it was easier to handle, the aggregate version gained sway over the larger part of the neoclassical school, and general equilibrium was left to the purists. Even some of those who were not happy with it on analytical grounds were disposed to regard it as an expedient short cut. But gradually allegiance to it faltered as the problems inherent in the measurement of the aggregate variables became appreciated, and then dramatically in the mid-1960s it was shown that it was easy to construct counterexamples to the supposed laws that were one of its main attractions in the first place. Since then the general equilibrium model has been the undisputed core of neoclassical capital theory.

Unfortunately the demise of the aggregate version encouraged some of the Cambridge school to believe that the neoclassical approach as a whole had foundered. Some appear to have taken this view because they were unaware of the content of the general equilibrium approach, ignorance which in part testifies to the durability of the influence of Marshall, whose teaching on capital theory was already outdated by the time of Clark. Although it is doubtful whether it ever made much impression outside England, it dominated Cambridge to such an extent that it remains a significant element in the debate on capital theory today. Marshall's suggestion that 'waiting' (a revised version of Senior's (1836) concept of 'abstinence') should be treated as a factor of production was accepted in England long after his death, despite receiving little support elsewhere. And when even Cambridge came to abandon it, its influence was not spent. Indeed it gained a new lease of life,

---

[1] For example, see the preface to Robinson (1956) and Robinson (1962), Chapters 1 and 3.

for when the last generation to be taught it, including some of the leading participants in the current debate, finally rebelled, this was the only version of neoclassical theory with which they were familiar,[2] and for them it has remained their target. Thus Robinson (1972), referring to her *An Essay on Marxian Economics* (1942), states:

> When I had written a chapter on Marx's theory of profits, I thought I had to write a chapter on the orthodox theory for comparison, and blest if I could find one high or low. Ever since I have been enquiring and probing but I still cannot find out what it is. We have Marshall's theory that the rate of interest is the 'reward for waiting' ...,

and she continues with Marshall as her Aunt Sally.

Other members of the Cambridge school, notably Pasinetti (1969, 1972), Garegnani (1970) and Rymes (1971, 1972), have taken the line that the general equilibrium approach, like the aggregate approach, is logically defective. They are under obligation to find fault with the logic of Debreu (1959), a rigorous if limited exposition of the general equilibrium approach, but none has ever challenged it. However such diversions, which draw attention away from the main points and create confusion in what is already a complex debate, are becoming less frequent with the gradual recognition by most members of the Cambridge school that the real issues at stake are empirical.[3]

A third source of friction has been the reluctance of the neoclassicals to take the Cambridge school seriously. Their attitude has been close to the condescending indifference reserved by the medical profession for acupuncturists, herbalists and osteopaths. At best the Cambridge school has been treated with the neglectful tolerance accorded to the fringe that any establishment must expect and with which it must learn to live; at worst it has been dismissed, with quick debating points, as a clique of lightweights.

It must be added, as a fourth source of friction, that the Cambridge school has been equally provocative, no doubt partly in response. Indeed at times they seem to have gone out of their way to make it difficult for those holding contrary positions to appreciate the value of their contributions. The

---

[2] 'When I came up to Cambridge, in October 1921, and started reading economics, Marshall's *Principles* was the Bible, and we knew little beyond it. Jevons, Cournot, even Ricardo, were figures in the footnotes. We heard of 'Pareto's Law', but nothing of the Walrasian general equilibrium system. Sweden was represented by Cassel, America by Irving Fisher, Austria and Germany were scarcely known. Marshall was economics.' (Robinson, 1973b). And unfortunately, in the opinion of Keynes (1924), Marshall's theory of distribution and profit was the 'least complete and satisfactory' part of his work.

[3] For example Nuti (1976) says 'I am convinced that the line of attack developed by Eatwell, Nell, Garegnani and Pasinetti has not only been ineffectual, but has also prevented the development of more powerful lines of attack. Ineffectual criticism acts like vaccination, and provides the most effective protection of neoclassical economics by breeding complacency and lessening the urgency of a more cogent attack; behind the smokescreen erected by the neo-Ricardian critics, neoclassical economics is thriving today as never before.'

magisterial style and the *ex cathedra* pronouncements favoured by some of its leading figures can hardly be expected to be persuasive. All too often they seem to be more concerned with rallying the faithful, like an embattled band of early Christians in a heathen world. Descriptions of the neoclassicals, in response to some of the first Cambridge criticism, as being 'cooped up... repelling all attacks with blank misunderstanding. Then, growing bold, they descend to the plains ...' (Robinson, 1970a), references to the 'confusions and sophistries of current neo-neoclassical doctrines', and the suggestion that 'the economics of equilibrium is a Moloch to which generations of students are still being sacrificed' (Robinson, 1973b) make for colourful reading in a subject that is all too solemn, but it hardly encourages goodwill and mutual understanding.

And of course these sources of friction have been mutually reinforcing. The reluctance of either side to be receptive to what is positive in the other has led to an entrenchment of attitudes,[4] and has encouraged both political mistrust and criticism which is unsound.

1.2 Reconciling neoclassical micro and macro theory

If the neoclassicals largely ignore the Cambridge school, as they do, this does not mean that they are complacent with their framework. Their main preoccupation at the present time is the problem of bridging the chasm between the general equilibrium foundations and the Keynesian macro-economic theory to which the majority of them subscribe. Like biologists who divide their discipline into botany and zoology, neoclassical economists have divided their basic analysis into micro and macro theory, with about as much contact between the two halves. A topic like capital theory which straddles them has been regarded as an awkward anomaly that strains the time-honoured classification, rather than as a possible avenue to integration.

Not only are the two halves uncoordinated, they are actually at times contradictory. In the conventional general equilibrium model involuntary unemployment does not exist by assumption, there is no place for money except as a medium of account, and such important macroeconomic structures as the consumption function are completely invisible. If it has not been evidence of schizophrenia, adherence to both bodies of thought simultaneously has required either an act of faith or a lack of appreciation of the difficulties involved.

However a movement towards uniting the two is now gathering force. In the first place the role of money has received attention that was long overdue. In early general equilibrium analysis, money did not appear at all

---

[4] Lamented, for example, by Solow (1962): 'I have long since abandoned the illusion that participants in this debate actually communicate with each other.'

and the models were simply those of barter economies. Less severe analysis, drawing on the quantity theory of money that reaches back as far as Cantillon and Hume, admitted money as a medium of exchange and focused on the transactions demand for cash. The consensus of opinion, exemplified by Fisher (1907, 1911), and held to this day by Friedman (1956) and his followers, was that in the long run real factors – tastes, technology and scarcity – determined relative prices and the real ('natural') rate of interest, while monetary factors determined the absolute level of prices and the money rate of interest. In the short run monetary factors could be responsible for the behaviour of the economy in disequilibrium, but they could hardly acquire a life in their own right. This tradition provided the starting point for one branch of the new literature and it even pretended to answer such difficult questions as the relationship between money and growth and the optimal amount of money. But after this fresh wave of enthusiam subsided there was a widespread feeling that the new models represented only a superficial advance on the old ones and that the deeper problems posed by money in its role as a store of value had not been touched.

The first major attempt to tackle this issue was the work of Patinkin (1956, 1965), who effectively treated money as just another commodity, real balances (holdings of money deflated by the general price level) being desired for their own sake. The elegant analysis that arose from this framework looked at one point as if it might contend with the Keynesian approach for the hegemony of neoclassical thinking on money (the Friedmanites at that time being a minor force), and the argument over the neutrality or non-neutrality of money was given a new lease of life. But in the world of efficient markets and perfect foresight created by Patinkin, as in the classical world criticized by Keynes,[5] it was hard to explain why anyone would actually wish to hold money as an asset, and this approach, too, eventually had to be set aside.[6]

The latest approach, initiated by Clower (1965) and Leijonhufvud (1968), represents a more radical break. Like those that have gone before it, it assumes that oversimplification is at the root of the failure to capture the nature of money. But whereas the former supposed that the problem could be remedied by extending the existing general equilibrium framework and adding detail to it, the present approach has undertaken to rebuild the framework itself.

Most crucially, the properties of alternative notions of equilibrium are being examined. The Walrasian notion, in which all bargains are struck simultaneously, has ceased to be dominant. Work is now progressing at an

---

[5] 'Why [in classical theory] should anyone outside a lunatic asylum wish to use money as a store of wealth?' Keynes (1937).

[6] For a critique of Patinkin, see Hahn (1965).

accelerating rate on models with non-simultaneous adjustment, quantity adjustment, and imperfect information, especial attention being paid to the formation of expectations since the seminal work of Muth (1961).

Not only does this offer the hope of supplying money with a meaningful role, but it also holds out the prospect of providing a choice-theoretic foundation for short-run macroeconomic theory, another goal high on the neoclassical agenda. And, in addition, shedding the Walrasian straitjacket may permit the exploitation of Keynesian insights that have been neglected by the neoclassicals since the publication of the *General Theory*.

And so at last there is reason to believe that a genuine integration is under way.[7] Whether this will have any impact on empirical macroeconomic research and on policy-making in the foreseeable future is another matter. In the same way as the earlier analysis of the existence and stability of equilibrium only yielded information about the assumptions required by a general equilibrium model, so may the present work prove for the time being to be introspective and more concerned with its descriptive plausibility than its-predictive power. It is, in the sense of Lakatos (1970), a research programme, the natural direction of development of the neoclassical approach and it is in its first phase. But it may eventually emerge as the first substantial step forward for a generation and in the process it may answer some of the shriller Cambridge critics.

1.3   The contribution of Irving Fisher

In the meantime there remains the problem of what the neoclassicals actually believe, here and now. Because such important issues as the principles governing taxation and public investment depend upon them, there is a pressing need for provisional answers to such questions as what determines the rate of profit and the rate of interest, and what is the nature of the link between the two. Since the formal theory is still in an experimental state, it must be accompanied, at least temporarily, by an informal theory that can make fuller use of the wealth of empirical studies that has accumulated over the years and that can take immediate account of those hypotheses that have been accepted by the neoclassical approach even though they have not been assimilated within its organizing framework.

At the risk of oversimplifying a complex process, the formal theory may be viewed as working downwards from general principles and the informal theory as working upwards from the data and from intuition born of experience, both being improved by interaction between them. As time goes by and analytical and empirical progress is made, the formal and informal

---

[7] For a recent survey of the new literature, see Weintraub (1977). Hahn (1977) discusses the relationship between the old Keynesian macroeconomics and the new developments.

theories on any topic should merge and attention turn to new issues. But
at any given moment there is no way of telling whether the current informal
theory is destined to be absorbed or whether it will prove to be as ephemeral
as the falsework in the construction of a bridge.[8]

In the present context, the informal theory is still largely based on the
work of Irving Fisher. Fisher was the inheritor of two traditions, one of substance, the other of technique. It was his recognition of the possibility of
applying the latter to the former, his success in achieving it, and, equally,
his lucid expositorial style, that gave him his pre-eminent position in the
history of the development of neoclassical capital theory.

Technically, Fisher's work may be summarized as giving a temporal
dimension to the general equilibrium analysis formulated by Walras. Walras,
in his enthusiasm for his own analysis, had compared its significance for
economics with that of Newton's *Principia* for mechanics, and did not dis-
courage those who suggested that it qualified him for consideration for a
Nobel Peace Prize.[9] The leading historians of theory of the previous and
present generations have been hardly less flattering: Schumpeter (1954,
p. 827) declares that '... so far as pure theory is concerned, Walras is in my
opinion the greatest of all economists. His system of economic equilibrium ...
is the only work by an economist that will stand comparison with the achievements of theoretical physics' and Blaug (1968, p. 588) describes his theory as
the 'Magna Carta of modern economics'.

But these remarks cannot refer to his contribution to capital theory, which
was not on the same level as the rest of his work. In his *Elements*, Walras gives
an explanation of how consumer preferences, expressed in the form of a
utility function, determine the relative prices of commodities and services
at a particular moment in time. He was well aware that, in order to provide
a rigorous explanation of saving and the rate of profit, he would need to
consider consumer preferences for future commodities and services. But
instead, in his first three editions, he contented himself with postulating a
savings function to be determined empirically. In his fourth edition (1900,
Lesson 23) he made a more serious attempt to explain the determination of
saving and the rate of profit, and indeed believed that he held the key to the
problem (Jaffé, 1965, C. 1410), but the analysis is artificially simplified and
leads to insuperable difficulties.

Pareto (1896) developed the Walrasian system in a number of respects,
but his treatment of the determination of saving was scarcely less superficial.

It was left to Fisher to demonstrate, in *The Rate of Interest* (1907), that

---

[8] The same, of course, is true of formal theory. As Hahn (1973) puts it in a concise statement of its
role and value, 'the student of GE [Arrow-Debreu general equilibrium theory] believes that he
has a starting point from which it is possible to advance to a descriptive theory' (p. 324) rather
than 'a description of an actual economy' (p. 329).

[9] Walras (1874, Lesson 58), Jaffé (1965, C. 1589).

exactly the same principles that had been used by Walras to determine relative prices of different commodities at a given moment in time could also be used to determine the relative prices of commodities at different points in time, and hence the rate of interest and the rate of profit from one moment to the next.

The Rate of Interest is dedicated to a forerunner 'on whose foundations I have endeavored to build' and, from what has just been said, one would expect the name of Walras. But the tribute is to Böhm-Bawerk, and it is extended to include Rae in the dedication to *The Theory of Interest*, the revised version of the treatise with a greatly improved exposition published in 1930.

Rae and Böhm-Bawerk are the most important figures of the other tradition that contributed to Fisherian theory, the confused struggle between what Fisher termed the 'productivity' and 'subjective' approaches to the determination of the rate of profit. To put it briefly, one side claimed that the rate of profit, and hence the rate of interest, were somehow determined by an inherent productivity of capital goods, while the other maintained that the primary factor was subjective discounting of the future. The achievement of Böhm-Bawerk (1889) was to demonstrate that one could construct a theory of the rate of profit by combining the two elements. But his analysis suggests that he did not fully realize that this was the critical issue, and appreciation of his theory is usually obscured by the explanation of the choice of technique (the 'period of production') that appears to be the dominant theme of his work. The looseness of his argument does not help.

Fisher's theory may be regarded as a refinement of Böhm-Bawerk's with a much more lucid perception of the roles and importance of the various elements of the model and a number of substantial theoretical improvements. Two of these may be traced back to Rae (1834): a rigorous stock/flow distinction between capital and income, and a prototype of the concept of the rate of return. It was for these specific contributions that Fisher singled Rae out as a forerunner. His theory as a whole suffers from his failure, common among theorists of the time, to distinguish clearly between factors responsible for saving and factors responsible for investment. He wraps the two together in what he calls the 'effective desire of accumulation', often illustrated by examples in which the two processes are identical.

His work seems to have attracted very little attention when first published, and it was probably Mixter's (1897, 1902) articles and the new edition edited by Mixter (Rae, 1905) that brought him to the notice of Fisher after sixty years of ill-deserved obscurity. The book has had an unlucky history, for it seems to have been almost as neglected since then as before. Apart from an appreciative comment by Schumpeter (1934, p. 11n), little reference has been made to it. The neglect is hard to justify, for the major contribution of the book, apparently completely overlooked by Fisher, is its protectionist analysis of the relationship between the rate of profit, the accumulation of capital, and the rate of technical progress, an analysis which entitles him to be regarded as one of the progenitors of modern growth theory and which would not have seemed out of place had it been written a hundred years later.

In style, Fisher's work was intended from the start to be accessible and persuasive to as large an audience as possible, to politicians and businessmen as well as economists. While a mathematical treatment is provided for the latter, the main exposition is verbal and graphical, given flesh by innumerable everyday examples, and enlivened by a passing parade of Victoriana. The Panama Canal and Ecuadorian Salt Bonds, Sarah Bernhardt and Hetty Green, the horse-drawn carriage and the victrola make appearances where one is now more accustomed to finding set theory and fixed point theorems.

It is this last aspect of his work that is responsible for its enduring influence. Others may have since refined it mathematically, relaxing some of its unnecessarily strong assumptions, but they have done so at the price of making the analysis mechanical and remote from the observed world, inviting the charge of sterility. By contrast, Fisher's writings on theory lead directly to his writings on policy. He was positively evangelical on the subject of taxation, being the guiding hand behind a bill for radical reform submitted to the United States Congress in 1922, and he even took on the dictionary in a long campaign to alter the meaning of income. The immediacy and vigour of his writing have caused it to be absorbed into the bloodstream of neoclassical thought. Like Keynes's writing on the short run, it has become important as a source of ideas which transcend the limits of the original model.

1.4 Outline of the book

The aim of this book is to make an assessment of the current state of informal capital theory, focusing on the issue of what determines the rate of profit in a modern market economy, and comparing the Fisherian tradition with the leading alternatives. As far as it goes, it is intended to be complementary with Hirshleifer (1970), which shares the same framework but is more concerned with investment analysis, and Bliss (1975), a recent impressive exposition of formal neoclassical theory.

The first task is to review the basic Fisherian model and to explore some of its implications. Although it may have been an adequate expression of informal theory in its time, and although it is still indispensable reading now, the fact remains that *The Theory of Interest* antedates Keynes's *General Theory* and even the most fervent enthusiast must concede that after almost fifty years it needs to be updated in some respects.

In particular it is necessary to introduce factor markets explicitly. Since they are not primary to his analysis and he had no wish to distract attention from its more important elements, Fisher sidestepped them by assuming that production and investment are undertaken by the self-employed, and his examples characteristically relate to farmers. But for a modern economy dominated by the corporation such a model is now unacceptably simplistic and one can no longer avoid an explicit treatment of the markets for capital goods and labour.

A second and more technical problem with *The Theory of Interest* is that the exposition, at first sight, appears to employ a one-commodity model. Indeed Fisher usually dispenses with physical units altogether and conducts the analysis in terms of dollars. Now it is well known that results that have been obtained with a one-commodity model do not automatically remain valid when the analysis is generalized to a model with many commodities. It is therefore of crucial importance to demonstrate that the Fisherian results are capable of such a generalization.

The first part of this book, after a chapter which demonstrates the inadequacy of the aggregate neoclassical approach, gives an outline of the Fisherian model which is extended to take account of these problems. The analysis of capital markets follows the spirit of that of Hirshleifer but adopts a slightly different framework. Next there is a discussion of aggregation, reswitching and the stationary state – topics which have become important in the literature on capital theory. Finally, in Chapters 5 and 6, the implications of the Fisherian model for two of its most obvious applications, taxation and the choice of public investment criteria, are investigated.

The second task of this book is to evaluate how well the Fisherian model survives when its assumptions are relaxed and when the current empirical literature is taken into account. In particular, Chapter 8 discusses the most crucial issue of all, the extent to which the econometric studies on saving and investment give support to the Fisherian explanation of their equilibration.

The third task is to balance the picture by evaluating in the same way some of the non-neoclassical models that have attracted attention. Obviously it would be quite impossible to explore all the different hypotheses and their variants that have been put forward, and attention has consequently been restricted to three very different, but possibly representative, models: those of Kalecki, Kaldor/Pasinetti, and Wood.

The final task is to attempt to obtain a perspective on the whole controversy and to judge how far the case for each approach depends on its consistency with the available empirical evidence rather than the exercise of sympathetic intuition.

2
The aggregate neoclassical approach

In the course of time the whole of the human body is replaced – even the brain cells are unceasingly being rebuilt – and yet one has no hesitation in speaking of the continuous existence of the individual. This is effectively the attitude towards capital of Clark. Capital is permanent, save calamity, even though the capital goods that constitute it are ephemeral. It 'lives, as it were, by transmigration, taking itself out of one set of bodies and putting itself into another, again and again' (1899, p. 120). Indeed since individual capital goods are subject to the inexorable attrition of economic obsolescence, they 'not only *may* go to destruction, but *must* be destroyed, if industry is to be successful ... seed-wheat must perish that wheat may abide' (p. 117).

Clark's conception of capital was only one of several neoclassical variants jostling for attention at the end of the nineteenth century, but it is representative of the aggregate approach as a whole, and through the writings of Knight it has remained influential until the present day.[1]

Essentially the approach asserts that aggregate capital may be regarded as a scarce resource in the short run and that the rate of profit – its price – is determined by its marginal product. Knight (1944) likens the capital stock to a plant which grows at a constant proportional rate, this rate determining

---

[1] For a fairly recent Knight-orientated textbook see Dewey (1965). The approach seems to have been discovered and independently rediscovered several times in the course of the nineteenth century, Longfield (1834) and Thünen (1850) being important forerunners of Clark. For a general discussion of its origins see Schumpeter (1954) and for Thünen's theory, see Leigh (1946).

Because it has been consigned to the boneyard of economic thought, the Austrian theory of capital, sketched by Jevons (1871) and developed by Böhm-Bawerk (1889) and Wicksell (1893) will not be treated here. For a perspective on its place in the development of neoclassical capital theory, see Kuenne (1963, Chapter 4).

the rate of profit. He discounts the importance of diminishing returns to investment in the long run on the grounds that capital can be used to augment the other factors of production and that technical progress appears in practice to offset the effects of their nonaugmentable characteristics. One thus has a version of George's theory in which the ties with nature are cut and capital is endowed with an autonomous reproductive capacity of its own, the rate of profit being wholly technologically determined and the role of subjective preferences being limited to the determination of the size of savings and hence the growth of the capital stock.

The more conventional version of the Clark approach assumes diminishing returns to investment, the effects of technical progress being treated separately. The model is completed by assuming that the supply of saving is a function of the rate of profit, and in long-run equilibrium the rate of profit and the stock of capital per worker are determined by the condition that the supply of saving be equal to the amount of investment required to offset depreciation and the widening effect of population growth. As in Knight's version, the rate of profit is equal to the marginal product of capital, but its long-run value is determined by the interaction of technology and subjective preferences as expressed in the savings function. In the short run, however, the rate of profit is determined by the marginal product of capital since the flow of investment is small compared with the size of the existing capital stock.

Put in such broad terms, the model may appear plausible. But as soon as one looks at its microeconomic side, cracks begin to appear. Figure 2.1 shows in schematic form the logic behind the first proposition of all, that the marginal product of capital determines the rate of profit.

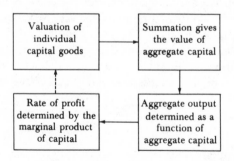

Figure 2.1

The first step is the valuation of the individual capital goods in existence in the economy. Whatever their approach, virtually all economists agree that the value of an individual capital good, *V*, is given, as a first approximation, by

$$V = a_0 + \frac{a_1}{1+i} + \ldots + \frac{a_T}{(1+i)^T} \qquad (2.1)$$

where i is the real rate of interest, assumed to be equal to the rate of profit, ρ, in equilibrium; a_t is the profit (quasi-rent) attributable to the good in year t; and T is the number of years for which it lasts. Of course, in a world of uncertainty the a_t and T are estimates rather than known figures, and hence V is itself an estimate. (Risk aversion may introduce further complications in the determination of V, but they are incidental to the issues under discussion here.)

The second step is simply the definition of the value of aggregate capital, K, as the summation of the values of all the individual capital goods.

The third step is to suppose that the size of aggregate output, Y, depends on K. For example, this may be expressed by means of an aggregate production function

$$Y = f(K, L) \qquad (2.2)$$

where L is the aggregate supply of labour.

Finally, the rate of profit is determined by the marginal product of capital:

$$\rho = \frac{\partial Y}{\partial K} = \frac{\partial f}{\partial K} \qquad (2.3)$$

A number of criticisms may be levelled against this structure. The first is one which is not well grounded, but is nevertheless worth mentioning because it is repeated so often. It is frequently alleged that it involves circular reasoning: that it pretends to offer an explanation of the determination of the rate of profit, and yet begins by assuming knowledge of the rate of profit (or, equivalently, its proxy, the real rate of interest) in the very first step, in the valuation of the individual capital goods.

But the suggestion that if one variable depends upon a second, and the second depends upon the first, then both are necessarily undetermined, is obviously complete nonsense. It is like saying that if one has two relations

$$y = 2x \qquad (2.4)$$

$$x = y - 1 \qquad (2.5)$$

with y depending upon x in one, and x depending upon y in the other, then neither x nor y is determinate.[2]

However, it should be noted that the simultaneity of the model makes it impossible to state unequivocally that the rate of profit is *determined by* the

---

[2] For a discussion of the Cambridge assertion of circularity in neoclassical capital theory, see Ng (1974).

marginal product of capital, any more than one could state that x determines y, or *vice versa*, in equations (2.4) and (2.5). This is not a point that would bother adherents of the general equilibrium version of the neoclassical approach, who are content to describe all relationships as equilibrium conditions rather than statements of causality, but it is a definite setback to their aggregate counterparts.

A more serious charge concerns the question of whether one can write Y as a function of K, both being measured in value terms. Provided that the change in the stock of capital goods is so small that relative prices and the interest rate are unaffected, there is no difficulty. In a marginal comparative statics exercise, the ratio of the increase in Y to the increase in K will be equal to the rate of interest. But as Wicksell (1893, 1901) points out, as soon as one leaves the safety of virtual displacements, discrepancies (known as Wicksell effects since being so named by Uhr (1951)) arise. Two simple points will illustrate the problem. First, from (2.1) it can be seen that if the rate of interest changes, the value of any individual capital good, and so that of aggregate capital, will change. Thus the same set of capital goods may in principle have a wide range of values of K associated with it. The value of aggregate output will also be affected by changes in the rate of interest, if only because output includes capital goods as well as consumption goods. But there is no reason to suppose that Y and K will be affected in such a way that they maintain the simple functional relationship that is required in the third step of the model.

Equally devastating is the state of affairs illustrated in Figure 2.2, which shows the output of a commodity, y, as a function of the amount of a capital

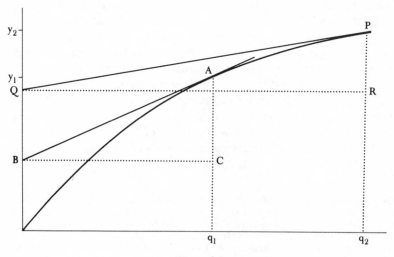

Figure 2.2

good employed, q (both y and q being measured in physical units). Consider first the point A, where q_1 units of the capital good produce y_1 output. The marginal product of the capital good, and hence its rental in a competitive economy, is given by the slope of the tangent AB to the curve at A, that is, by AC/BC. The total rental payment to the q_1 units of the capital good is thus $(AC/BC)\,BC$, which is AC. And so the value of the capital employed, assuming an infinite time horizon and no change, is AC/i.

Next consider the point P, where q_2 units of the capital good produce y_2 of output. Following the same reasoning, the value of the capital employed is PR/i. Now in the diagram diminishing returns have had the effect of making PR smaller than AC, and so one has the paradox that the value of capital at P is lower than that at A, even though it is greater when measured in physical units.[3]

In principle this might be representative of the economy as a whole, and so one cannot expect to find a monotonic functional relationship between Y and K, even if the rate of interest and rate of profit were to remain constant. The logical structure of Figure 2.1 therefore collapses.[4]

For a long time the response of the aggregate neoclassical approach was to attempt to redefine K as a measure of aggregate 'real' capital instead of capital value. This was not only essential, for the reasons just outlined, but also desirable since it should eliminate the element of simultaneity present in Figure 2.1. But no satisfactory formula could be found. As Harcourt (1972), who has chronicled it in detail, aptly put it, it proved to be the search for a will o' the wisp, the high points perhaps being Champernowne's (1954) chain index and Samuelson's (1962) attempt to skirt the problem with his surrogate production function.

The search was definitively put to an end by the discovery of reswitching by Pasinetti (1966b),[5] one of the few tangible advances that has been made in capital theory in the present century. Its nature and implications will be discussed at length, together with the significance of the so-called factor price frontier, in Chapter 4 (where it is shown that, contrary to the opinions expressed in Pasinetti (1969, 1972), it does not in any way undermine the logical validity of the Fisherian approach).

Here it will suffice to state the central result, that it is in general impossible to find a direct relationship between choice of technique and the rate of interest. To be precise, one might encounter the following apparent paradox:

---

[3] In the terminology of Bhaduri (1966), the price Wicksell effect outweighs the real Wicksell effect.
[4] For a general analysis of Wicksell effects, see Swan (1956) and Bhaduri.
[5] Credit for the discovery has variously been ascribed to Cohen (Robinson, 1956, p. 109), Robinson, Champernowne and Sraffa (Harcourt, 1972, p. 124), and even, appropriately and ironically enough, to Fisher (Velupillai, 1975). But Pasinetti was the discoverer in the sense of being the first to understand and exploit its significance.

technique A (with a given set of capital goods) may be the most efficient technique when the rate of interest is equal to i; if the rate of interest were higher, say equal to i', technique B is the most efficient; if it were higher still, equal to i'', technique A is again the most efficient. This discovery dealt a fatal blow to the proposition of the aggregate neoclassical approach that a more capital-intensive technique would be associated with a lower rate of interest, if only because there was no longer any means of ordering techniques according to capital intensity. It followed that it was impossible to construct an index of real capital that could be counted on to be well-behaved in an aggregate production function, and hence the third, and so also the fourth, links in the chain in Figure 2.1 were broken. The aggregate neoclassical approach had been given the *coup de grâce* and the arena has since been left to the general equilibrium theorists and their Cambridge critics.

3
Time preference, profit and interest

3.1 Introduction

In the following exposition of Fisherian theory the technical analysis will
be kept to a minimum for two reasons. In the first place, it exactly parallels
the standard neoclassical model of production, consumption and exchange in
an atemporal economy. As Samuelson (1967) has observed, 'the Fisher 1907
system, which antedates the work of Slutsky (1915) or W.E. Johnson's
classic exposition of indifference curves (*Economic Journal*, 1913), is completely isomorphic to the microeconomic model of general equilibrium in
J.R. Hicks, *Value and Capital* (1939).' It will be seen, in particular, that the
discussion of equilibrium in a two-period, single consumption commodity
economy is, with appropriate labelling changes, identical to that of equilibrium in a single-period economy with two consumption commodities.
And since the development of the intertemporal model mirrors that of the
atemporal model, there is very little point in discussing it in much detail.

The other reason for restricting the technical analysis is that much of it is
uncontentious. For example, the exposition is greatly simplified by the use of
very strong – unnecessarily strong – assumptions with regard to the production possibilities frontier and the intertemporal indifference curves. If the
question of how far these assumptions could be relaxed without affecting the
existence of equilibrium is neglected, this is not because it is unimportant. Indeed existence and stability analysis has been and remains a vital tool in the
development of general equilibrium analysis. It is neglected because it is
not an aspect of the neoclassical model that has drawn fire from its critics.
Their objections are generally on a different, and more radical, level. For
instance, to most of them it makes no difference whether the intertemporal
preference orderings are handled with strong or weak assumptions – they

dispute their practical relevance in any form. Similarly, the assumptions about the nature of the production possibilities frontier are of little concern to those who do not believe that firms pursue profit-maximizing investment policies.

Instead the discussion will be directed towards the more intuitive aspects of the Fisherian model which, after all, were the reasons for studying it in the first place. But one technical issue that cannot be ignored is Pasinetti's (1969) claim that the Fisherian model is in reality a one-commodity model which is incapable of being generalized and is therefore subject to the same problems as the Clark model reviewed in Chapter 2. This will be shown to be false.

3.2   Consumption and capital

For the definition of consumption and capital, from a Fisherian point of view it is hard to improve on the definition of Rae, who held that consumption is the flow of commodities (including services) which are desired by individuals, and that capital is the stock of commodities which influence this flow. To repeat an example given by him, a ham sandwich is counted as consumption when it is eaten, but as capital until that moment.[1]

For ease of exposition, it will be assumed initially that there is only one consumption commodity. This assumption, which is not, and never has been, considered to be important in capital theory, will be relaxed in Section 3.8.

But no such assumption will be made with regard to capital goods. Throughout the exposition it will be assumed that there are a large, unspecified number of them. However, although the analysis depends upon their existence, they will not appear explicitly in the basic exposition of Fisherian theory. This may be disconcerting to those who expect to have their capital goods counted and labelled. And it may be hard for some to accept that analysis with an undefined number of capital goods is capable of being both conceptually and analytically simpler than analysis in which one or two are treated explicitly. For the price of generality is usually an increase in complexity, not the reverse. It is a feature of the analysis that would seem to require emphasis, for so eminent a critic as Pasinetti has been deceived by this apparent sleight of hand and has come to the conclusion that it is a one-commodity model, and not a one-consumption-commodity model, that is

---

[1] Rae was not the first to make this distinction. Adam Smith includes stocks of consumption commodities as 'the first of the three portions of stock' – those that do not yield revenue – but promptly excludes it from his investment and production orientated analysis. Jevons (1871) also adopted Rae's definition, but with less logical precision and no application to his theory.

being described.[2] And this, if correct, would be extremely damaging, for as those familiar with the implications of the reswitching phenomenon (see Section 4.6) will be aware, one can prove propositions within a one-commodity model which are incapable of being generalized within a model with many capital goods.

How is it that capital can be absent from an exposition of capital theory? The answer (from a Fisherian point of view) is that the latter is a misnomer, the essence of the subject being the efficient production and pricing of a stream of consumption goods over time. The concepts of capital, investment, even income are not only superfluous but actually dangerous, at least to the extent that they distract attention from the main issues. Nor does one (even) have to introduce the concepts of rates of profit and interest, since one can conduct the analysis of value exclusively in terms of price streams. But for heuristic reasons it will be convenient to do so.

In view of the definition of consumption as a flow, one might expect it to be written as a continuous variable, say $C(t)$, over the time interval in question. However, it will simplify the analysis to use a discrete time framework. For example, a stream received in periods 1 through T will be written $\{C_1, ..., C_T\}$ with the convention that the amount received in any period comes as a pulse at its end. As far as the basic exposition of Fisherian theory is concerned, the distinction is insubstantial: the length of the period is a matter of convention, and so continuous time may be approximated by making it arbitrarily small. Frequently the word 'year' will be used instead of 'period', but this should not be taken literally, at least during the basic exposition.

The corresponding price stream will be written $\{p_1, ..., p_T\}$, where p_t is

---

[2] See Pasinetti (1972). Fisher's own exposition (1907, 1930) was indeed effectively conducted within a one-commodity model. To focus attention on the determination of prices through time, he assumed that the relative prices of different commodities at any given moment in time were fixed (enabling him to measure quantities of commodities in terms of current dollars). He was aware that such a dichotomy was illegitimate, but was confident that there would be no difficulty in integrating his analysis with that of the determination of atemporal pricing to form a complete model:

Theoretically any analysis of one part of the economic organism must include an analysis of the whole, so that a complete interest theory would have to include also price theory, wage theory and, in fact, all other economic theory.

But it is convenient to isolate a particular element by assuming the other elements to have been determined. So this book is a monograph, restricted, so far as may be, to the theory of interest, and excluding price theory, wage theory and all other economic theory. Afterward it will be easy to dovetail together this interest theory, which assumes price predetermined, with price theory which assumes interest predetermined, thus reaching a synthesis in which the previously assumed constants become variables. But all the principles remain valid. (Fisher 1930, p. 131n.)

And a rigorous dovetailing, to form the general equilibrium system that he had in mind, has been given by Debreu (1959). The present set of assumptions (which seems to have been first used by Solow (1963)) permits a great gain in generality with no change of substance to Fisher's exposition.

the price that would be given at the end of year 1 for the delivery of one unit of the consumption good at the end of year t, and the numeraire is a unit of consumption available at the end of year 1 (so that $p_1 = 1$). The rate of interest, measured in terms of the consumption good, that rules during period t will be denoted i_t and is given by

$$i_t = \frac{p_{t-1} - p_t}{p_t} \tag{3.1}$$

Before proceeding further with the definitions it will be convenient to introduce the model that will be developed in this and the next three chapters.

3.3 The consumption possibilities frontier

Initially, it will be assumed that the economy contains only one individual and that his planning horizon is two years. He is equipped with an initial stock of capital goods at time zero and he uses it and his own labour (assumed to be supplied in fixed quantities in the two years) to produce surpluses of the consumption good at the end of each year: the original stock is transformed by means of labour in the first year into a consumption surplus C_1 and (in general) a different set of capital goods, and the latter is then transformed by the labour supplied during the second year into a consumption surplus C_2 and a terminal stock of capital goods. The complete two-year process will be referred to as a production activity, and the pair $\{C_1, C_2\}$ as the consumption stream yielded by it.

By varying his choice of production activity, the individual is able to vary the consumption stream that he obtains. The set of consumption streams yielded by all the feasible production activities will be described as the production set of the individual. For the time being it will be assumed to be convex and its boundary will be described as the consumption possibilities frontier.

It should be stressed that the extent of the production set, and so the location of the consumption possibilities frontier, will, in general, depend on the stock of capital goods supplied at time zero. Neither the initial capital goods, nor those whose production and utilization constitute part of the production activity, will appear explicitly in this preliminary exposition of Fisherian theory, but it should not be forgotten that they are lurking in the background. This point should be emphasized, lest it be thought that a one-commodity model is being described. Since the capital goods are not specified, there may be any number of goods in the economy.

3.4 Time preference

It is assumed that the individual is capable of ranking the potential consumption streams according to a weak preference ordering, and it will be convenient (but not essential) to suppose that this may be represented by a series of convex indifference curves. This ranking will determine his choice of production activity, since he will choose that which yields him the best feasible consumption stream.

The rate of time preference in year t, R_t, will be defined to be the extra amount of consumption in year t that the individual would have to receive in order to compensate him for a loss of consumption in year $t - 1$, measured as a proportion of the latter, in a marginal exchange. As an illustration, suppose that in the two-year model the individual is indifferent between two consumption streams $\{C_1^\alpha, C_2^\alpha\}$ and $\{C_1^\beta, C_2^\beta\}$ which are only marginally different. Then his rate of time preference during year 2 (the only year for which it is defined in this model[3]) is given by

$$R_2 = \frac{C_2^\beta - C_2^\alpha}{C_1^\alpha - C_1^\beta} - 1 \tag{3.2}$$

This is illustrated graphically in Figure 3.1. The points X and Y represent the streams α and β respectively. The quantities $(C_1^\alpha - C_1^\beta)$ and $(C_2^\beta - C_2^\alpha)$ are measured by the lines ZX and ZY respectively, and so it can be seen that R_2 is given by $(ZY/ZX - 1)$. Note that, since ZX and ZY are both (infinitely) small,

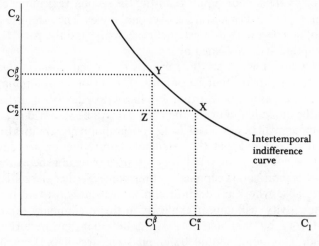

Figure 3.1

---

[3] In order for the rate of time preference to be defined during year 1, the individual would have to be able to consider marginal exchanges of consumption at time 1 for consumption at time zero, and this has been excluded by convention. It could be included without altering the analysis by assuming C_0 to be fixed and that such marginal exchanges could not actually take place. C_0 would then be regarded as influencing subsequent production and consumption decisions only in the same way as other initial conditions.

the ratio ZY/ZX represents the absolute magnitude of the slope of the indifference curve through α and β (again, since α and β are very close, the slope will be the same at both points). Hence it may be seen that, in general, the rate of time preference is given by the absolute value of the slope of the indifference curve through the point representing the stream, less unity (the slope being measured, of course, at the point in question).

From this it should be evident that the rate of time preference depends upon the amounts of consumption received at the ends of years 1 and 2. If C_1 is small compared with C_2, the individual may be keen to increase the former at the expense of the latter and be willing to accept a high discount in order to be able to do so; in this case the rate of time preference would be high. If the disparity is smaller, so in general is the rate of time preference. If C_1 is greater than C_2, it is possible that the individual might be willing to accept a discount in order to postpone consumption, in which case the rate of time preference would actually be negative. The three cases are illustrated by the points P, Q and R in Figure 3.2. The slope of the indifference curve is steep at P, less steep at Q, and smaller than unity (in absolute magnitude) at R.

If the consumption stream is rising, as represented by the point P, individuals may be expected to have positive time preference and it will be rational for them to discount future consumption. Nevertheless, occasionally one encounters what appears to be vigorous opposition to this proposition. Discounting 'later enjoyments in comparison with earlier ones' is 'a practice which is ethically indefensible and arises merely from the weakness of the imagination' (Ramsey, 1928). That 'generally speaking, everybody prefers

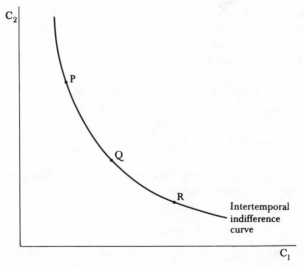

Figure 3.2

present pleasures or satisfactions of given magnitude to future pleasures or satisfactions of equal magnitude, ... implies only that our telescopic faculty is defective' (Pigou, 1920). 'Pure time preference' is 'a polite expression for rapacity and the conquest of reason by passion' (Harrod, 1948).

In fact these attacks turn out to be directed, not against the notion of time preference itself, but against a positive bias in it. If an individual is indifferent between consumption streams $\{C', C''\}$ and $\{C'', C'\}$, for any values of C' and C'', that is, if all his indifference curves are symmetric about the 45° axis, he may be described as possessing unbiased time preference. If, on the other, he prefers $\{C', C''\}$ to $\{C'', C'\}$ whenever C' is greater than C'' (as is the case with the indifference curve in Figure 3.2), he may be said to exhibit positively biased time preference; and similarly, if he prefers $\{C', C''\}$ to $\{C'', C'\}$ whenever C' is less than C'', he exhibits negatively biased time preference. Ramsey, Pigou and Harrod argue, not that planners should not use a discount rate, but that the discount rate should not be influenced by a positive bias in time preference.

3.5   A digression on the treatment of time preference in optimal growth models

The Fisherian notion of time preference, and its relationship with Böhm-Bawerk's earlier treatment, may be illustrated by reference to the criteria of optimality employed in the literature on optimal growth that has grown so rapidly over the last two decades.

Such analysis has investigated some aspects of optimal growth (optimal savings policy, optimal monetary policy, optimal trade policy, to name but a few), maximizing some function of the consumption stream yielded over the planning period. Two objective functions have predominated, both appearing some times in discrete, sometimes in continuous form:

$$\phi = \sum_{t=0}^{n} C_t (1 + \lambda)^{-t} \quad \text{or} \quad \phi = \int_0^{n+1} C(t) e^{-\lambda t} dt \tag{3.3}$$

and

$$\phi = \sum_{t=0}^{n} U(C_t)(1 + \lambda)^{-t} \quad \text{or} \quad \phi = \int_0^{n+1} U(C(t)) e^{-\lambda t} dt \tag{3.4}$$

Provided that certain integrability conditions are satisfied (Houthakker, 1950), the Fisherian intertemporal indifference curves may be regarded as isoquants of a concave ordinal utility function

$$\phi = \phi(C_1, C_2) \tag{3.5}$$

(retaining the discrete time framework). The rate of time preference in year 2, R_2, associated with a consumption stream $\{C_1, C_2\}$ is then given by

$$1 + R_2 = -\frac{\partial C_2}{\partial C_1} \qquad (3.6)$$

where $\partial C_2/\partial C_1$ is measured with ϕ held constant.

If the utility function is treated as cardinal, one has

$$1 + R_2 = \frac{\partial \phi/\partial C_1}{\partial \phi/\partial C_2} \qquad (3.7)$$

where $\partial\phi/\partial C_1$ and $\partial\phi/\partial C_2$ are measured with C_2 and C_1 constant, respectively.

Objective functions of type (3.3) may be regarded as linear forms of (3.5), and so (taking n equal to 2), the rate of time preference is given by

$$1 + R_2 = \frac{1}{1/(1+\lambda)} = 1 + \lambda \qquad (3.8)$$

The rate of time preference in such models is thus equal to λ regardless of the level of consumption in each year. This has two implications. One is that, since the rate of time preference is equal to λ when C_1 is equal to C_2, λ may be ascribed to a positive bias in time preference, and, as the quotes from Ramsey, Pigou and Harrod suggest, this is a controversial matter. It is arguable whether a planning authority ought to exhibit such a bias even if individuals do, and whether individuals do must itself be an open question.

The second implication is that such models are likely to yield bizarre solutions. Since the distribution of consumption over time does not affect the rate of time preference, applied models have shown a tendency to 'flip-flop', concentration on investment for most of the planning period leading to a brief burst of consumption at the end (see, for example, Eckaus and Parikh, 1968).

Accordingly, (3.4), which alleviates both of these problems, has tended to be more popular (for examples of its use in different theoretical contexts, see Ramsey (1928), Tinbergen (1960), Goodwin (1961), Phelps (1962), Sidrauski (1967); for applications, see Kendrick and Taylor (1970) and Westphal (1971)). It may be regarded as being derived from an alternative approach to intertemporal preferences. The most polished and best-known analysis is that due to Böhm-Bawerk (1889), but it was earlier given formal treatment by Jevons (1871) and its origins can be traced back at least as far as the 'calculus of pleasures and pains' of Bentham (1789). Essentially it consists of assuming that consumption C_t in year t gives rise to an amount of instantaneous pleasure $U(C_t)$ (U being a convex function), and that, given a consumption stream $\{C_1, ..., C_T\}$, the individual evaluates the corresponding stream of pleasure $\{U(C_1), ..., U(C_T)\}$ according to a concave utility function which will be written $\psi[U(C_1), ..., U(C_T)]$.

If the latter is written in the linear form (3.4) (as was assumed by Böhm-

Bawerk), the rate of time preference in the two-year model is given by

$$1 + R_2 = \frac{\partial \psi / \partial C_1}{\partial \psi / \partial C_2} = \frac{\partial U / \partial C_1}{(\partial U / \partial C_2)/(1 + \lambda)} = (1 + \lambda)\frac{\partial U / \partial C_1}{\partial U / \partial C_2} \qquad (3.9)$$

The rate of time preference in this formulation depends on two factors, λ and the ratio of the marginal pleasure[4] from consumption in the two years. If C_1 and C_2 are equal, R_2 is equal to λ, since the marginal pleasure will be equal in the two years. Hence λ may again be taken as representing a positive bias in time preference. The second factor picks up the effect on time preference of the curvature of the intertemporal indifference curves, as shown in Figure 3.2. Even if λ is equal to zero (as Ramsey assumed in his model), there will still be positive time preference if C_2 is greater than C_1. The greater the disparity, the greater it will be. Thus models with this type of objective function possess a built-in stabilizer which reduces the tendency to flip-flop, although the problem may still arise (for example, in Goodwin (1961); for a general discussion, see Koopmans (1967)).

In what follows, Fisher's approach has been preferred to Böhm-Bawerk's. It is doubtful whether the additional complications introduced by the latter can make other than a heuristic contribution to the analysis, and even this is suspect. Jevons asserted that, in his calculus of pleasures and pains, the individual would take account not only of the instantaneous pleasure derived from an event but also the pleasure derived from anticipating it (1871, Chapter 2). The latter component is not easy to handle and he omits it from the mathematical statement of his theory. It would seem that one must either add such pleasure of anticipation to the function explicitly, or else redefine the function U to include it. The former course would complicate the analysis enormously, the latter would alter the meanings of the weights and undermine the concept of pure time preference. Thus even in principle one finds oneself returning to the relatively abstract Fisherian formulation.

3.6   The rate of interest

The next stage in the analysis is to suppose that there are many individuals in the economy and that they interact by forming a market in which consumption in year 1 can be traded for consumption in year 2. Each individual now has two decisions to make: he has to choose a production activity, and then decide how to modify the resulting consumption stream by trading in the market. It will be assumed that the activities of any one individual have a negligible effect on the rate of interest ruling in the market.

---

[4] This is often described as 'marginal utility'. U is of course a cardinal utility function, but the term 'pleasure' has been retained to distinguish instantaneous utility from overall utility.

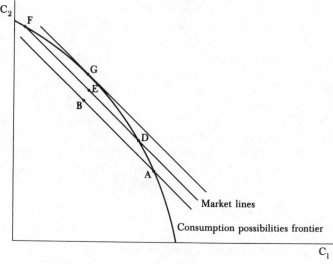

Figure 3.3

A possible pair of decisions is shown in Figure 3.3. The individual can choose the point A in his production set, which yields him the consumption stream $\{C_1, C_2\}$. He then exchanges x of consumption in year 1 for $x(1 + i_2)$ in year 2, where i_2 is the rate of interest ruling in year 2,[5] and so ends up with a consumption stream $\{(C_1 - x), (C_2 + (1 + i_2)x)\}$, represented by the point B. It is important to note that the slope of the line AB is equal to $-(1 + i_2)x/x$, that is, to $-(1 + i_2)$, and hence is independent of the value of x. This implies that the individual is in fact able to reach any other point on the line by varying the amount that he trades in the market. For this reason, using Fisher's terminology, it will be described as the 'market line' through A. It may further be noticed that the slope is also independent of the levels of C_1 and C_2. Thus *every* market line through a point representing a production activity will have that slope, and hence be parallel to that through A.

Obviously B is inefficient, for if the individual chose production activity D and traded to E he could obtain more consumption in both years. Equally obviously, the optimal production activity is given by G, the point in which the consumption possibilities frontier is tangential to a market line, for the market line in question is the highest that can be attained.

If he had complete information concerning his production set, the individual would choose G directly. But it will be supposed that he has to locate

---

[5] Since (by convention) consumption is assumed to be delivered as a pulse at the end of the year, i_2 will be the relevant interest rate when C_1 and C_2 are traded for one another. i_1 is not defined in this model for the same reason that R_1 is not – that C_0 is not defined.

it by trial and error. The individual will be assumed to begin by considering some arbitrary production activity and then to compare it with some alternative. Whichever of the two lies on the higher market line becomes his candidate plan and is compared in turn with another alternative, the process being continued until the point G and the highest attainable market line are reached. The comparison test for two alternatives may be described as follows. Given any two production activities α and β, with consumption streams $\{C_1^\alpha, C_2^\alpha\}$ and $\{C_1^\beta, C_2^\beta\}$, respectively, the values of the two streams, in terms of consumption in year 1, will be $C_1^\alpha + C_2^\alpha/(1 + i_2)$ and $C_1^\beta + C_2^\beta/(1 + i_2)$. But these values determine the points in which the corresponding market lines cut the C_1 axis in a diagram like Figure 3.3. Hence the market line for β will be higher than that for α if and only if

$$C_1^\beta + \frac{C_2^\beta}{1 + i_2} > C_1^\alpha + \frac{C_2^\alpha}{1 + i_2} \tag{3.10}$$

Assuming, without loss of generality, that C_2^β is greater than C_2^α, this may be rewritten

$$i_2 < \frac{C_2^\beta - C_2^\alpha}{C_1^\alpha - C_1^\beta} - 1 \tag{3.11}$$

that is,

$$i_2 < r_{\alpha\beta} \tag{3.12}$$

where

$$r_{\alpha\beta} = \frac{C_2^\beta - C_2^\alpha}{C_1^\alpha - C_1^\beta} - 1 \tag{3.13}$$

$r_{\alpha\beta}$ is, of course, what Fisher described as the 'rate of return over cost' on adopting β in place of α.[6] (3.13) may be recast in the form

$$C_1^\alpha + \frac{C_2^\alpha}{1 + r_{\alpha\beta}} = C_1^\beta + \frac{C_2^\beta}{1 + r_{\alpha\beta}} \tag{3.14}$$

which yields the alternative definition of the rate of return as that rate of discount which equates the present discounted values of the two streams.

The introduction of the concept of the rate of return over cost thus permits an attractive simplifiction of the decision rule for the individual: he should adopt β instead of α if and only if the rate of return over cost obtained by the change is greater than the rate of interest. It should be stressed, though, that the validity of this version of the rule depends upon the validity of that represented by (3.10) from which it is derived, and that the concept of the rate of return (as it is now usually called) is not an essential part of the

---

[6] *The Theory of Interest*, (Fisher 1930, p. 155). In *The Rate of Interest* he described it as the 'rate of return on sacrifice'.

Fisherian apparatus.[7] Indeed, in Section 3.7 it will be shown that there are circumstances in which it cannot be employed.

The definition of the rate of return implies that it is measured by

$$r = -s - 1 \tag{3.15}$$

where s is the slope of the line joining the (marginally distant) points representing the production activities being compared. From (3.13) it may be seen that for marginal movements along the consumption possibilities frontier the rate of return is given by the steepness of the slope of the latter at the point in question. Hence, for example, in Figure 3.3 one can see that at the point D the slope of the consumption possibilities frontier is greater than that of the market line through D, implying that the rate of return for a movement along the frontier is greater than the rate of interest, and so that such a movement would be desirable. Conversely, at F the rate of return is less than the rate of interest and the individual should choose a point lower down the frontier. At G, the optimal point, the rate of return is equal to the rate of interest, since the consumption possibilities frontier is tangential to the market line through G.

So far there has been no mention of the rate of profit. This is defined with reference to the production equilibrium adopted by the economy, in this case the point G. It is defined to be equal to the greatest rate of return obtainable on any marginal movement from the equilibrium position. In the present model it is measured by the rate of return on a marginal movement along the consumption possibilities frontier, since it may easily be verified that the rate of return on a movement from G to a neighbouring interior point of the production set is lower. Thus one has the well-known Fisherian proposition that, when all the appropriate assumptions are satisfied, the rate of profit is equal to the rate of interest.

Having determined his optimal production decision, the individual has to decide how to modify the resulting consumption stream by trading in the market. Suppose that he were to consider trading to the point H in Figure 3.4. He would find that the rate of time preference associated with it would be higher than the market rate of interest, and hence that he could improve his position by moving further down the market line and exchanging more consumption in year 2 for consumption in year 1. If he were at a point like J, he should do the reverse, since at that point his rate of time preference is lower than the market rate of interest. He is thus led to the point at which his rate of time preference is equal to the market rate of interest, that is, to the point K

---

[7] Indeed, as Samuelson (1967) has observed, there is no need for it to appear in an exposition of Fisherian theory. However, for heuristic reasons (which will become more evident in the context of a many-individual model), Fisher chose to express the decision rule in the form (3.12) rather than the more basic form (3.10), thus giving the concept a prominent role in his theory.

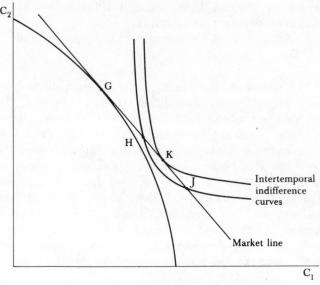

Figure 3.4

where the market line is tangential to an indifference curve, and this, in view of the assumed convexity of the indifference curves, represents his optimal position after trading.

How is the market rate of interest, so far assumed to be exogenous, determined? Before answering this question it will be necessary to investigate the relationship between the market rate of interest and the amount borrowed or lent by a given individual. Suppose that in Figure 3.4 the market rate of interest is increased. The market lines become steeper than before, with the result that a point lower than G on the consumption transformation frontier is selected. The optimal position for the individual lies on the market line through this point and is located as before at the point where it is tangential to an indifference curve. The amount borrowed is altered and can be seen to depend upon the rate of interest.

If the rate of interest rises sufficiently the individual will neither borrow nor lend. This will be referred to as the nil-borrowing rate for the individual. The optimal point will then be that point on the consumption transformation frontier which is tangential to an indifference curve, and their common slope at this point will then be equal to that of the market lines. If the rate of interest rises any higher the individual will reach his optimal position by lending in the first year.

Figure 3.5 illustrates cases in which the individual borrows, lends, and does neither, with the optimal points labelled K, L and M in the three cases respectively.

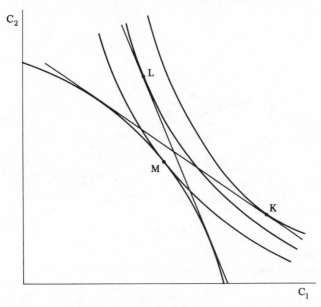

Figure 3.5

It is thus possible to construct a schedule showing how the amount bor-rowed by the individual varies with the market rate of interest. For all levels of the rate of interest below the nil-borrowing rate the individual will borrow a positive amount, and for all levels above it he will borrow a negative amount, that is, lend.

Such a schedule may be constructed for each individual in the economy. These schedules may then be combined to obtain an aggregate borrowing schedule for the economy as a whole, and it is this aggregate schedule that can be utilized to locate the equilibrium market rate of interest. For although any individual may borrow or lend, the economy as a whole cannot and the market rate of interest must be such as to make aggregate borrowing equal to zero. That such an equilibrium rate of interest exists can easily be demons-trated. If the market rate of interest were above the highest nil-borrowing rate of all the individuals, each individual would desire to lend and thus the aggregate schedule would be positive. If the market rate of interest were below the lowest nil-borrowing rate, each individual would desire to borrow and aggregate borrowing would be negative. Since aggregate borrowing varies continuously with the interest rate, it must be equal to zero somewhere between the highest and the lowest nil-borrowing rates.

Fisher appears to have assumed that the equilibrium market rate of interest must be unique, but this is not necessarily the case. For, as Fisher himself was aware (1930, p. 286), the amount borrowed by an individual does not neces-

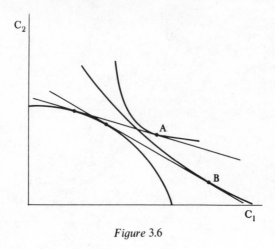

Figure 3.6

sarily fall monotonically as the market rate of interest rises. The change in the amount borrowed depends upon an income effect and a substitution effect, determined by the shape of the intertemporal indifference curves, and the substitution effect along the consumption possibilities frontier. The substitution effects cause the amount borrowed to fall with a rise in the rate of interest, but the income effect may go in the opposite direction.

Figure 3.6 illustrates a case in which a reverse income effect outweighs the two substitution effects and the individual borrows more in reaching optimal point B than he does in reaching optimal point A even though the market rate of interest has risen.

It is therefore possible for the individual borrowing schedule to have the form shown in Figure 3.7. It should be noted that, since in general the nil-

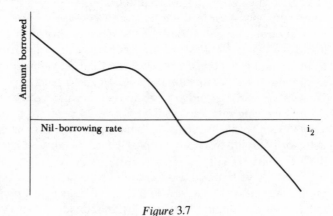

Figure 3.7

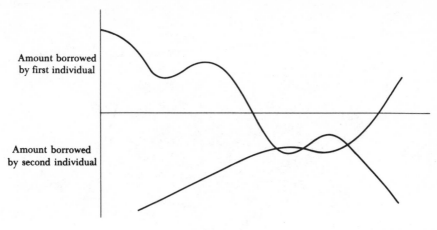

Amount borrowed
by first individual

Amount borrowed
by second individual

Figure 3.8

borrowing rate is unique, the schedule can cross the horizontal axis only once.

If it is now supposed that the economy consists of just one other individual (and that both individuals are price-takers, and so do not exploit the situation of bilateral monopoly), it is possible to locate equilibrium rates of interest by superimposing the latter's borrowing schedule upside-down on Figure 3.7 and noting the points where the schedules cut, for these points indicate zero aggregate borrowing.

In Figure 3.8 three such equilibrium points exist. And clearly multiple equilibria could persist when one generalizes to a market with many individuals. Note that there is no guarantee that the saving schedules, either individual or aggregate, are necessarily monotonically increasing functions of the rate of interest, as has sometimes been assumed by neoclassical writers.[8]

At this point one may answer two questions that have recurred time and again in the literature: why is the rate of interest positive, and which is more important in its determination, technology or subjective preferences?

The Fisherian answer to the first is that it may be due to a bias in favour of later consumption in the trade with nature represented by the consumption possibilities frontier, or to a positive bias in time preference of the individuals in the economy, or to a combination of both.

Suppose initially that the consumption possibilities frontier and the intertemporal indifference curves of each individual are unbiased, that is, symmetric about the 45° line through the origin. Under these conditions the rate of interest will be zero and no trading will take place.

---

[8] For a discussion of the effects of the rate of interest on saving, see Bailey (1957, 1959a) and Buchanan (1959). For empirical references, see pp. 121–5 above.

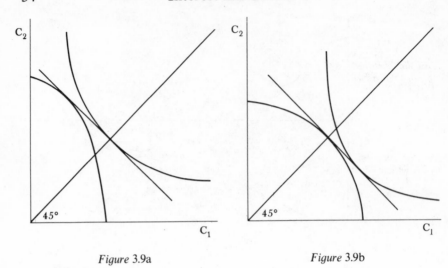

Figure 3.9a   *Figure* 3.9b

Next suppose that some, or all, of the consumption possibility frontiers are biased in favour of later consumption. If the rate of interest were zero, the individual in question would wish to borrow, as shown in Figure 3.9a. Hence in aggregate there would be excess borrowing, and the rate of interest would have to be positive for equilibrium to be established.

Alternatively, suppose that the consumption possibility frontiers are unbiased, but that some, or all, of the individuals possess positively biased time preference. Again, if the rate of interest were zero, such individuals would wish to borrow, as in Figure 3.9b, and to establish equilibrium the rate of interest would have to be positive.

The Fisherian answer to the second question is that both technology and time preference are important, since the equilibrium rate of interest is determined jointly by the shape of the consumption possibility frontiers and shape of the intertemporal indifference curves. 'To adopt a simile of Alfred Marshall, both blades of a pair of scissors are needed to make the scissors work' (Fisher, 1930, p. 282), and it is impossible, in general, to isolate their separate influence.

However, as Hayek (1941a) points out (cf. also Fisher, 1930, p. 282), one could be said to dominate if its curve were relatively straight. This is most easily shown with reference to the one-individual model. In Figure 3.10a the rate of profit is determined by the constant slope of a straight consumption possibilities frontier. The shape and location of the intertemporal indifference curves merely determine the optimal consumption stream, the individual choosing that point on the consumption possibilities frontier where his rate of time preference is equal to the predetermined rate of profit. As Hayek

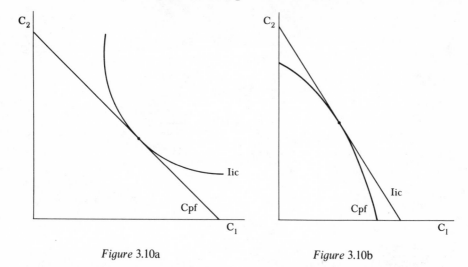

Figure 3.10a   *Figure* 3.10b

points out, Knight's approach to capital theory may be interpreted as belong-ing to this special case (see, for example, Knight 1931), and Hayek favours it himself.

In Figure 3.10b, where the intertemporal indifference curves are straight (as in Figure 3.10a, only one has been shown, for convenience), preferences are dominant. The slope of the intertemporal indifference curves determines the rate of time preference and hence, when the optimal point has been located with the aid of the consumption possibilities frontier, the rate of profit. Fisher acquired a reputation for leaning towards this special case, but it would appear that this was merely a reaction to his insistence on the role of time preference, largely absent in the theories of Clark and Wicksell.

There do not appear to be any empirical studies addressed to the question of whether the general case, or one of the extreme cases just considered, is a better representation of the interaction between preferences and technology. But an indication of the opinion of many economists is implicit in the wide acceptance of Friedman's (1957) permanent income approach to the deter-mination of aggregate consumption. This assumes that individuals aim to consume a fixed proportion of their 'permanent', that is, estimated long-run, income, and therefore that their intertemporal indifference curves display a high degree of complementarity, as shown in Figure 3.11.[9]

---

[9] Friedman himself makes the weaker assumption that the curves are homothetic, but this is insufficient, for homotheticity by itself could result in individuals making plans in one year which they know they will revise in the next. For a discussion of temporal consistency in planning, see Strotz (1956).

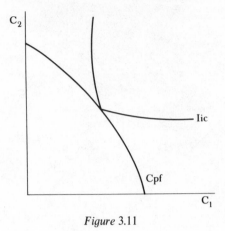

Figure 3.11

Figure 3.11 is a variation on Figure 3.10a and leads to the same conclusions. In the limit the indifference curves would be right-angles and time preference undefined.[10]

3.7 Nonconvexity

It has been assumed so far that the production set of each individual is convex. Figure 3.12 illustrates a case where this assumption is not satisfied.

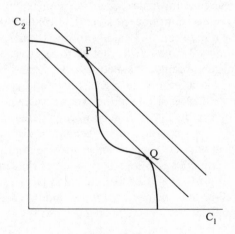

Figure 3.12

---

[10] A further variation on this theme is the Coué model of Chakravarty and Manne (1968), who also assume strict complementarity but suggest that, *ceteris paribus*, a monotonic rise in the consumption stream may be desired.

The optimal production activity is represented by the point P, and comparing the rate of return with the market rate of interest will lead the individual to it provided that he is aware of all his efficient production possibilities. But if he is myopic, and starts his search with a technique represented by a point on the lower part of the curve, he might wind up at Q, a local optimum.

Fisher assumes that in this situation the individual would in fact possess sufficient information to detect re-entrant bulges in the consumption transformation frontier. (1930, pp 279–80) Since this does not appear to be a contentious issue, the same assumption will be adopted here.

3.8   Generalization of the model

Generalization to many, say T, time periods involves nothing more than the replacement of the two-dimensional diagrams of the preceding analysis by T-dimensional ones. A production activity now encompasses T periods and yields a consumption stream $\{C_1, ..., C_T\}$. The consumption possibilities frontier becomes a $(T-1)$-dimensional surface, and so do the intertemporal indifference curves. Similarly the market lines become $(T-1)$-dimensional hyperplanes, whose orientation is determined by the $(T-1)$ interest rates. As before, the individual achieves his optimal consumption stream by locating the point on his possibilities frontier where it is tangential to a market hyperplane and travelling on this hyperplane, by lending or borrowing, until he reaches the point in which it is tangential to an intertemporal indifference surface. This double tangency requires that in each time period his rate of profit in production and his rate of time preference are equal to the rate of interest. The rates of interest in every time period are determined jointly by the simultaneous requirement that aggregate borrowing in every time period be zero. There is no reason to suppose that the rate of interest will be the same from one time period to the next.

Generalization to many, say M, consumption commodities offers no further conceptual difficulties. The geometry of the problem is essentially unchanged, but now the coordinate framework must have MT axes, one for each commodity in each year. The production set has MT dimensions, and the consumption possibilities frontier and the indifference surfaces have $(MT-1)$. The individual reaches his optimal point by choosing that production activity which is represented by the point at which his consumption possibilities frontier is tangential to a market hyperplane, and then trading along the hyperplane until he reaches the point in which it is tangential to an indifference surface. The orientation of the hyperplane, which will now have $(MT-1)$ dimensions, is determined by the prices of the commodities and the rate of interest. If one particular commodity is chosen as numeraire in each year, there are $(M-1)$ relative prices per year, and hence $T(M-1)$ in all, in addition to the $(T-1)$ rates of interest (these rates being defined in terms of the numeraire) to be determined. Corresponding to these $(MT - 1)$ quantities, there are the MT conditions that the market for every commodity should be cleared in every year, which yield $(MT - 1)$ independent constraints after taking account of Walras's Law.

Hence one again has all the elements one needs to establish equilibrium. As in the single consumption commodity case, and for the same reasons, the tangency conditions imply that the rate of profit on production, in terms of the numeraire-equivalent, is equal to the numeraire rate of time preference of each individual, in every year, both of these rates being equal to the market rate of interest, in terms of the numeraire, for the same year.

Verbalizing the description of equilibrium further would be a tedious matter at best and it will be halted at this point. As was noted in Section 3.1, the generalization from two time periods to many is formally equivalent to the generalization of traditional atemporal equilibrium analysis from two commodities to many. The next stage unites them, and a rigorous treatment will be found in Debreu (1959).

It should however be mentioned that some care is needed in the handling of the rate of return in a many-time-period model. Supposing that there is only one consumption commodity, an individual who is considering a candidate consumption stream $\{C_1^\alpha, ..., C_T^\alpha\}$ and an alternative $\{C_1^\beta, ..., C_T^\beta\}$ will prefer the latter if and only if

$$c_1^\beta + \frac{c_2^\beta}{1 + i_2} + ... + \frac{c_T^\beta}{(1 + i_2)...(1 + i_T)} > c_1^\alpha + \frac{c_2^\alpha}{1 + i_2} + ... + \frac{c_T^\alpha}{(1 + i_2)...(1 + i_T)}$$

$$(3.16)$$

where i_t is the rate of interest in the tth time period.[11] The two sides of the inequality measure the total amounts of consumption in year 1 for which the respective streams could be exchanged in the market, that is, their present discounted values in year 1.

This inequality corresponds to (3.10) in the two-period case. It may be observed, though, that there is no simple way of generalizing the analysis that followed (3.10), for one cannot rewrite (3.16) in the form (3.11), nor can one extend (3.13) to define a 'rate of return' on moving from α to β. Hence in this situation one is unable to begin a generalization of the decision rule that β should be adopted instead of α if the rate of return is greater than the rate of interest.

It might be thought that one could nevertheless obtain a 'multiperiod rate of return' by generalizing (3.14) and defining it to be that rate of interest

---

[11] Note that since (as a matter of convention) it has been assumed that consumption in any period is received at the end of the period, and C_1 is the earliest consumption that is traded in the market, there is no need to introduce i_1 into the analysis.

which makes the present discounted values of the two streams equal to one another:

$$c_1^\alpha + \frac{c_2^\alpha}{1 + r_{\alpha\beta}} + \dots + \frac{c_T^\alpha}{(1 + r_{\alpha\beta})^{T-1}} = c_1^\beta + \frac{c_2^\beta}{1 + r_{\alpha\beta}} + \dots + \frac{c_T^\beta}{(1 + r_{\alpha\beta})^{T-1}} \quad (3.17)$$

But, in general, $r_{\alpha\beta}$, as thus defined, has no significance. In the two-period case, definition (3.14) was valid only because it was a simple transformation of (3.13), and (3.13) was useful because it was the right-hand side of (3.11), a transformation of the basic criterion inequality (3.10). Equation (3.17) has no such foundations, and so, in general, the statistic $r_{\alpha\beta}$ is meaningless.[12]

The impossibility of devising a multiperiod rate of return is reflected in the absence of any answer to the following question: even if one could define such a rate of return, with what would one compare it? For instead of there being a single rate of interest, as in the two-period case, there are now $(T - 1)$ of them, and there is no reason why these should not all be different.[13]

However, since definition (3.17) is used very frequently in cost-benefit analysis, it is worth noting that comparing the rate of return, thus defined, with the market rate of interest will lead to the correct decision provided that (3.17) has a unique solution and that the market rate of interest may be assumed to be constant. In most practical applications the first assumption is satisfied and the second is as reasonable as any other, and so the rate of return comparison and the present discounted value criterion are equivalent. But it is possible that there might be several solutions to (3.17) and therefore multiple 'rates of return', in which case the present discounted value criterion should be used.[14]

3.9 Testing the Fisherian triple equality

The Fisherian model, in its simplest version, predicts that in every time period the rate of interest will be equal to the rate of time preference and the rate of profit, a proposition which in principle should form the basis of a test. Unfortunately the practical execution of such a test is beset by several

---

[12] This point is made by Hirshleifer (1958, 1970), Solow (1963) and Samuelson (1967). As is argued in Dougherty (1972), Fisher himself was aware of the problem and avoided using a definition of the form (3.17), although this has sometimes been described as his definition of the rate of return (notably, Pasinetti, 1969).

[13] One solution to the whole problem is to generalize the search procedure in a less ambitious way than that proposed above, at each step testing the candidate stream against another which differs only in two components, as described in Dougherty (1972). Another procedure is described by Bailey (1959b).

[14] Comparison of multiperiod rates of return may also lead to an incorrect decision in the case of the evaluation of mutually exclusive projects. The possible conflict between the two investment criteria has given rise to a large and rather pedantic literature. For an early and lucid discussion, see Hirshleifer (1958).

problems, the chief one being the measurement of the rate of time preference. Since there do not exist any suitable data for measuring it directly, recourse must be made to an indirect method, and the only one to have received serious attention in the literature has evolved as a byproduct of Friedman's (1957) theory of the aggregate consumption function. Requiring a measure of 'permanent income' (income purged of its transitory component) he uses the adaptive expectations mechanism pioneered by Cagan (1956) to estimate it as the weighted sum of current and past measured income. Writing Y_t^p and Y_t for permanent and measured income at time t, the adaptive expectations mechanism (expressed here for sake of simplicity in a trendless form):

$$\Delta Y_t^p = \beta(Y_t - Y_{t-1}^p) \tag{3.18}$$

yields

$$Y_t^p = \beta Y_t + \beta(1 - \beta)Y_{t-1} + \beta(1 - \beta)^2\, Y_{t-2} + \dots \tag{3.19}$$

and Friedman interprets the reaction factor β as the subjective rate of discount. From this it is but a short step to interpret β as the rate of time preference (Friedman, 1960, 1963, and several subsequent studies by other writers).[15]

The main problem with this procedure is that it is not at all obvious why the way in which an individual discounts *past* income for prediction purposes should have any connection with the way in which he discounts *future* consumption in his intertemporal preference ordering. And the estimates of β have on the whole been too high to permit the easy acceptance of this double interpretation. Even Friedman, with his estimate in the region of 0.35 per year, concedes that one would need to broaden the notion of the rate of time preference for it to be plausible, and although some writers have obtained similar estimates (Laumas, 1969; Landsberger, 1971), others have obtained much higher ones. Wright (1969b) suggests that it lies between 0.7 and 0.8, and Holbrook (1967), using quarterly data, obtains figures ranging from 1.3 to 3.3.

The variability of the estimates of β in any case severely limits the discriminatory power of the test of the triple equality. Additional, if lesser, problems arise in the estimation of the rate of profit. In principle this should be estimated *ex ante*, as the expected rate, rather than *ex post*, as actually measured, and (*ex post*, at least) it displays wide variations over time (Christensen and Jorgenson, 1973).

Further problems are introduced in practice by the presence of taxation, particularly the personal income tax and the corporation tax. Even in a perfectly competitive economy these would be responsible for discrepancies

---

[15] Darby (1974) presents an ingenious argument for equating β and the long-run expected rate of return on wealth, but it depends on several strong assumptions.

between the rate of profit, the rate of interest and the rate of time preference. The effects of these taxes are discussed at length in Chapter 5, and they are sufficiently complex to have given rise to a debate which is far from concluded.

For these reasons a direct test of the triple equality is not a realistic proposition. In its place an indirect, component-by-component evaluation will be presented in Chapter 8. First, however, it is desirable to develop the model further and discuss some of its implications.

4

Extensions of the Fisherian model

4.1 Capital

Capital was defined in the previous chapter to be the set of physical endowments that could influence the subsequent production of a consumption good. Two aspects of this definition should be stressed immediately. First, its physical nature. The capital goods in the background of the preceding analysis have been conceived of in physical terms. The question of the values to be attached to them is considered for the first time in this chapter.[1] Secondly, its generality. There is no need to assume the existence of a finite classification of capital goods. Capital is not limited to sets of machines or stocks of intermediate goods. It is anything which is useful in a specific production process and to which one can tie a label. Hence, for example, it includes land in a broad sense. It is not assumed that any two items are alike, either at a given point or at different points in time. The last consideration implies that a capital good that has been used for a year is subsequently regarded as a completely distinct type of good.

It will be convenient to begin the discussion of the determination of the value of a capital good in the context of the two-period one-consumption-commodity many-individual economy of Section 3.6.

Suppose that an individual, whose production set has frontier AA', as shown in Figure 4.1, is deprived of one of his initial stock of capital goods. One may again evaluate all his feasible production activities and derive his production set. This must be a subset of the original set, since every activity

---

[1] It therefore goes without saying that aggregate value capital and the 'marginal product' of capital play no part in Fisher's theory of interest, despite Kregel's (1976a, p. 86) and Pasinetti's (1969, p. 511) suggestions to the contrary.

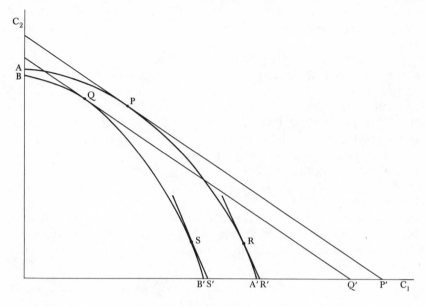

Figure 4.1

available to him now was available to him previously, and so no part of the new consumption possibilities frontier, BB′, may lie outside AA′. BB′ may lie wholly within AA′, as shown in Figure 4.1, or be tangential to it in places. Since the activities of a single individual are assumed to have a negligible effect on the market rate of interest, the market line tangential to AA′ at P, the old optimal point, will be parallel to that tangential to BB′ at Q, the new optimal point.

If P and Q represent points $\{C_1^\alpha, C_2^\alpha\}$ and $\{C_1^\beta, C_2^\beta\}$, respectively, the deprivation of the capital good would cause the individual to lose a stream $\{(C_1^\alpha - C_1^\beta), (C_2^\alpha - C_2^\beta)\}$. Note that it is not necessarily true that both elements of the stream are positive: Figure 4.1 illustrates a case in which $(C_2^\alpha - C_2^\beta)$ is negative, implying that the removal of the capital good induces the individual to take a loss in year 1 which he can partly recoup in year 2.

The value of the capital good to the individual, in terms of consumption delivered at the end of year 1, is thus

$$(C_1^\alpha - C_1^\beta) + \frac{C_2^\alpha - C_2^\beta}{1 + i_2} \qquad (4.1)$$

It may be seen that this quantity is measured by the distance $P'Q'$, where P' and Q' are the points in which the market lines through P and Q cut the C_1 axis.

It should be noted that the value of the capital good is not necessarily an inverse function of the market rate of interest. In Figure 4.1, P and Q represent the optimal production activities at a fairly low rate of interest. R and S represent the corresponding optimal activities at a higher one. It can be seen that $R'S'$ is greater than $P'Q'$, from which it follows that the value of the capital good is higher at the higher rate. This could conceivably be the case for every capital good held by every individual, and so in aggregate. One does not need to appeal to the reswitching phenomenon to demonstrate the invalidity of the old proposition that the value of aggregate capital varies inversely with the rate of interest.[2]

Generalization to T periods is perfectly straightforward. If the individual obtains optimal consumption stream $\{C_1^\alpha,...,C_T^\alpha\}$ when the capital good in question is included among his initial stocks, and $\{C_1^\beta,...,C_T^\beta\}$ when it is not, its value is given by

$$(C_1^\alpha - C_1^\beta) + \frac{C_2^\alpha - C_2^\beta}{1 + i_2} + ... + \frac{C_T^\alpha - C_T^\beta}{(1 + i_2)...(1 + i_T)} \tag{4.2}$$

Note that in general all T terms will be nonzero, even if the life of the capital good is much shorter than T: the presence or absence of the capital good may well have repercussions on the optimal production activity long after it has ceased to exist.

Finally, suppose that there are M distinct consumption commodities produced each year, so that there are MT in all. One could treat them as a single vector and index them in such a way that $C_{M(t-1)+m}$ would refer to a delivery of commodity of type m in year t. In actual fact it will be convenient to follow the more usual practice of matrix indexing with double subscript, so that $C_{m,t}$ refers to the commodity just mentioned. Similarly $P_{m,t}$ will be used to denote the value of that commodity in terms of commodity 1, chosen as numeraire, delivered in that year.

Now the optimal consumption stream will have the form $\{(C_{1,1}^\alpha,...,C_{M,1}^\alpha),$ $...,(C_{1,T}^\alpha,...,C_{M,T}^\alpha)\}$, so that it can be treated as a stream of annual baskets. The stream that the individual obtains when deprived of the initial capital good will be of similar form with superscript β. The difference that the capital good makes to the consumption stream is thus a stream of baskets $([C_{1,t}^\alpha - C_{1,t}^\beta],...,[C_{M,t}^\alpha - C_{M,t}^\beta]), t = 1,...,T$, and so its value is given by

$$\sum_{t=1}^{T} \frac{([C_{1,t}^\alpha - C_{1,t}^\beta] + p_{2,t}[C_{2,t}^\alpha - C_{2,t}^\beta] + ... + p_{M,t}[C_{M,t}^\alpha - C_{M,t}^\beta])}{(1 + i_2)...(1 + i_t)} \tag{4.3}$$

---

[2] The present Wicksell effect context is, of course, very different from that of reswitching analysis, which will be discussed below.

This disaggregated approach to the valuation of a capital good is both general and powerful. There is no presumption that either the structure of the consumption basket or that of relative prices will be constant from year to year, and so the expression is free to reflect changes in production and market conditions over time.

Equally important, the expression is free to reflect changes in the capital good itself. It may be observed that physical depreciation has automatically been taken into account, the consumption streams being defined net of it. If the individual decides to maintain a capital good in mint condition, that will be identified as an element of one activity; if he decides to do nothing to arrest its deterioration, that will, *ceteris paribus*, count as another activity; and any intermediate policy, *ceteris paribus*, will count as yet another activity. The associated consumption streams will be distinct points in the production set. The most efficient maintenance policy with regard to that particular capital good is, by definition, that which is adopted in that activity which yields the optimal consumption stream.

In this way one sidesteps the problem of what is meant by 'maintaining capital intact', an issue in capital theory that is as unnecessary as it is intractable. Unnecessary because the analysis does not presuppose that any given type of capital good will be produced in more than one year, which makes for realism in a world of continuous technological change. And intractable because, except under restrictive assumptions, physical depreciation must be calculated in value terms, is thus logically posterior to an analysis of prices, and is therefore inextricably intertwined with the equally unnecessary and intractable concept of economic obsolescence.[3]

Even depreciation, the sum of physical deterioration and economic obsolescence, is not well-defined. For an individual capital good it may be convenient to define it as the difference between its capital value at the beginning and the end of the year. But this convention may be regarded as satisfactory only in the cases of relatively durable goods. With a short-lived good which changes its character substantially during the year, one may have the alternatives of considering the good either to be partly depreciated but still in existence as such, or to be wholly depreciated, what is left of it being counted as part of gross output. It follows that the definitions of both aggregate depreciation and aggregate gross output are purely matters of convention. Fortunately, but consequentially, theory can do without the concepts.

So far only the exogenously given initial stocks of capital goods have been assigned values, but one may readily extend the analysis to cover the stocks on hand at the beginning of the second and subsequent years as the optimal production activity unfolds through time. To derive the value of a specific capital good on hand at the beginning of, say, year t, suppose that the indivi-

---

[3] For a valiant attempt to wrestle with the problem, see the proposals of Pigou (1935, 1941); and for a dissection of his argument, see Hayek (1941b).

dual is deprived of it at the point and has to modify as best he can his optimal activity, having followed it until then. The value of the capital good is determined by the difference between the original and the new consumption streams, that is, a series of consumption baskets beginning at the end of year t, and this can be expressed in terms of the numeraire at the end of year t using the price system as before.

4.2   Labour

One of the most common criticisms of Fisherian analysis is that it pays inadequate attention to the role of labour. Since wages and profits together make up national income, so this line of argument goes, a treatment that concentrates exclusively on the determination of the rate of profit at the expense of that of the wage rate is unbalanced, to say the least.

This criticism is often voiced by those who are still thinking in terms of the aggregate neoclassical approach to capital theory and the answer to it is that it fundamentally misunderstands the nature of Fisherian analysis. The focus is not on factor rewards (as is implicitly suggested by such critics) but on intertemporal consumption patterns, and the rate of profit is essentially a subordinate variable, the key one being the rate of interest. Certainly the rate of profit has implications for income distribution, but these are a by-product, as in the non-neoclassical theories of Kalecki and Wood discussed in Chapters 9 and 11.

Nevertheless, since income distribution is such an important topic, it is useful to investigate how labour fits into the Fisherian model. There are two alternative (but equivalent) ways of handling it, and both will be considered in turn. Initially it will be assumed that each individual has discretion over the amount of labour that he supplies.

One approach, which may be traced back to Jevons (1871), effectively treats labour as if it were a 'discommodity'. In the same way as the consumption of a commodity affords utility, work, on the whole, gives rise to disutility. A little light work may actually be considered desirable by an individual, but beyond a certain point disutility sets in and the marginal disutility increases with the work rate. The individual, consulting his calculus of pleasures and pains, chooses that work rate at which the marginal disutility of labour is equal to the utility of the commodities that can be bought with the wages earned.

Treating labour as a negative consumption commodity involves adding a negative dimension in each time period to the consumption possibilities frontier, the intertemporal indifference curves and the market hyperplanes, and the wage in any time period is determined as a price relative to the numeraire like any true commodity. Since this is precisely the standard treatment in static analysis, very little more need be said. Looked at this way, the determination of total wages appears almost independent of the determination of total profits.

The other way of handling labour within the Fisherian framework is to treat it as an exogenous input like a capital good and to consider the effects on the consumption possibilities frontier of reducing it by one unit in a given time period. The analysis is parallel to that of Section 4.1. If $\{C_1^\alpha, ..., C_T^\alpha\}$ is the original optimal consumption stream, and $\{C_1^\beta, ..., C_T^\beta\}$ is the best consumption stream available after the removal of a unit of labour in period 1, the value of a unit of labour in that period, w_1, is given by the present value of the difference:

$$w_1 = (C_1^\alpha - C_1^\beta) + \frac{C_2^\alpha - C_2^\beta}{1 + i_2} + ... + \frac{C_T^\alpha - C_T^\beta}{(1 + i_2)...(1 + i_T)} \qquad (4.4)$$

This way of valuing labour explicitly takes account of the intertemporal repercussions of a change in the labour supply, whereas the previous one is restricted to the current-period trade-off between consumption and labour, labour being valued in terms of the numeraire commodity in the current period. But for marginal adjustments the difference in frameworks is immaterial and arbitrage ensures that both methods give the same results.

The discretion over the amount of work supplied by an individual assumed so far is clearly at variance with what one observes in the more advanced economies today, where the majority of the labour force is subject to contracts which specify so many hours of work per week and so many weeks per year.

If one assumes instead that labour inputs are fixed institutionally, the first of the two approaches described above breaks down, but the second is unaffected. Since the supply of labour no longer depends on intertemporal preferences, the wage rate does not reflect the subjective marginal rate of substitution between labour and consumption. But the tangency condition remains in operation on the production side, and so expressions of the form (4.4) remain valid.

To assume that the individual has no, rather than absolute, discretion over the amount of work he supplies, is itself an extreme assumption. For he may have a choice of occupations offering more pay for greater effort; if not, he may have opportunities to moonlight; in addition, in many occupations, overtime of one form or another may be available; and in a few occupations, notably self-employed craftsmen and professionals, there is Jevonian scope for the work rate.

Since it accommodates both types of supply assumption, the second way of handling labour will be adopted in what follows. It has the further advantage that, as far as production is concerned, the initial capital goods and labour are placed on the same footing, together comprising the set of exogenous inputs. Indeed from the Fisherian point of view the distinction between the two subsets of exogenous inputs is of negligible consequence, and any suggestion that one is more 'primary' than the other is unwarranted.

4.3   Firms and factor markets

Having investigated the roles and rewards of capital goods and labour, one may pull the threads together to obtain a formal theory of distribution. But first it will be convenient to increase the generality of the analysis by sketching the consequences of relaxing an assumption that will all along have seemed highly artificial – the assumption that each individual produces in isolation and that markets exist only for consumption goods.

There is no need to dwell on the fact that the contribution to the production process of most individuals is restricted to their labour, and that the greater part of the aggregate output of goods and services is produced by enterprises which pool the resources, capital and labour, of many individuals. It may therefore seem surprising that it was not until very recently, with the pioneering study of Hirshleifer (1970), that these facts of economic life were treated explicitly within the framework of Fisherian theory.

Why has this development taken so long? The basic reason must be that the extent of the gap between a body of economic theory and the phenomena that it is supposed to explain depends largely on the trade-off between the increasing complexity of the former and improved understanding of the latter. Those who accept Fisher's theory at all seem to have felt that *The Rate of Interest* and *The Theory of Interest*, simple though their presentation of the theory may be, state the essentials of the problem, and that further elaboration might only serve to divert attention from them. This is an attitude which, as far as production is concerned, has certainly been fostered by the existence of an independent, well-articulated neoclassical theory of the firm which would serve to reduce the gap. But with recent developments in capital theory, the time has come to extend Fisher's model in this as well as other directions.

The first change that will be made will be to follow Hirshleifer's lead and assume that firms, rather than individuals, are responsible for all production. It will be supposed that, at time zero, the individuals have in their possession the stocks of capital goods with which the economy is initially endowed, and that the firms possess nothing. The individuals then sell the initial stocks of capital goods to the firms, and supply them in the course of time with their own labour, receiving in exchange titles to streams of consumption goods.[4]

Since labour is a variable input to a firm, it must be taken into account

---

[4] This treatment is rather different from that of Hirshleifer, who does not bring factor inputs and markets into the picture explicitly. He assumes that firms are endowed with production opportunities, and that individuals own shares in the firms.

explicitly in the characterization of the latter's production set. In the previous chapter, where the individual was responsible for production, it was shown that this involved adding an extra dimension to his production set in each year. In the present context the production set must likewise be extended dimensionally, but now by as many dimensions in each year as there are different types of labour, since the firm may employ each and every type available. It will be assumed that these are finite in number and that each is traded in a perfect market.

Similarly, capital goods, both those bought initially from the individuals and those produced subsequently, will also be introduced explicitly into the production set. No distinction will be made between outputs, which will yield income to the firm in the same way as the sale of consumption goods, and inputs – the latter will simply be treated as negative outputs. Again, it will be assumed that the number of capital goods in finite and that perfect markets exist for each of them.

Each activity available to a firm will now yield what may be termed a production stream, rather than a consumption stream, since in addition to the consumption goods it will list the surpluses of the capital goods produced in each year and the amounts of the different kinds of labour utilized. Given a set of market prices, the firm will then select that activity which will leave it on the highest possible market hyperplane, that is, which will maximize its net profit.

It will be assumed that the production set of each firm is convex and that therefore, in an intertemporal sense, constant returns to scale prevail.

Decreasing returns can only occur if some factor contributing to production is neglected when the effects of changes in scale are considered. In the present analysis, that factor is identified as a capital good, however far it may be from the usual notion of fixed capital, and it is taken into account in the specification of the production set. Rent, as such, does not make an appearance, unless the term is used to denote the gross rental earned by certain specialized capital goods (for example, land and patents).

Increasing returns may likewise be discounted if, as Koopmans (1957) suggests, they may be attributed to indivisibilities. For although indivisibilities may significantly affect the behaviour of a firm, and perhaps that of an industry, they are unlikely to have much influence on the aggregate consumption possibilities set and the equilibrium rate of interest.[5]

There still remains the question of what determines the size of any particular firm when several are using the same technique, a question which will be left open. To answer it one would have to construct a theory of how equilibrium prices are discovered, and at this point this is hardly worth the effort, in view of the critique of Fisherian analysis in Chapters 7 and 8. Suffice to say

---

[5] For a contrary view, see Kaldor (1972).

that the very condition of constant returns to scale which is responsible for the indeterminacy makes it immaterial how production is allocated among firms.

Returning to the determination of prices, one may derive further insights by looking at the economy in aggregate. If one considers every activity available to every firm, taking into account the interdependence imposed by the finiteness of the supplies of the initial capital goods and labour, one may derive aggregate production streams, and hence an aggregate production frontier, by summing the individual streams. Since the capital goods produced as outputs by some firms as inputs to others disappear in aggregate,[6] the aggregate production stream will be that much simpler than those of the individual firms. Further, in aggregate the use of the exogenous inputs, that is, the initial capital stocks and the different types of labour in each year, is fixed, and so these may be treated as parameters rather than variables. One might do both and define, in addition to the aggregate production possibilities set, an aggregate consumption possibilities set. The former has MT dimensions for the consumption commodities and an additional dimension for each of the exogenous inputs, treated as variables, while the latter just has the MT dimensions for the consumption commodities, the levels of the exogenous inputs being treated as parameters.

The values of the exogenous inputs, determined above with reference to the individual firms employing them, may also be determined by considering either of these aggregate sets. On the one hand, looking at the consumption set, if one removed one unit of one of the inputs from the economy, the consumption possibilities frontier would shrink and a new equilibrium point would be established. The value of the input is then given by the difference between the streams of consumption baskets represented by the old and the new equilibrium points.

On the other hand, one could derive the value of an input directly from the orientation of the price hyperplane sustaining the equilibrium point on the aggregate production possibilities frontier. Given the assumption that each of the micro-level production activities is subject to constant returns to scale, it follows that the aggregate production possibilities set is likewise subject to constant returns to scale. Consequently, given any equilibrium point, the value of the aggregate stream of consumption baskets (valued at equilibrium prices) will be exhaustively allocated among the exogenous inputs, that is, among the initial stocks of capital goods and the labour supplied by the individuals during the different years.

---

[6] Terminal capital stocks will be neglected since they are assigned zero value.

4.4 Aggregation

In a much-quoted passage, Robinson wrote

> The student of economic theory is taught to write $Y = f(L,K)$ where L is a quantity of labour, K a quantity of capital and Y a rate of output of commodities. He is instructed to assume all workers alike, and to measure L in man-hours of labour; he is told something about the index-number problem involved in choosing a unit of output – and then he is hurried on to the next question, in the hope that he will forget to ask in what units K is measured. Before he ever does ask, he has become a professor, and so sloppy habits of thought are handed on from one generation to the next. (1953, p.81. The symbols have been changed to conform with current usage.)

Partly as a result of this and the subsequent contributions by herself and others discussed in Chapter 2, the present-day student of capital theory is keenly aware of the fact that aggregate capital is a perilous construct. He knows, for example, that if he comes across an old-fashioned neoclassical theorist (of the aggregative type) who thinks that the rate of profit is determined by the marginal product of capital, all he has to do is to point out that the value of aggregate capital depends upon the rate of profit. Circularity exposed. Collapse of stout party. If the neoclassical is less naive, and talks in terms of equilibrium conditions rather than causality, then the reswitching phenomenon is a handy stick to beat him with.

These lessons have been so well taught that the student, unless he is unusually unreflective or obdurate, is likely to subscribe to the widespread feeling that the aggregation of capital goods involves complex problems originating in mysteries understood only by a few initiates. In contrast to the aggregation of output, which, in the general view, gives rise to an index number problem that becomes of interest only in such uncontroversial issues as the comparison of standards of living in different countries, and that otherwise may be dismissed as a minor nuisance responsible for an inelegant but mild indeterminacy in the measurement of some macroeconomic statistics. And as for the aggregation of labour, it is frequently considered a sign of weakminded pedantry not to finesse it or ignore it altogether.

Nevertheless, this asymmetry in attitude towards the three aggregates is largely unjustified, as Bliss (1975) has demonstrated in a formal treatment of the aggregation conditions.[7] In this section it will be shown that, within a Fisherian framework, there are no conceptual differences, apart from a matter of convolution, in the status of the three aggregates in a world where

---

[7] Hicks (1961) asserted this in a defence of the aggregate production function, but his argument would not satisfy a general equilibrium theorist.

expectations are held with certainty and fulfilled. It follows that such differences as do exist may be attributed to the effects of uncertainty.

To forestall unnecessary controversy, it should be stressed that the analysis should not be interpreted as an attempt to rehabilitate aggregate capital as a factor of production. Quite the opposite – it shows that the other two variables are nearly as defective, and thus adds to the case against the use of the aggregate production function as an element of theoretical analysis.[8]

Conducting the analysis over a specific interval of time, rather than in the context of a stationary state, has had several obvious advantages. Consider first the significance of aggregate capital. No attempt has been made here to define the marginal product of it, or even the marginal product of a particular type of capital good, as a flow (for example, on an annual basis). Indeed, in a world where physical depreciation and economic obsolescence are the rule, it would appear to be impossible to attach unambiguous meanings to such concepts. They could, of course, be defined as net rentals, that is, the product of the capital value and the current rate of interest, but then they would be *ex post* constructs and could not be used in any positive analysis.

Instead, it has been shown that a capital good may be regarded as the present embodiment of a future stream of baskets of consumption goods – its marginal product taking all T years together. Since the sum of a number of streams is a stream of sums, aggregate capital may likewise be regarded in this way.

It has been argued that the value of the services of any particular kind of labour, and hence of aggregate labour, in any year may be treated in exactly the same way. Of course the aggregate labour input is usually estimated in terms of manhours, not the wage bill, at least ostensibly. But unless the heterogeneity of labour is being ignored, this means calculating 'equivalent manhours' in efficiency units – and the customary weights are relative wages, so one is effectively calculating the wage bill with one kind of labour chosen as the numeraire.

Before examining the significance of aggregate output, one must first discuss the well-known but easily-neglected problem of its definition. For, unlike capital, labour and consumption, the definition of output is purely a convention. The two most common variants may briefly be labelled the services and surplus concepts.[9] The former regards it as the flow of services enjoyed by individuals, in other words, what is now normally called consump-

---

[8] For a summary of the assumptions involved in the use of aggregate capital (and aggregate output) as arguments in production functions, see Green (1964) and Gorman (1968).

[9] Another concept which has received attention (but which will not be considered here) is the 'standard stream' defined by Fisher (1906, pp. 396–8) and advocated briefly by Hicks (1939). For a similar consumption-orientated definition see Hayek (1935 and 1941a, Chapter 25).

tion. The latter, which corresponds to the usual, everyday sense of the term, defines it to be the maximum amount that could be consumed which would leave the capital stock intact; it is thus equal to actual consumption plus the increase in the value of the capital stock, that is, consumption plus net investment as measured.

It may seem strange that there should have been an enduring controversy over what is clearly a matter of semantics. The most obvious reason is that it was a subsidiary issue in the campaign to replace the income tax with a consumption tax to avoid the double taxation of savings. The case, discussed in Section 5.2, would plainly be strengthened if income were redefined in this way.[10] A second motive, also psychological, may have been to reinforce the notion that consumption, in its broadest sense, is the ultimate objective of economic activity.

In what follows, the more conventional surplus concept will be adopted. If one defines the value of aggregate consumption produced at the end of year t to be C_t, the payment to labour at the end of year t to be W_t, and the value of aggregate capital on hand at the end of year t to be K_t, all measured in units of the numeraire commodity delivered at the end of year t, the value of Y_t is given by

$$Y_t = C_t + K_t - K_{t-1} \qquad (4.5)$$

the sum of consumption and net investment in year t.

By virtue of the exhaustion of the value of the product, discussed in Section 4.3, the value of the stock of capital goods at the end of year $t-1$ is equal to the discounted value of the stock of capital goods at the end of year t plus the discounted value of the surplus of consumption over wages at the end of year t:

$$K_{t-1} = \frac{K_t}{1+i_t} + \frac{C_t - W_t}{1+i_t} \qquad (4.6)$$

Hence

$$Y_t = K_{t-1} i_t + W_t \qquad (4.7)$$

which demonstrates that the surplus concept is also equivalent to the sum of wages and the net rental on the capital stock, that is, to income as usually defined.

(4.5) states formally that aggregate output is just a mixture of consumption goods and capital goods, that is, of present and future consumption goods,

---

[10] The most fervent advocate of the services concept was Fisher (for references see Section 5.2). Among the more energetic defenders of the surplus concept one may note Cannan (1897), Lindahl (1933) and Simons (1938).

and hence, like both capital and labour, it may be viewed as a sum of streams of consumption baskets.

It thus follows that the three aggregates – capital, labour and output – are cut from the same cloth, and therefore, in the present context, they must necessarily be as satisfactory or unsatisfactory as each other.

For example, consider an obvious issue – the choice of numeraire. In the present context this is quite arbitrary and can make no difference to the quantitative, disaggregated side of the analysis.[11] But on the other hand it may have a substantial effect on, say, the estimate of the growth of aggregate consumption over time – aggregate consumption might appear to have a positive growth rate with one numeraire and a negative growth rate with another.[12] To obtain a 'true' picture one might use a weighted average of commodities, instead of a single commodity, as numeraire, and perhaps change the weights over time. But sauce for the goose is sauce for the gander and there is no reason why adjustments applied to the estimates of aggregate consumption should not be applied equally to the three aggregates derived from it.[13] And the same considerations apply in the case of more general index numbers, for it is inconsistent to use different techniques when constructing measures of 'real' output, capital and labour.

Of course, a key assumption of the foregoing general equilibrium framework is that expectations are held with certainty and fulfilled. In the absence of futures markets, this implies that each individual must have a broad knowledge of production conditions and subjective preferences over time if the model is to approximate the workings of an actual economy. Needless to say, such knowledge is not possessed in detail, but it could be argued that a general idea of the overall rate of technical progress and possible shifts in preferences may be adequate for the purpose.

Even with this simplification, the average individual is unlikely to have

---

[11] For that matter, it would make no difference if one type of labour were adopted as the numeraire. It is therefore difficult to understand the contention of Robinson (1953, 1956) and Rymes (1971) that aggregate capital measured in labour units has greater significance than aggregate capital measured in commodity units. Robinson suggests that choice of technique may usefully be analyzed by examining the relationship between output per worker and 'real' capital (capital valued in labour units) per worker, but she does not attempt to demonstrate that the change of unit makes any fundamental difference to the analysis. Rymes makes the same assertion in a discussion of the measurement of technical progress.

[12] The classic illustration of this point is Wicksell's discussion of the consequences of adopting pig-iron (whose price used to be highly cyclical) as numeraire: Wicksell (1935, pp. 210–11).

[13] In their case, however, the calculations will involve an extra degree of convolution. To measure the composite commodity value of, say, aggregate capital at time zero, one must estimate the composite commodity value of each of the consumption baskets in the stream attributable to it through time, and then discount them at the own rate of interest of the composite commodity. If one wished to construct a time series for capital, this process must be repeated from scratch for the stock of capital goods on hand at the beginning of each year. The same applies to aggregate labour and output.

more than a general feel for future developments, a feel which becomes increasingly vague and unstable the further he looks ahead. And so the determinism of the model must be relaxed to allow for shifts in expectations, shifts which are likely to occur for most individuals simultaneously and thus have substantial aggregate effects.

Such shifts are likely to have especial impact on estimates of aggregate capital. They will alter the valuation of a capital good in two ways: in the estimate of the series of consumption baskets attributable to it – its dis-aggregated physical productivity – and in the prices that are likely to be attached to the components of the baskets and the rates of interest used to discount them. The volatility of stock market indices suggests that the combined effects are substantial and rapid. As a consequence, the market valuation of capital goods is reduced in significance, being based on the restless sands of conjecture. Real indices may be slightly better off, but only to the extent that they eliminate the need to forecast changes in relative prices – which, of course, is a measure of their arbitrariness; it will, in general, still remain necessary to obtain some estimate of the physical, consumption basket, productivity.

Exactly the same considerations apply to aggregate output, in view of the capital goods component. If K_{t-1}^{t-1} and K_t^{t-1} are the values of the sets of capital goods in existence at the end of year t and $t + 1$, respectively, valued according to the expectations ruling at the end of year $t - 1$, then the surplus concept of output given by (4.5) becomes

$$Y_t = C_t + K_t^{t-1} - K_{t-1}^{t-1} \tag{4.8}$$

It is thus dependent in the same way as aggregate capital on the ex-pectations ruling at the beginning of year t. In the case of output, however, there is the further difficulty caused by the possibility of changes in expecta-tions occurring *during* the period of output. The actual value of capital at the end of year t, K_t^t, will in general be different from K_t^{t-1} and so one has two further versions of the surplus concept:

$$Y_t = C_t + K_t^t - K_{t-1}^{t-1} \tag{4.9}$$

and

$$Y_t = C_t + K_t^t - K_{t-1}^t \tag{4.10}$$

K_{t-1}^t being the value that the capital stock at the end of year $t - 1$ would have had with the expectations ruling in year t. Of the three versions, (4.9) is the only one susceptible to measurement, but it has been generally criticized in the literature on the grounds that it includes windfall capital gains. (4.8) and (4.10), advocated by Lindahl (1933)[14] and Hicks (1941), respectively, represent

---

[14] Lindahl's 'income as interest' was expressed in the form of (4.7). But this is equivalent to (4.8).

attempts to define output net of this element.[15] It hardly needs to be said that the final choice of surplus concept is thus a convention within a convention, and that whichever is chosen, it is subject to the effects of uncertainty in the same way as aggregate capital.

Finally labour. When measured in efficiency units, instead of by a body-count,[16] it is affected by uncertainty in the same way as aggregate capital since, as has been argued above, wage weights may be regarded in the same way as the prices of capital goods.

These considerations suggest that the making of endogenous valuations, rather than the effects of uncertainty, the point at issue, the long-standing controversy over qualitative differentiation between the three aggregates has been doubly misleading. It has both focused on the wrong problem, and, more seriously, taken the wrong form: it has tried to take a purely logical approach to an empirical problem that should be decided *ad hoc* in any given context.

4.5   The factor price frontier

Before elaborating on these conclusions, it will be convenient to examine the logical foundations of the supposed counterpart of the aggregate production function, the 'factor price frontier', as it is usually called. This shows the maximum wage rate, given any rate of profit, that can be sustained in an economy experiencing steady-state growth with a fixed set of techniques, and thus defines a trade-off between the rate of profit and the wage rate which is frequently described as the dual of the trade-off between capital and labour given by the aggregate production function. In view of the demise of the latter it is truly remarkable how well the notion that the former may be regarded as its dual has survived. It will be argued that the factor price frontier is a misleadingly oversimplified construct and that it would be better to dispense with it and pay more attention to the basic intertemporal Euler equation from which it is derived.

---

[15] Windfall capital gains being defined as $(K_t^t - K_t^{t-1})$ in the Lindahl case and $(K_{t-1}^t - K_{t-1}^{t-1})$ in the Hicks case. For a discussion of the problem and surveys of the literature, see Parker and Harcourt (1969), Introduction, and Kaldor (1955), Appendix to Chapter 1 (reprinted in Parker and Harcourt).

One might be tempted to speculate that the Lindahl and Hicks concepts could be made to converge by working in continuous time, but this could occur only if K_t^t were a continuous function of time, and there is no reason to suppose this to be the case. Even if it were continuous, the measures of output and capital gain over any finite time interval would be line integrals dependent on the path by which expectations had been transformed during the interval, and so an arbitrary element in the division would remain.

[16] Which, like an index of 'real' capital, substitutes arbitrariness for the effects of uncertainty.

A. THE INTERTEMPORAL EULER EQUATION

At the end of Section 4.3 it was observed that the total value of the aggregate consumption stream, taking the T years of the model together, is equal to the total value of the exogenous inputs (the initial capital stocks and labour), under the assumption of constant returns to scale. Thus, if there are N different types of initial capital good, but only one kind of consumption good and one kind of labour, as will be assumed for the time being, and if S_n is the initial stock of the nth capital good, and if C_t and L_t are consumption and employment respectively in year t, one obtains an intertemporal Euler equation of the form

$$q_1 S_1 + \ldots + q_N S_N + w_1 L_1 + \frac{w_2 L_2}{1 + i_2} + \ldots + \frac{w_T L_T}{(1 + i_2)\ldots(1 + i_T)}$$

$$= C_1 + \frac{C_2}{1 + i_2} + \ldots + \frac{C_T}{(1 + i_2)\ldots(1 + i_T)} \tag{4.11}$$

where q_n is the value of a unit of the n th capital good, measured in terms of consumption delivered at the end of year 1.

(4.11) is a disaggregated and explicitly intertemporal reformulation of (4.6), both of them being alternative ways of stating the Wicksell–Wicksteed exhaustion theorem. It defines a consistency relationship, of which the so-called factor price frontier is an artificial special case, between the interest rate in each period, the wage rate in each period, and the prices of the initial capital goods.

Its role may be illustrated by the following exercise in comparative dynamics. Consider two economies which are identical in all respects, except that in one the individuals exhibit a relatively high degree of bias in time preference in favour of early consumption. In this economy one would expect the rate of interest to be relatively high. According to the reasoning behind the traditional presentation of the factor price frontier, one would also expect the wage rate to be relatively low in this economy. But examination of (4.11) reveals a number of other possibilities which ought to be considered. First, it is likely that the relatively high rate of interest will be partly offset by relatively low prices for the capital goods: the higher the rate of interest, the smaller will be the later terms in (4.2). Second, the relatively high rate of interest may be partially offset by the adoption of a production activity which yields a relatively early consumption stream, which, after all, is intuitively what one would expect in an economy dominated by the impatient. Although these effects are likely to be accompanied by a fall in the wage rate in each year, in principle they could more than compensate for the rise in the interest rate. Just as it was demonstrated in Section 4.1 that it is possible for the price of a capital good to rise with the rate of interest, so, adapting the same example, one may demonstrate that the wage rate may, in theory, rise. This, of course, makes life awkward for those who would interpret the relationship (or the factor price frontier derived from it) as a factor price trade-off.

B. A NUMERICAL EXAMPLE

At this point, it may help to illustrate the analysis with the aid of a numerical example.[17] An economy, which lasts for 30 years, contains a number of individuals whose combined supply of labour in each year is fixed and constant and defined to be one unit. There are two goods, a consumption good and machines, and both are produced by fixed-coefficient processes which require labour and stocks of machines: in order to produce one unit of the consumption good, 0.05 units of labour and a stock of 4 machines are required, and in order to produce one machine, 0.10 units of labour and a stock of 2 machines are required. Thus

$$0.05C_t + 0.10M_t \leq 1 \qquad \text{(labour constraint)} \qquad (4.12)$$

$$4C_t + 2M_t \leq S_{t-1} \qquad \text{(capital constraint)} \qquad (4.13)$$

where

M_t = number of machines produced in year t

S_t = stock of machines at the end of year t

Capital depreciation in any year is equal to 10 per cent of the capital stock at the end of the previous year. The stock of machines at the end of year t is equal to the stock at the end of previous year less depreciation plus the production of new machines:

$$S_t = S_{t-1} - 0.1S_{t-1} + M_t = 0.9S_{t-1} + M_t \qquad (4.14)$$

The initial stock of machines, S_0, is assumed to be 30.

It will be assumed that the intertemporal consumption preference orderings of the individuals are such that equilibrium is established with a constant rate of interest of 5 per cent.[18] Equilibrium is then established with the

---

[17] For a comprehensive analysis of models of the following kind, see Bruno (1967).

[18] For example, it might be supposed that the ordering for each individual is derived from a utility function of the form

$$U = U(C_1 + bC_2 + b^2C_3 + \ldots + b^{29}C_{30})$$

with the parameter b taking the same value in each case. The indifference surfaces for each individual are then hyperplanes of the form

$$C_1 + bC_2 + b^2C_3 + \ldots + b^{29}C_{30} = \text{constant}$$

and so the equilibrium point on the aggregate consumption frontier is sustained by such a hyperplane. It follows that the rate of interest in each year is equal to $\left(\dfrac{1}{b} - 1\right)$.

Table 4.1

year	C_t	M_t	S_t	q_t	u_t	w_t
1	3.33	8.33	35.33	1.053	0.158	7.37
2	5.11	7.44	39.24	1.053	0.158	7.37
3	6.41	6.79	42.11	1.053	0.158	7.37
4	7.37	6.31	44.22	1.053	0.158	7.37
5	8.07	5.96	45.76	1.053	0.158	7.37
6	8.59	5.71	46.89	1.052	0.158	7.37
7	8.96	5.52	47.72	1.052	0.158	7.36
8	9.24	5.38	48.33	1.052	0.158	7.36
9	9.44	5.28	48.77	1.052	0.158	7.36
10	9.59	5.20	49.10	1.052	0.158	7.36
11	9.70	5.15	49.34	1.051	0.158	7.35
12	9.78	5.11	49.52	1.051	0.158	7.34
13	9.84	5.08	49.65	1.050	0.158	7.33
14	9.88	5.06	49.74	1.049	0.159	7.31
15	9.91	5.04	49.81	1.047	0.159	7.29
16	9.94	5.03	49.86	1.044	0.159	7.26
17	9.95	5.02	49.90	1.041	0.160	7.21
18	9.97	5.02	49.92	1.035	0.161	7.14
19	9.97	5.01	49.94	1.028	0.162	7.04
20	9.98	5.01	49.96	1.017	0.164	6.90
21	9.99	5.01	49.97	1.002	0.166	6.69
22	9.99	5.00	49.98	0.980	0.170	6.40
23	9.99	5.00	49.98	0.949	0.175	5.99
24	9.99	5.00	49.99	0.904	0.183	5.39
25	10.00	5.00	49.99	0.840	0.193	4.54
26	10.00	5.00	49.99	0.749	0.209	3.31
27	10.00	5.00	50.00	0.617	0.231	1.56
28	12.50	0.00	45.00	0.442	0.250	0.00
29	11.25	0.00	40.50	0.238	0.250	0.00
30	10.12	0.00	36.45	0.000	0.250	0.00

remaining variables taking the values shown in Table 4.1. The price system is given in terms of current prices. The price of a machine is q_t. The gross rental in year t, u_t, is given by $(-0.9q_t + [1 + i_i]q_{t-1})$. The wage rate is w_t. The current price of the consumption good is, by definition, unity in each year.

The behaviour of the economy can loosely be divided into three phases. In an initial phase lasting about ten years the economy begins by devoting most of its resources to the production of machines and then gradually shifts over to consumption as the stock of machines is increased.

There ensues a period of stability, which lasts through year 27. Towards the end of this period the absence of any value on the terminal stock of machines is beginning to make itself felt: the value of a machine depends exclusively on the services that it provides within the thirty-year horizon of the model, and so it falls as the terminal date approaches and the time available for the provision of such services contracts. As a consequence the value of output is reduced and the wage rate falls as well.

Eventually, as the terminal date comes into sight, it becomes no longer worthwhile to produce machines at all, and in a final phase of three years the economy gives itself over to a burst of consumption, living off its capital. The reduction in output is sufficiently severe that not all labour is employed and the wage rate falls to zero.

First, it may be observed that the intertemporal Euler equation (4.11) is satisfied: the value of the consumption stream is 140.32, and this is equal to the value of the wage stream, 107.17, plus the value of the initial capital stock, 33.16.[19]

Second, by varying the interest rate (but, for the sake of simplicity, keeping it the same in each year), one may show that the price of the initial capital good, and the wage rate in each year, are implicit functions of it. For example, if the interest rate were increased to 20 per cent, q_0 would fall from 1.05 to 0.857, and the wage rate is in each year would be lower (2.86 instead of 7.37 in year 1, 2.76 instead of 6.90 in year 10).

Third, the model may be used to illustrate the valuation of a capital good in terms of the consumption stream attributable to it, discussed in Section 4.1. Suppose that the initial capital stock were 29 instead of 30. The consumption stream would now be lower than before, the difference being {0.33, 0.24, 0.18, 0.13,...}. The value of this stream is 1.105, as it should be. Likewise, if the stock of labour were reduced by 10 per cent in year 1, the consumption stream is reduced[20] by a series {− 067, 0.44, 0.33, 0.24, 0.18,...}, equal in value to 10 per cent of the wage rate, 7.37, in year 1.

It has already been observed that in years 10–20, that is, in the years relatively unaffected by initial and terminal conditions, the economy enjoys a period of stability. In fact it is obvious that it is approximating a stationary state, and it can readily be verified that if the stock of machines were 50, the economy could continue indefinitely producing 10 units of consumption together with the 5 machines that are just sufficient to offset depreciation;

---

[19] These values are expressed in terms of consumption delivered at the end of year 1. q_0 is equal to 1.105 since the value of a machine on hand at time zero is equal to the value of 0.9 of a machine on hand at the end of year 1 (allowing for physical depreciation) plus the rental paid at the end of year 1.

[20] In the first year the output of consumption is actually increased, the production of the relatively labour-intensive machines being cut back sharply (by 1.33 of a machine) in response to the reduction of labour in that year.

and that it would maintain this structure, given an exogenous rate of interest of 5 per cent, if the price of a machine were constant at 1.053. This last condition underlines the fact that one could not expect a stationary state to ensue if one merely increased the initial stock of machines from 30 to 50: there would still be the problem of the gradual fall in the value of a machine to zero. Given the inflexibility of the model (only one technique in each sector), a stationary state would initially be maintained in physical terms, but q, u, and w would gradually alter, with the result that eventually it would not be worthwhile to produce machines and there would be a final phase of concentration on consumption. But the larger is T, the longer and the closer will be the approximation to a stationary state. And if T, becomes infinitely large, the stationary state may be regarded as representing the long-run behaviour of the economy, whatever the initial stock of machines.

It has been noted above that the wage rate in each year varies with the interest rate when T is finite, and the same is true when T becomes infinite. Hence one may write the stationary state wage rate as a function of the interest rate.[21] Table 4.2 gives some example values. It also shows the stationary-state price of the capital good.

A plot of the wage rate against the rate of interest would yield an example of the wage rate/rate of interest frontier (the factor price frontier[22]) so often encountered in the literature.

---

[21] The intertemporal Euler equation (4.11) becomes in stationary state

$$w\left(\frac{1+i}{i}\right) + q^S = C\left(\frac{1+i}{i}\right)$$

where q is the value of a unit of the capital good on hand at the beginning of the year in terms of consumption delivered at the end of the year.

If one defines q' to be the value of a unit of the capital good in terms of current consumption, one has $q = q'(1+i)$, and hence the Euler equation may be rewritten

$$w + iq'^S = C$$

In this example the relationship becomes

$$w + 50iq' = 10$$

To obtain the wage rate/rate of interest frontier, one must eliminate q' from this equation, for example by solving for q' in terms of w using the condition that the price of a unit of consumption and of a machine should equal their respective costs of production

$$1 = .05w + 4u$$
$$q' = .10w + 2u$$

where u, as before, is the gross rental earned by a machine. One obtains $q' = .075w + 0.5$ and hence the wage rate/rate of interest frontier

$$w = \frac{20 - 50i}{2 + 7.5i}$$

[22] One should, however, note that the term 'factor price frontier' has also been used to describe the relationship between the wage rate and the net rental rate on capital goods, that is, $i\phi$ where ϕ is a capital goods price index.

Table 4.2

i(%)	w	q
0	10.00	1.25
10	5.45	0.91
20	2.86	0.71
30	1.18	0.59
40	0.00	0.50

However, this frontier has been obtained in a model with just one set of techniques and one capital good. Suppose that there were alternative techniques in the consumption and capital good sectors and that there were many capital goods. A number of different stationary states would then be possible, each with its own frontier. The frontier for the whole economy is then usually defined to be the envelope of the individual frontiers. For example, the frontiers for three alternative stationary states are represented in Figure 4.2, and the frontier for the whole economy is then said to be the envelope ABCD.

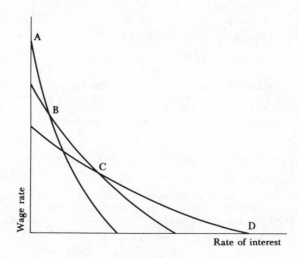

Figure 4.2

4.6 Static and dynamic choice of technique

What is the significance of such a frontier? Does it really, as is usually assumed without question, indicate which set of techniques will be adopted at a given rate of interest? If so, can it be used to order sets of techniques in terms of the rate of interest? Is it necessarily downward sloping? Does it necessarily take the form of a simple line?

First, the question of whether it indicates the set of techniques that will be adopted. One may quote Pasinetti[23] for the usual view: 'Clearly, on grounds of profitability, that technology will be chosen which – for any given wage rate – yields the higher rate of profit. Or alternatively (which comes to the same thing) that technology will be chosen which – for any given rate of profit – yields the higher wage rate.'

Before one can consider the validity of this proposition, one must clarify two crucial points. First, what assumptions are made concerning the initial stocks of capital goods? Second, having achieved one stationary state, is it possible for the economy to traverse to another, and if so, under what terms?

Let it be supposed, for expositional simplicity, that there is just one (price-taking!) firms running the economy and that its efforts to maximize its profits are responsible for the choice of technique.[24] As before, the individuals in the economy possess the initial endowments of capital goods, and they sell these and their own labour to the firm at such prices that the firm makes a zero profit. It will be assumed throughout that the intertemporal consumption preferences of the individuals interact with the activity of the firm in such a way that the rate of interest, whatever its level happens to be, is the same in each year.

Suppose that the firm has to choose between establishing two possible stationary states, A and B. Initially it will be supposed that the initial endowments of capital goods are exactly those required to maintain stationary state A. It will be supposed that the rate of interest sustaining A is i_a and that annual consumption is C^a. The firm has the choice of maintaining this state of affairs, an alternative which will be described as activity α. Or it can undertake the traverse to B, a process which will require a period of transition, say v years, during which it arranges its production in such a way as to adjust the stocks of capital goods to the new stationary state levels. This will be described as activity β. It will be supposed that consumption is $\tilde{C}_t$ in year t of the transition, and that it is C^b once the stationary state B has been established.

For the time being it will be supposed that the alteration in the consumption vector in each year is marginal, that is, that $(C^a - \tilde{C}_t)$ and $(C^a - C^b)$ are so small that the interest rate is not affected.

Given this assumption, the firm will undertake the transition to B if

---

[23] Pasinetti (1966b, p. 507). The remark is made in the context of a discussion of choice between two stationary states which could be maintained with alternative sets of fixed-coefficients techniques.

[24] The firm, of course, represents the corporate sector as a whole.

$$\sum_{t=1}^{v} (\tilde{C}_t - C^a)/(1 + i_a)^{t-1} + \sum_{t=v+1}^{\infty} (C^b - C^a)/(1 + i_a)^{t-1} > 0 \qquad (4.15)$$

For if this condition were satisfied, the firm could make a positive profit, after paying the individuals the same amounts as before for their capital goods and labour, by switching to β.

The values[25] of i_a for which the inequality becomes an equality are of special interest because they mark the critical levels of the rate of interest at which the firm switches its decision from one activity to the other. These switching points will not in general be the same as those in which the wage rate/rate of interest frontiers of A and B intersect. To keep the two sets apart, the former will be described as D-switching points and the latter as S-switching points, referring to their dynamic and comparative statics framework, respectively.

Figure 4.3 gives an example in which there are two S-switching points and two D-switching points.[26] The heavy line indicates the choice of technique. Note, in particular, that if the interest rate lies between S_1 and D_1, or between S_2 and D_2, the economy will remain in A even though B appears to be more efficient; the explanation is that the cost of the transition outweighs the subsequent benefit in terms of increased consumption, even though this is in perpetuity, at those rates of interest.

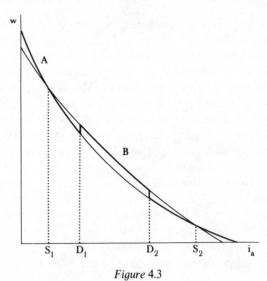

Figure 4.3

---

[25] Values, since there may be more than one. When (4.21) becomes an equation in i_a, it may have up to v real roots.

[26] The distance between the two frontiers has been exaggerated: they should be almost coincidental, since the states are only marginally different.

It should be emphasized that the diagram has been drawn on the assumption that the existing capital goods are those appropriate to A. If, instead, they were appropriate to B, and one were considering the conditions under which the economy could make a transition to A, one could draw a similar diagram with the same frontiers for A and B, but now the D-switching points, if they existed, would lie to the left of S_1 and to the right of S_2, and the heavy choice-of-technique line would be adjusted accordingly.

Under what conditions will the D-switching rates of interest be the same as the S-switching rates given by the intersections of the wage rate/rate of interest frontiers? No attempt will be made to answer this question comprehensively here.[27] However, a fairly obvious sufficient condition is that the economy should be able to divert resources from employment in the set of techniques corresponding to one stationary state directly to employment in the set corresponding to the other without underutilizing them. Suppose the economy is in stationary state A and the rate of interest is that of an S-switching point with stationary state B. Assuming the rate of interest to be constant, if B were established, without resources being wasted or lying idle, the firm could maintain the stationary state wage rate throughout the transition. The transition to B would thus be fully competitive with the alternative of continuing with A, and so the S-switching rates would also be the D-switching rates.

By way of illustration of this point, a numerical example constructed by Samuelson (1966) will be borrowed and extended. In an economy with a single consumption good and a single type of labour, there are two techniques of production. With the first, seven units of labour are employed in year t to produce an intermediate good which, without further attention, transforms itself into a unit of consumption at the end of year $t + 2$. With the second, two units of labour in year t produce an intermediate good which requires the further application of six units of labour in year $t + 2$ before turning itself into a unit of consumption in year $t + 3$.

The stationary states employing the two techniques will be labelled A and B, respectively. If in stationary state A the interest rate is i_a and the wage rate is w_a, the value of a unit of consumption, in terms of its labour input, is $7w_a (1 + i_a)^2$. But by definition this is unity, and so one has the relationship

$$7w_a(1 + i_a)^2 = 1 \qquad (4.16)$$

Similarly, if in stationary state B the rate of interest is i_b and the wage rate is w_b, the value of a unit of consumption, in terms of its labour input, is $2w_b(1 + i_b)^3 + 6w_b(1 + i_b)$, and so one has

$$2w_b(1 + i_b)^3 + 6w_b(1 + i_b) = 1 \qquad (4.17)$$

---

[27] For discussion of some aspects of this question in the context of the evaluation of the social rate of return on switching between stationary states, see Solow (1967) and Burmeister (1968). See also Spaventa (1973).

These frontiers intersect each other twice, the S-switching points being given by rates of interest of 50 per cent and 100 per cent.[28]

Let the actual process of switching from A to B now be considered. To keep the arithmetic simple, it will be supposed that 56 units of labour are supplied each year. It will be supposed that A is maintained until the beginning of year 1 and that in that year the firm diverts some of the labour to the initial stage of the B technique. If it tried to divert all 56 units of labour, it would find that in year 3, when this batch requires its second application of labour, it would need the impossible quantity of 178 units of labour to continue the production process. So to avoid either a labour shortage or labour wastage, it should perform the transition in two steps, diverting 14 units of labour from the A technique to the first stage of the B technique in year 1 and then the remainder to the second stage of the B technique in year 3.

The output of consumption, beginning in year 1, is thus $\{8, 8, 6, 6, 0, 0, ...\}$ from the technique used in A, and $\{0, 0, 0, 7, 7, 7, ...\}$ from that used in B. If the firm makes the transition, the total consumption stream will be $\{8, 8, 6, 13, 7, 7, 7, ...\}$. If it does not makes the transition and remains in stationary state A, the consumption stream will be 8 in each year. Thus the D-switching rates for the transition are given by

$$(8 - 8) + \frac{(8 - 8)}{1 + i} + \frac{(6 - 8)}{(1 + i)^2} + \frac{(13 - 8)}{(1 + i)^3} + \sum_{t=4}^{\infty} \frac{(7 - 8)}{(1 + i)^t} = 0 \qquad (4.18)$$

which simplifies to

$$2i^2 - 3i + 1 = 0 \qquad (4.19)$$

---

[28] It may be noted that here one has an example of capital reversal, that is, the value of capital per worker increasing with the rate of interest, contrary to the prediction of the aggregate neoclassical approach. In stationary state A the value of capital per worker in the form of semifinished product is $\{w_a + w_a (1 + i_a)\}$, which is equal to 3/28 when the rate of interest is 100 per cent. In stationary state B the value of capital per worker is $\frac{1}{8}(2w_b + 2w_b(1 + i_b) + 2w_b(1 + i_b) + 6W_b)$, which is equal to 5/56 at that rate of interest. Thus the switch from B to A which occurs at that level of the interest rate entails an increase of 1/56 in the value of capital.

However another prediction of the aggregate approach, that $\Delta Y / \Delta K$ should be equal to the interest rate, survives. Output per worker in stationary state A is 1/7, and in B it is 1/8, so the increase in output is also equal to 1/56 and $\Delta Y / \Delta K = i$ at the switch point. This follows from equation (4.7), which states that

$$Y_a = K_a i_a + W_a$$
$$Y_b = K_b i_b + W_b$$

It may be shown that at an S-switching point commodity prices, as well as the wage and interest rates, are the same in both stationary states, and hence one may write

$$\frac{Y_b - Y_a}{K_b - K_a} = i, \quad \text{or} \quad \frac{\Delta Y}{\Delta K} = i$$

For a more formal presentation of this result see Malinvaud (1953).

and again yields rates of 50 per cent and 100 per cent.

In this example all the resources, capital goods (in the form of work in progress) and labour, were fully utilized and the S-switching and D-switching points coincide. Suppose now that one considers a variation: the model is the same as before, except that when labour is transferred from A to B it works at only 98 per cent efficiency during the first year. The stream derived from technique B becomes $\{0, 0, 0, 6.86, 7, 7, 7, \ldots\}$ and the total stream becomes $\{8, 8, 6, 12.86, 7, 7, 7, \ldots\}$. The D-switching points are then given by

$$(8 - 8) + \frac{(8 - 8)}{1 + i} + \frac{(6 - 8)}{(1 + i)^2} + \frac{(12.86 - 8)}{(1 + i)^3} + \sum_{t=4}^{\infty} \frac{(7 - 8)}{(1 + i)^t} = 0 \qquad (4.20)$$

which yields rates of interest of 70 per cent and 72 per cent. Under these conditions, the firm will find it profitable to undertake the transition only if the rate of interest lies in the narrow range between these two figures.

If the stationary states A and B are more than marginally different, they will in general be sustained by different equilibrium interest rates and sets of relative prices, and criterion (4.15) loses its validity. Under these conditions neither the S-switching nor the D-switching rates would have any significance for choice of technique, even if it were possible to calculate them.[29] This is also the case if the initial stocks of capital goods do not correspond to either stationary state.

4.7 Implications

Despite the fact that it assumes an economy experiencing steady-state growth, and is therefore a wholly artificial construct with no practical relevance, the wage rate/rate of interest frontier has become a well-worn tool in the hands of the critics of neoclassical theory. One reason, of course is that it furnishes counterexamples to some of the more important propositions of the Clarkian view of capital and has therefore administered the *coup de grâce* to it. Given the contradictions arising from Wicksell effects, the aggregate neoclassical approach was already a terminal case, but it was a long time expiring. The foregoing analysis demonstrates that all the findings damaging to the Clarkian view that have been derived from the potential multiplicity of S-switching rates of interest continue to hold when one discards the comparative statics framework adopted in most of the reswitching literature, and gives the propositions the more natural inter-

---

[29] Equilibrium could only be determined by direct reference to production possibilities and intertemporal preferences, unless there existed a set of intermediate stationary states which provided a series of marginally different stepping stones between A and B. It would then be possible to evaluate the desirability of a traverse from A to B by evaluating the desirability of shifting to the first stepping stone from A, then to the second stepping stone from the first, and so on. For a discussion see Dougherty (1972).

pretation of referring to the long-run behaviour of a given economy with given endowments. For, as has been shown, it is possible to provide examples in which the D-switching rates and the S-switching rates are identical.

A second reason for the attention given to the frontier is that it appeared to offer a simple means of presenting one version of the Cambridge approach to functional income distribution. It was noted at the beginning of Section 4.6 that it was originally described as the 'factor price frontier' and that when derived in early numerical examples it was invariably smooth and monotonically declining, which seemed to corroborate, even to encapsulate, the notion that the higher is the reward for capital, the lower is the reward for labour. According to some Cambridge theorists, it defines the set of efficient possible outcomes, and the actual outcome is determined by political and institutional factors – collective bargaining and the like.

There has, however, been one notable study which, if its implications had been fully digested, would have helped to undermine this view. Nuti (1970) demonstrates that the wage rate/rate of interest frontier (as he is careful to call it) is not necessarily monotonically declining and, without stating the conclusion in so many words, goes much of the way to showing that the factor price interpretation is untenable.

It might be tempting to dismiss the Nuti bumps and grinds as aberrations and to suppose that the downward sloping curve is the representation of 'reality'. But such an attitude would be a throwback to the idea that the interest rate clears the "market for capital". Once it has been recognized that the role of the rate of interest (however much disguised) is to clear the market for intertemporal consumption loans, this view should be dispelled. Why should a price which clears a transfer market bear any relationship at all to a price which clears a factor market?[30]

The true significance of the frontier – that it is a special form of the intertemporal consistency relationship between the wage rate, the rate of interest, and the prices of capital goods – was obscured by the limitation of the analysis to steady-state growth and the failure to make any conceptual distinction between the rate of profit and the rate of interest.

In Section 4.4 it was argued that, until empirical considerations are adduced, there is no reason to suppose that aggregate capital should be

---

[30] Irving Fisher is particularly lucid on this point:

> The student should also try to forget all former notions concerning the so-called supply and demand of capital as the causes of interest. Since capital is merely the translation of future expected income into present cash value, whatever supply and demand we have to deal with are rather the supply and demand of future income. It will further help the student if he will, from the outset, divest himself of any preconception he may have acquired as to the role of the rate of interest in the distribution of income. It may be well here to point out that interest is not, as traditional doctrine would have it, a separate branch of income in addition to rent, wages and profits ... (It is) the most pervasive price in the whole price structure. (Fisher, 1930, pp. 32–3).

any less satisfactory a construct than its little-criticized counterpart, aggregate labour. There is, however, one important difference–the fact that, as Joan Robinson observed in the passage quoted at the beginning of that section, there is no natural physical unit for capital. And here would seem to be the origin of the confusion over the meaning of the wage rate/rate of interest frontier. Had there been an intuitively appealing unit for capital, something which would have made it possible to talk of a supply of capital in the same misleadingly precise way that one talks of a supply of labour, the dual of the aggregate production function would have been sought in the form of a relationship between the *price* of the capital good and the wage rate (as the *price* of the labour input), with the interest rate playing a parametric role. Or, a little less crudely, in the form of a relationship between the capital price index and the wage index, subject to the same kind of controversy as that surrounding the aggregate production function. And the wage rate/ rate of interest stationary state consistency relationship would never have acquired the supposed significance that it is only now beginning to shed.

5
Taxation

5.1 Introduction

In this chapter the intertemporal aspects of taxation will be examined, focusing on the incidence and effects of two of the more common forms – the income tax and the corporation tax – and on those of a third that has been forcefully advocated but never implemented on a large scale[1], the expenditure tax.[2]

Until relatively recently the great majority of studies of incidence and response employed the traditional Marshallian partial equilibrium framework. Satisfactory though such analysis may be for such limited exercises as investigating the effects of an excise tax on a single commodity, it has long been acknowledged that its validity, even as an approximation, for more broadly-based taxes is questionable. But the Gordian knot (McLure, 1975) of replacing the Marshallian framework with a general equilibrium model that was analytically tractable remained uncut until Harberger (1962) introduced a model which, with extensions and detailing, has become the standard tool of incidence analysis (McLure 1975; Homma, 1977). With the division of the economy into two productive sectors (usually identified as personal and corporate) both employing capital and labour, it permitted the

---

[1] The tax has been adopted by Ceylon. It was also introduced in India in the 1960s, but soon abandoned (Kay and King, 1978).

[2] The discussion therefore neglects atemporal aspects, for example the question of equity, and such topics as the effects of an excise tax. For an introduction to the literature, see Sandmo (1976). The discussion is further limited in that it does not consider the effects of a capital gains tax, which would be included in a fuller treatment. Analysis of capital gains taxation is greatly complicated by the fact that in practice it is usually levied on realized rather than accrued gains, which substantially reduces its impact.

systematic evaluation of the repercussions of a tax and the investigation of their dependence on such structural characteristics of the economy as the relative factor-intensities of sectoral production functions.

But in cutting one Gordian knot, its simplifying assumptions tied another. For the Harberger model's use of aggregate capital as an economic variable makes it inadequate for the analysis of the incidence of a tax which affects factor shares, for exactly the same reasons that such a framework is inadequate for explaining factor shares in the first place. Both the income tax and the corporation tax fall into this category. The same applies of course to any other model which employs aggregate capital, and equally to any that attempts to dodge the problem altogether by assuming that the interest rate is fixed. Much of the recent incidence literature has completely ignored the controversy over the measurement of capital discussed in Chapter 2, this blind spot affecting so many contributors that it would be invidious to select examples.

To analyze the effects of an income tax or a corporation tax rigourously it is therefore necessary to employ a disaggregated general equilibrium framework, and the Fisherian model in particular is well suited. Besides being more rigorous, the Fisherian analysis is simpler in some cases. For example, it handles especially well the incidence of a tax on the income from capital, to be considered in the next section. Admittedly in other cases the results can only be stated in the most general qualitative terms, but little satisfaction can be gained from precision if it is reached via dubious simplification.

Further complexity in the discussion of taxation is inevitably introduced by differing opinions over appropriate behavioural assumptions. Recently even the neoclassical mainstream has been paying increasing attention to legal and institutional constraints, but a consensus has yet to be established and in this respect any analysis must be considered conditional.

5.2 Income taxation and the 'double taxation of savings'

In his *Principles of Political Economy* (1848), John Stuart Mill asserted that

the proper mode of assessing an income-tax would be to tax only the part of income devoted to expenditure, exempting that which is saved. For when saved and invested (and all savings, speaking generally, are invested) it thenceforth pays income-tax on the interest or profit which it brings, notwithstanding that it has already been taxed on the principal. Unless, therefore, savings are exempted from income-tax, the contributors are twice taxed on what they save, and only once on what they spend. To tax the sum invested, and afterwards tax also the proceeds of the investment, is to tax the same portion of the contributor's means twice over.

This appears to have been the opening shot in a controversy which continued in fits and starts for a hundred years. The literature[3] makes curious reading, for at no point do the participants pause to consider whether or not the tax might be shifted, not even Fisher (1897, 1906, 1927, 1937, 1942), a tireless expositor of Mill's argument.[4] And yet, with the tools that he has provided, it is easily shown that a tax on interest will be completely shifted, apart from possibly minor effects on choice of production technique, if interest payments are tax-deductible (as is the case in the U.K. for firms, and also for the interest component of mortgage payments on housing, the major form of personal borrowing).

For in the taxless Fisherian model, the rates of interest in all periods are co-determined by the requirement that the loans market be cleared in all periods. If a tax is imposed, and if the market rate of interest increases so that the rate after tax is the same as before, lending and borrowing plans will be unaltered, and so the loans market will continue to be cleared in all periods.

Despite the fact that nowadays it ought to occur almost as a reflex, this simple point does not appear to have been raised in the debate over the double taxation of savings, not even when it is discussed in comparisons of the relative merits of the income and expenditure taxes.[5] But it implies that if the income tax is inferior to the expenditure tax, as is so frequently asserted, its inferiority must reside in its distortionary effects on the production decision, not the consumption decision.[6]

---

[3] For an extensive bibliography, see Fisher and Fisher (1942), pp. 249–60.

[4] The following illustration of the argument is based on an example in Fisher (1927). Similar examples may be found in Guillebaud (1935) and Meade (1978, pp. 36–7).

  Two individuals, A and B, receive income of £100. Income tax is paid at the rate of 50 per cent. A consumes the remaining £50 of his income immediately, while B invests his in a perpetual bond which yields 20 per cent per year. B thus receives £10 per year, of which £5 is paid in tax, and he consumes the remainder. The table summarizes the consumption and tax streams of the two individuals, and gives the respective present values, discounting at 20 per cent.

Year	1	2	3	4	...	Present Value
A: consumption	50	0	0	0	...	50
A: tax	50	0	0	0	...	50
B: consumption	0	5	5	5	...	25
B: tax	50	5	5	5	...	75

  By saving, B has made himself liable not only for the initial taxation of £50 in year 1 but also for a perpetual stream of £5 tax per year subsequently. The present value of his taxation is thus £75, as opposed to £50 for A, and the present value of his consumption stream is correspondingly £25 lower.

[5] For the current textbook treatment, see Musgrave and Musgrave (1973). See also Meade (1978).

[6] The fallacy in the numerical example in the footnote above originates in the use of the pre-tax rate of interest as the discount factor. Since it is the post-tax rate which is relevant to lending and borrowing decisions, the individual reaches his optimal consumption stream when his activities in the loans market have made his rate of time preference equal to the post-tax rate in all time

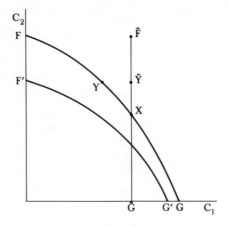

Figure 5.1

So far the production side of the analysis has been ignored. First consider the case of peasant producers with no firms. The analysis is similar to that of Section 3.6. In Figure 5.1, FG represents the production frontier for the individual, and F'G' represents the set of consumption streams available to the individual after the payment of income tax.

As a first approximation, one might expect that F'G' may be drawn simply by shrinking FG proportionately towards the origin by a factor $(1 - \theta)$. If one were considering the effects of an expenditure tax, this would be the case.

But the effects of an income tax will be slightly different. The exact consequences will depend upon the definition of income adopted, and as has been discussed in Section 4.4, this is inevitably somewhat arbitrary. Indeed, it has sometimes been suggested that income is what is defined as such by the tax authorities.

Since the usual concept of income defines it as consumption plus net investment, the relationship between the consumption stream and the income stream is likely to resemble that shown in the figure. X represents a production programme where no net investment takes place in year 1, and hence the income stream and the consumption stream are identical. Next suppose that the consumption stream Y is generated by the same production programme as X, except that there is less consumption in year 1 and correspondingly more net investment (as defined by the tax authorities). Income in year 1 will be the same as before, but income in year 2 will be greater by the amount of the

---

periods. The latter should therefore be employed as the discount factor. If this rate (10 per cent) is used in the numerical example, the present value of B's consumption stream is 50, the same as that of A. The present value of his total income is 150, as opposed to 100 for A, but the difference is absorbed by his higher tax, 100 as opposed to 50.

additional consumption generated, and hence the income stream corresponding to Y will be represented by the point $\bar{Y}$ horizontal with Y and vertically above X.

If differences in the time profile of the output of consumption could be ascribed simply to differences in the amount of net investment in year 1, the income curve corresponding to FXG would thus be the vertical line $\bar{F}X\bar{G}$.[7]

Income tax, although levied at the same rate in both years, is thus likely to weigh proportionately more heavily on consumption streams above X on the consumption frontier and less heavily on those below it. In the extreme case where the income curve is the vertical line $\bar{F}X\bar{G}$, the amount of income tax will be the same for all streams in year 1, and so the proportion of year 1 consumption absorbed will be greater than θ for streams represented by points above X, less than θ for points below it. The proportion absorbed in the second year will be θ for all streams since there is no saving. The combined effect is to make the curve F'G' in Figure 5.1 slightly flatter than FG.

The optimal production decision requires that the individual should choose the activity which generates a point on F'G' where that frontier is tangential with a market line, that is, where the post-tax rate of profit is equal to the post-tax rate of interest. This implies that, as compared with the no-tax case, the production choice of the individual should shift in the direction of C_1. For it was shown above that, if one neglected production effects, the post-tax rate of interest should be equal to the no-tax market rate of interest. Hence, if it were not for the flattening of F'G' the same technique should be chosen as before. The flattening of F'G' thus implies a shift from C_2 to C_1.

This in turn implies that each individual will typically wish to lend more or borrow less, and therefore that the aggregate lending-borrowing schedule will shift upwards. Consequently the post-tax rate of interest will be lower than the rate of interest in the no-tax case.

Hence one has an amended version of the triple equality: the rate of time preference for each individual and the post-tax rate of profit obtained by him in production should both be equal to the post-tax rate of interest.

The pre-tax rate of profit will be approximately equal to the pre-tax rate of interest. The income tax thus drives a wedge between the rate of time preference of the individuals in the economy and the pre-tax rate of profit, and thus is responsible for misallocation of resources. Present consumption is being favoured at the expense of future consumption.

The analysis is similar when firms are introduced into the picture, provided that retained earnings do not escape income tax and that there is no separate

---

[7] However, the different points on FG are also likely to reflect the adoption of different production techniques. If one may make the assumption that the non-marketed investment goods and services generated by the firm in year 1 are not fully recognized as net investment, this will have the effect of making the curve $\bar{F}X\bar{G}$ slope downwards from left to right.

corporation tax. If retained earnings were exempted, as would be the case if firms were allowed free depreciation,[8] F'G' in Figure 5.1 would be exactly the same as FG scaled down, and hence there would be no difference between the post-tax and pre-tax rates of profit.[9] The same production programme as in the no-tax case would be selected and the triple equality between the rate of time preference, the rate of profit and the post-tax rate of interest would be restored.

Of course, in most advanced economies the analysis is further complicated by the imposition of a corporation tax, and the effects of this will now be considered.

5.3 The corporation tax and the cost of capital

In the theory of financial management, the cost of capital is defined to be that rate of discount which, when used to evaluate potential investment projects, leads to the acceptance of those which increase shareholders' wealth and to the rejection of those that do not. Since it is a familiar and convenient concept, the optimal decision rules will be framed in terms of it, wherever possible.

In practice, the cost of capital is usually held to be given by the rate of discount implicit in the valuation of a firm's shares, given the expected stream of dividends. For example, if a firm is expected to maintain a dividend D per share indefinitely in the future, and P is the price of a share, the implicit discount rate applied by the market, x, is given by

$$P = \sum_{t=1}^{\infty} \frac{D}{(1+x)^t} = \frac{D}{x} \tag{5.1}$$

and so the cost of capital is given by D/P, the dividend yield. If the dividend were expected to grow at a rate g, the implicit equation would be

$$P = \sum_{t=1}^{\infty} \frac{D(1+g)^t}{(1+x)^t} = \frac{D}{x-g} \tag{5.2}$$

and so in this case x is given by $(D/P + g)$, the sum of the dividend yield and the growth rate.

In the riskless, taxless model of Chapters 3 and 4, the cost of capital is simply the market rate of interest, since its use as a discount rate leads to the optimal production decision. Risk is usually handled, in principle, by adding a risk premium to the rate of interest to obtain the cost of capital, so that

---

[8] That is, if they were allowed to offset investment expenditure against profits for tax purposes, as is currently the rule in the United Kingdom.
[9] It is assumed that firms do not use retained earnings to participate in the loans market.

$$x = \frac{D}{P} + g = \text{interest rate} + \text{risk premium} \qquad (5.3)$$

Of course neither g nor the risk premium are directly measurable, and so both approaches to the cost of capital contain an element of subjective judgement.

To take account of the effects of taxation on the cost of capital one has to return to first principles. Throughout, the cost of capital will be defined to be the discount rate to be applied to post-tax profits in project evaluation, and the risk premium will be neglected.

Three factors complicate the analysis of the effects of a corporation tax. Two of them, the deductibility of interest payments and the legal provisions concerning the treatment of depreciation, have already figured in the discussion of the income tax. The third, the question of whether borrowing is a marginal form of finance, has perhaps not received the same attention in the economic literature as it has in the financial literature and appears to have caused a certain amount of confusion.

Initially it will be assumed that firms are entirely financed by equity and that only 'true' economic depreciation may be offset against profits for tax purposes. The consequences of borrowing (and lending) and of accelerated depreciation will then be considered in turn.

A. ALL-EQUITY FINANCING

At first sight, at least, a further complication would appear to be introduced by the fact that there is no single obvious way of taxing firms. Historically the design of corporate taxes has depended on the extent to which tax authorities have considered firms to be separate entities rather than extensions of their shareholders, the extent to which they have decided to use corporate taxation as a policy instrument, and the extent to which they have simply seen corporate income as an expedient source of revenue. In the United Kingdom at least five different systems have been in force since 1947 (King, 1975a).

However, in practice it turns out that the more common variations are in fact virtually equivalent to one another, for, as King (1974) has pointed out, the most important distinguishing characteristic, the degree of discrimination against dividends, should in theory have no effect on the behaviour of the firm.[10]

Consider first the case where there is no discrimination against dividends, the 'imputation system' in force in the United Kingdom at the time of writing. Corporations are allowed a tax credit for the personal income tax paid on

---

[10] However it should be noted that several studies assert that tax discrimination does have an effect in practice. For references, see pp. 125–7 above.

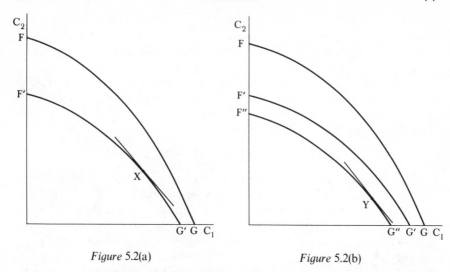

Figure 5.2(a)   *Figure* 5.2(b)

dividends, and hence the total taxation of dividends is the same as that for retained earnings. For simplicity, it will be assumed that the firm is owned by a single shareholder-manager and that his personal taxation is considered simultaneously. As usual, it is assumed that the firm acquires its inputs of capital goods at time zero and that investment in year 1 is financed by retained earnings.

Figure 5.2(a) illustrates this case. FG is the production frontier before corporation tax and F'G' after corporation tax. As in the case of Figure 5.1, F'G' is flatter than FG owing to the double taxation of retained earnings. The shareholder will choose the point X where F'G' is tangential to one of the individual's post-income-tax market lines.

Next consider the case where all corporate income is taxed at the same rate, and then dividends are additionally subjected to personal income tax (the system in force in the United Kingdom from 1965 to 1973). This is shown in Figure 5.2(b). FG and F'G' have the same significance as before. F"G" represents the possible dividend streams of the individual after the payment of corporation and personal income tax. He will choose the point Y where F"G" is tangential to a post-income-tax market line.

F"G" must be a proportionately scaled-down version of F'G', the proportional factor being $(1 - \theta)$ where θ is the rate of income tax. It therefore follows that Y must be generated by the same production activity as X, and hence that the choice of technique will be exactly the same as in the previous case.[11]

---

[11] To see this algebraically, suppose that in both cases the firm has just earned one unit of gross profit and is considering applying it to a one-year project with rate of return r.

Under the first system, immediate distribution would place $(1 - \phi)$ in the hands of the

This would also be the case if dividends were taxed more lightly than retentions. F"G" would now lie outside F'G', but it would again have the same shape, and hence the optimizing decision would lead to the use of the same production activity.

The optimal choice of technique requires that the post-corporation tax rate of profit should be equal to the post-income-tax rate of interest (and hence to the rate of time preference). If ρ is the pre-tax rate of profit and x the cost of capital, one has

$$x = \rho(1 - \phi) = i(1 - \theta) \qquad (5.4)$$

Thus, as in the case of the peasant producer discussed in the previous section, a wedge has been driven between the pre-tax rate of profit and the rate of time preference. If the rate of corporation tax is greater than the rate of income tax, the departure from pareto-optimality is more serious than before. Techniques yielding earlier consumption rather than later consumption will be even more heavily favoured. However, individuals will consequently be further biased towards lending rather than borrowing, and this should cause the rate of interest to fall, reducing this distortion.

If the rate of corporation tax is lower than that of income tax (which is only possible if the tax system is formally of the type shown in Figure 5.2(b)), the departure from pareto-optimality will be correspondingly less serious than before. Incorporation becomes a means of reducing the liability to tax of retained profits and the discrepancy between the pre-tax rate of profit and the rate of profit that would obtain in the absence of taxation diminishes.

Although, as will be seen in Chapter 8, retained earnings are the main source of equity finance, some firms occasionally resort to new issues. In terms of Figure 5.2(a), this may be justified if the optimal decision is represented by a corner solution, with the point X lying at F' and no dividend being declared in year 1. Neglecting the effects of risk, the firm must be able to

---

shareholder, where ϕ is the rate of corporation tax. Use in the project would yield $(1 - \phi)$ $(1 + r)$ gross profit at the end of the year and hence a dividend of $(1 - \phi)(1 + r)(1 - \phi)$. The rate of return on the shareholder's funds would thus be

$$\frac{(1 - \phi)^2 (1 + r) - (1 - \phi)}{1 - \phi} = (1 - \phi)(1 + r) - 1.$$

Under the second system the shareholder would receive $(1 - \phi)(1 - \theta)$ with immediate distribution, where θ is the rate of income tax. Use in the project would yield $(1 - \phi)(1 + r)$ gross profit at the end of the year, and a dividend of $(1 - \phi)(1 + r)(1 - \phi)(1 - \theta)$ after payment of corporation and income tax. The rate of return on the shareholder's funds would thus be

$$\frac{(1 - \phi)^2 (1 + r)(1 - \theta) - (1 - \phi)(1 - \theta)}{(1 - \phi)(1 - \theta)} = (1 - \phi)(1 + r) - 1$$

as before.

earn a post-corporation-tax rate of profit on such funds equal to the interest rate to be able to attract and pay subscribers, and hence the cost of capital for such funds is greater by a factor $1/(1 - \theta)$ than the cost of retained earnings, a fact which has been influential in several theories of investment behaviour discussed above, pp. 128–9.

It should be noted that it has been assumed that the basic rate of corporation tax is unaffected by the subsequent treatment of dividends. However, it may well be argued that, in a comparison of the effects of the different systems, it should be total yield of the taxation that should be held constant. In this case the rate of corporation tax in the system illustrated in Figure 5.2(b) would be lower than that of Figure 5.2(a), and the shape of F'G' (and F"G") in Figure 5.2(b) would be closer to that of FG. The distortions caused by taxation would correspondingly be reduced. By the same token, under these conditions discrimination in favour of dividends would have the opposite effects, and the distortions would be increased.

B. DEBT FINANCE AND LENDING

Now suppose that the firm is both able to borrow and lend. Initially it will be assumed that such activities merely alter the time profile of the dividend stream. Later the implications of borrowing for financing production will be considered. Throughout it will be assumed that interest payments are deductible from profits for tax purposes, as is the case in both the United

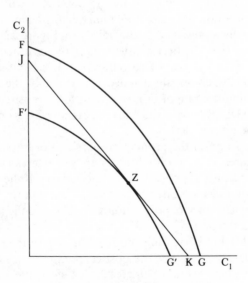

Figure 5.3

Kingdom and the United States. Equally, it will be assumed that interest received is subject to corporation tax. For simplicity, it will be assumed that the corporation tax is of the imputation type illustrated in Figure 5.2(a).

As before, FG will denote the production possibilities frontier of the firm and F′G′ the frontier after the payment of corporation tax on trading profits, as in Figure 5.2(a). Now the firm is able to modify any point on F′G′ by either borrowing or lending, effectively at the post-corporation-tax rate of interest. The optimal point on F′G′ will be that in which the post-corporation-tax rate of profit is equal to the post-corporation-tax rate of interest, the point Z in Figure 5.3. In the absence of legal restrictions, this point enables the firm to offer any of the dividend streams represented by the line JZK. The choice of a production activity associated with any other point on F′G′ would lead to a set of potential dividend streams represented by a line parallel to JZK and lower than it.

Since JZK is necessarily a straight line, the optimal point will be a corner solution, rather than the interior solution of Figure 5.2(a). J will be chosen if the rate of corporation tax is lower than the rate of income tax paid by the shareholder, and K will be chosen if it is higher. In the first case the shareholder will be able to accumulate capital faster by allowing the firm to lend on his behalf. In the second he will do better to take his dividends as soon as possible and to lend directly.

Next, one should recognize that in practice legal provisions prevent firms from borrowing to finance dividend payments. Taking this restriction into account, the potential dividend frontier becomes the line JZ and the curve ZG′. If the optimal solution is given by the point J, it will be unaffected, but if the rate of corporation tax is greater than that of income tax, the optimal solution will again be represented by the point X in Figure 5.2(a).

Finally, suppose that the firm is able to borrow in order to finance its production activity. If the rate of corporation tax is less than the rate of income tax, it will have chosen the activity represented by the point Z, where the post-corporation-tax rate of profit is equal to the post-corporation-tax rate of interest, and it will have no incentive to borrow. Thus one may confine the analysis to the reverse case.

Hitherto the position of the production possibilities frontier of the firm, FG, which measures gross profits before tax and interest payments, was determined by the equity supplied by the shareholders. If the firm is able to borrow, the position of FG ceases to be fixed. The more the firm borrows, the greater will be its choice of production activities, and the further the FG curve will lie from the origin.

For any given level of borrowing and position of FG, the point X on the corresponding curve F′G′, where the post-corporation-tax rate of profit is equal to the post-income-tax rate of interest, will indicate the optimal production activity. When the firm begins to borrow, X is likely to travel away from the origin. Under the assumption of constant returns to scale, it will travel outwards along a straight line through the origin.

In principle, the appetite of the firm for borrowing would be insatiable under these conditions. The post-corporation-tax cost of debt is $i(1 - \phi)$, but, as has just been seen, optimality requires that the pre-corporation-tax rate of profit, ρ, satisfy

$$\rho(1 - \phi) = i(1 - \theta) \tag{5.5}$$

where θ is the rate of income tax. Since ϕ is greater than θ, the cost of debt is less than the post-tax rate of profit, and the firm should finance all its investment by borrowing.

In reality, there is usually a limit to the leverage – the debt-equity ratio – that a firm can maintain, for reasons that will be discussed in Section 8.3. Thus, for a given amount of equity finance, the maximum amount of debt will be finite and debt becomes an intramarginal component of the finance of the firm. It may thus be neglected as a first approximation[12] and one returns once again to the position illustrated in Figure 5.2(a), the one change being that FG and F'G' now take account of the increase in the scale of production activities offered by the debt. The implications for choice of technique and efficiency remain the same.[13]

C. ACCELERATED DEPRECIATION

Accelerated depreciation will have much the same effect on a firm that it had in the absence of a corporation tax in Section 5.2. Free depreciation will cause the post-corporation-tax frontier F'G' in Figure 5.2(a) to have exactly the same shape as the pre-tax frontier FG. Consequently the post-corporation-tax rate of profit is equal to the pre-corporation-tax rate, and so the choice of technique is unaffected by the level of corporation tax. The rate of profit is equal to the post-income-tax rate of interest, and it has been demonstrated in Section 5.2 that this is equal to the market rate of interest that would obtain if there were no income tax, provided that production is unaffected. It thus follows that the introduction of a corporation tax with free depreciation has

---

[12] This result is approximative in the sense that it neglects the fact that a firm with maximum leverage will be able to increase its debt if it increases its equity, which will permit it to seek a lower pre-tax rate of profit on new issues, and also on retained earnings if the rate of corporation tax is greater than the rate of income tax. The financial text-books advocate the use of a hybrid cost of capital for investment financed by a mixture of equity and debt, calculated as a weighted average of the cost of equity and the cost of debt, typically on the ground that this seems 'common sense' (for example, Bromwich, 1976). But there is no justification for this. The correct procedure is to subtract the cost of servicing the debt from the cash flows and apply the appropriate cost of capital to the equity component as usual.

[13] This conclusion of course differs from that of Stiglitz (1973) and King (1975b), who base their analysis on the assumption that debt is the marginal form of finance.

the paradoxical effect of removing the distortions caused by an income tax, and the Fisherian triple equality between the rate of profit, the rate of time preference and the (post-income-tax) rate of interest is restored.[14] The imposition of a corporation tax under these conditions amounts to a once-and-for-all lump-sum tax on the shareholders of the firm.

As a corollary, an accelerated depreciation system which represents a compromise between true and free depreciation may be expected to go some way to removing the distortions.

5.4 Expenditure taxation

Fisher's advocacy of the expenditure tax followed from his view that consumption, rather than income as conventionally defined, should be regarded as a central objective of economic activity. It was part and parcel of a campaign which even included an effort to alter the English language by redefining income as consumption. Largely through his influence a bill for the restriction of taxation to expenditure was introduced to the United States Congress by Ogden L. Mills in 1921.[15]

This was not the first time that an expenditure tax had been officially considered, for as Kaldor (1955) relates, Mill had pressed his view before the Select Committee on Income and Property Tax of 1861. Kaldor's own carefully mounted advocacy of the expenditure tax is based on the grounds that consumption represents the exercise of economic power and indicates taxable capacity, an opinion which differs from that of Fisher perhaps more in emotion than substance. Like Fisher, he argues that an expenditure tax should replace corporate taxation as well as income taxation, in as much as the former is principally an extension of the latter. The effects of an expenditure tax will be investigated making this assumption.

Returning to Fisher's two-year model, suppose that an individual peasant producer has the production frontier FG in Figure 5.4. The optimal production decision is represented by the point X where FG is tangential to a market line PQ, and in the absence of taxation the optimal consumption stream is represented by the point A.

The imposition of an expenditure tax does not affect directly either the

---

[14] For a simple algebraic proof, see Stiglitz (1976, pp. 303–4). Flemming (1976) reaches similar conclusions but under a different set of assumptions: he assumes that debt is the marginal form of finance and his result depends upon the corporation and personal tax rates being equal, and upon interest being tax-deductible.

The result is at variance with that of Samuelson (1964), who regards free depreciation as bribery, but his discussion appears to overlook the distortions caused by income tax. Here one has a classic example of 'second best analysis', where a measure which would introduce distortions in an otherwise pareto-optimal system actually removes them in a system which is imperfect.

[15] See Mills (1921) and Fisher and Fisher (1942, pp. 208–9).

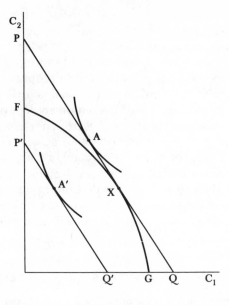

Figure 5.4

income from production or the interest from lending, and so its impact may simply be represented by a proportional inward shift of PQ to P'Q'. The new optimal consumption decision is given by the point A', provided that government expenditure is not perceived as a substitute for consumption in either year. P'Q' has the same slope as PQ since interest as such is not taxed.

If the indifference curves are homothetic, the result of the expenditure tax is just to scale down the individual's lending or borrowing plans proportionately. If the same is true for all the individuals in the economy, the original rate of interest will continue to clear the loans market. The rate of interest will thus alter only if the indifference curves are heterothetic or if government expenditure is non-neutral in its effects. There would appear to be no *a priori* reason for expecting a substantial bias in either direction, and hence the expenditure tax may be regarded as nearly perfect, in as much as it leaves the triple equality undisturbed: the rate of time preference of each individual and his rate of profit in production are both equal to the market rate of interest. In the absence of corporate taxation, this conclusion would not be altered by the introduction of firms.

When first conceived, the expenditure tax was dismissed as impracticable in the face of the apparently insuperable obstacle of assessment. Clearly it would be futile to attempt to persuade individuals to keep direct records of expenditure. But, as was eventually pointed out by Fisher, it is possible to measure expenditure implicitly using existing income returns supplemented by the statements of wealth that, with the advent of capital gains, wealth and gifts taxes, are in any case increasingly being incorporated in tax returns in the more developed countries. It is from this point of departure that Kaldor, and Kay and King, put forward their proposals.

In view of the heterogeneity of its advocates, it is perhaps rather strange that the campaign for the expenditure tax is dormant today.[16] It is one of the very few practical matters of significance where major neoclassical and non-neoclassical writers have found themselves in agreement. In principle, a flat-rate income tax together with a corporation tax subject to free depreciation should have similar effects, as has been demonstrated in the previous section. But it may be argued that imperfections in the capital market are likely to interfere with the necessary adjustment in the pre-tax market rate of interest, and in any case further complications will be introduced by progressive taxation.

5.5. The progressive income tax and the progressive expenditure tax

It is generally accepted, in theory if not always in practice, that the burden of taxation should fall proportionately more heavily on those individuals who are most able to afford it. The imposition of relatively high sales taxes on luxury goods may be seen as one means of implementing this principle, and perhaps also the corporation tax might be seen in this light, in as much as the personal ownership of shareholdings is largely confined to those who are richest.[17] But at best both of these methods of introducing progressiveness are clumsy and feeble. The traditional vehicle is therefore the personal income tax, despite the opportunities that it offers for evasion.

The following discussion will investigate the effects of first the progressive income tax, and secondly, its possible alternative, the progressive expenditure tax, on the rate of interest, the rate of profit and the behaviour of firms. To simplify the analysis, it will be assumed that individuals fall into two classes, the rich and the poor, the latter paying the tax at a standard rate and the former at a higher rate. It will be assumed throughout that government expenditure is neutral and that each individual possesses homothetic intertemporal indifference curves.

---

[16] However, the recent report of the Meade Committee (Meade, 1978) and the lucid advocacy of Kay and King (1978) may stimulate a renewal of interest. Kay and King note that the tax has recently been the subject of official studies in the US and Sweden.

[17] However, in the United Kingdom the proportion of total corporate equity held by institutions (pension funds, life assurance companies, etc.) is greater than the proportion held directly by individuals, and it is still growing (Moye, 1971; Revell, 1975; Erritt and Alexander, 1977).

A. THE PROGRESSIVE INCOME TAX

First, suppose that it is possible to neglect the production side of the analysis, assuming for example that each individual earns his income through supplying fixed amounts of labour. It was shown in Section 5.2 that if there were a single rate of income tax, the market rate of interest would rise to offset it exactly and leave the post-tax rate of interest unaltered.

If the rich are now taxed more heavily, their market lines will be flatter than before. Assuming as usual that income effects do not outweigh substitution effects, they will lend less or borrow more than before. In aggregate there will be excess borrowing and the rate of interest must rise. In equilibrium the post-tax rate of interest of the poor will be higher, and that of the rich lower, than the original rate of interest. This implies that, as a group, the rich will be lending less to the poor, or borrowing more from them, than before.

Next, consider the effects on production, assuming an economy of peasant producers. In Section 5.2 it was argued that if there were only one class of taxpayers, there would be excess saving if the post-tax rate of interest were maintained at the original rate. For the post-tax production frontier would be flatter than the pre-tax frontier, causing a bias towards techniques with higher C_1/C_2 ratios.

Figure 5.5 shows the situation with two classes of taxpayers. FG is the pre-tax production frontier, $F_p G_p$ the post-tax frontier if the individual is poor, $F_r G_r$ the post-tax frontier if he is rich. $F_r G_r$ is flatter than $F_p G_p$ and both are flatter than FG, owing to the effects of the double taxation of reinvested earnings.

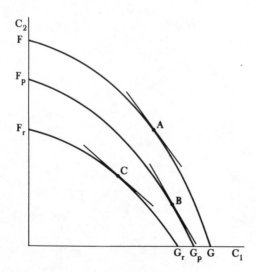

Figure 5.5

A represents the optimal production technique in the absence of tax, B the optimal technique for a poor individual and C for a rich one, assuming that the rate of interest has adjusted as in the fixed incomes case just described.

Since the post-tax rate of interest for the poor is higher than the old rate of interest, B is lower down $F_p G_p$ than before. Likewise since the post-tax rate for the rich is lower, C is higher up $F_r G_r$ than it would be if there were no poor. The bias towards techniques with a high C_1/C_2 ratio is thus increased for the poor, but decreased for the rich.

It is not obvious whether or not there is an increase in the overall bias towards a higher C_1/C_2 ratio, and hence excess saving and a lower rate of interest. It will depend, among other things, on the exact legal definition of income for tax purposes, the relative proportions of rich and poor, and their relative rates of income tax.

Finally, introduce companies and corporate taxation. It will be assumed that the latter is of the imputation type described in Section 5.3. FG and F′G′ in Figure 5.6 represent the production frontier before and after the payment of corporation tax. B and C represent the optimal production decisions from the point of view of the poor and the rich respectively, assuming for each class the post-tax rate of interest established in the fixed incomes case discussed at the beginning of this section.

If the company has both rich and poor shareholders, its management is unable to satisfy both groups simultaneously. The market line of the poor through C is lower than that through B, and that of the rich through B

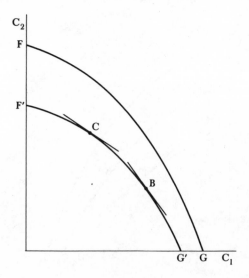

Figure 5.6

lower than that through C. Any compromise between the points B and C will leave both groups dissatisfied.

The natural outcome will be for companies to specialize. Those with the greater growth prospects may be expected to attract rich shareholders, while those offering a higher yield will attract the poor. As Wood (1975) has argued,[18] once a company has attracted a certain clientele, its management is likely to respond to its interests. The effect will then be to make the specialization complete, with shareholders who are being discriminated against switching to companies with more appropriate policies.

The general effects will thus be much the same as in the peasant producers case, with one small difference. The post-tax production frontier of a company with rich shareholders will not be as flat as it would be if the production were in the hands of a single rich peasant, because retained earnings reinvested will be taxed only at the rate of corporation tax, not the rate of income tax for the rich.[19] The production decision taken by the company may therefore be expected to be less biased in the direction of techniques with high C_1/C_2 ratios. This in turn implies that there will be a tendency for shareholders to lend less or borrow more, and hence there should be upward pressure on the rate of interest. Of course the same applies in reverse to companies owned by poor shareholders.

To summarize, the overall effect of the introduction of progressive income taxation will depend upon the relative proportions of rich and poor. If it may be assumed that the rich own the greater proportion of the means of production,[20] either in incorporated or unincorporated form, progressive taxation will result in the choice of techniques with low C_1/C_2 ratios, a tendency towards excess borrowing and a rise in the rate of interest.

It was shown that in the absence of production effects, the post-tax rate of interest of the poor would be higher, and that of the rich lower, than the rate of interest obtaining in the absence of all taxation. Taking into account the production effects, the post-tax rate of interest of the poor will be higher still, while that of the rich might be either higher or lower than the old rate.

B. THE PROGRESSIVE EXPENDITURE TAX

If the expenditure tax were levied at a flat rate, it could simply be collected in the form of a uniform sales tax applied to all final goods and services. However, if such a tax were to replace the personal income tax and the corporation

---

[18] See especially p. 49 *et seq.*

[19] It is implicitly assumed that the rate of income tax of the rich is greater than the rate of corporation tax. If this is not the case, the argument goes the other way.

[20] An assumption which is secularly becoming less valid in the United Kingdom with the increasing proportion of all shares owned by insurance companies and superannuation funds (see p. 84n).

tax, it would have to be progressive and therefore collected directly from the individual.

It was argued in Section 5.4 that a flat rate expenditure tax would be unlikely to have any significant effect upon the market rate of interest and choice of technique. Provided that intertemporal indifference curves are homothetic and government expenditure neutral, neither the slopes of the market lines of individuals nor the production frontiers of firms would be affected, and hence lending/borrowing plans would be the same as in the absence of the tax, except that they would be scaled down proportionately. The rate of interest would thus be unaltered.

By the same token, as a first approximation, a progressive expenditure tax would also leave the market rate of interest and the choice of technique unaltered. If there could be any effect, it would have to have its origin in the fact that some lending/borrowing plans are scaled down more than others, and would depend upon exploiting some association between the level of expenditure of an individual and the shape of his intertemporal indifference curves.

Dropping the assumption of homotheticity, one might hypothesize that the poor are relatively biased towards present consumption, compared with the rich (this would be an interpretation of the Duesenberry (1949) relative income hypothesis in the present context). If this is the case, taxing the rich more heavily should have the effect of reducing lending rather than borrowing, and accordingly one might expect a corresponding increase in the rate of interest.

Apart from the possibility of arguments of this nature, the expenditure tax remains ideal from the Fisherian point of view. The triple equality between the rate of time preference of each individual, the rate of profit in production, and the market rate of interest would be conserved, and it is difficult to argue that the equilibrium rate of interest would be substantially different from that obtaining in the absence of the tax.

5.6 Conclusions

The discussion in this chapter has been restricted to the standard two-year Fisherian model. Of course it could be extended to a multi-period framework, but it is doubtful whether this would change the results in qualitative terms. It is simpler to interpret the two years as 'the near future' and 'the medium-term future' and regard the analysis as determining average, medium-term rates of interest, profit and time preference.

The results that have been obtained depend, needless to say, on the validity of the Fisherian assumption – that individuals do possess some notion of time preference and are able to transform consumption streams by borrowing and lending, that companies do maximize the discounted value of their profits using the rate of time preference of their shareholders as a discount rate, and that money does not play a significant role – points which will be discussed at length in Chapters 7 and 8. One may make one specific point with regard to the second: if the management of companies is in fact willing to trade profitability for growth, as is suggested in Chapter 8, this would be represented in the present framework by a bias towards techniques with low C_1/C_2 ratios. The post-corporation-tax rate of profit is now lower than the post-income-tax rate of interest and therefore lower than the rate of time preference of the individuals owning the company; but the discrepancy between the rate of time preference and the pre-tax rate of profit has been reduced.

To summarize the results, it has been shown that, from a Fisherian point of view, a progressive expenditure tax (or almost equivalently, income tax coupled with a corporation tax offset by free depreciation) is superior to any other form of taxation in as much as it leaves the triple equality undisturbed and does not distort incentives. In particular, it does not give rise to the major inefficiency of income and orthodox corporate taxation, the driving up of the pre-tax rate of profit with its inhibiting effects on growth.

6
Public investment criteria

6.1 Introduction

It need hardly be said that the determination of public investment criteria is one of the most important applications of welfare economics. It is also one of the most difficult and contentious. One may readily find in the literature instances of contributors agreeing on basic principles and yet arriving at apparently irreconcilable conclusions.

The differences frequently originate in quite minor variations in assumptions, and a recent and welcome development in the literature has been the growing recognition that such discussions must specify explicitly both the notion of efficiency employed (if efficiency is a guiding principle) and a full-blooded model which permits a systematic evaluation of the effects of public investment from the standpoint of this notion. Such models help one to avoid the pitfalls of oversimplification and make it possible to locate the sources of differences of opinion.

Within the neoclassical approach, general equilibrium analysis almost automatically provides a suitable framework,[1] and the Fisherian model, which is especially convenient, will be employed here. The discussion will be close to that of Sandmo and Drèze (1971), who depart from the Fisherian model in only minor details.[2] James (1969) and Ramsey (1969) reach similar conclusions.

---

[1] It should, however, be emphasized that the general equilibrium analysis should be on Arrow–Debreu lines. The aggregate neoclassical model is as unsatisfactory in this context as it is in the analysis of the effects of taxation.

[2] For a comparison of the Sandmo–Drèze model with the well-known (aggregate neoclassical) analysis of Arrow (1966) (developed by Kay, 1972), see Drèze (1974).

The purpose of the discussion is to outline in general terms the issues at stake. It will be assumed throughout that a public investment project will necessarily absorb resources which would otherwise have been used in the private sector and that it is not large enough to affect prices and interest rates.

Under these conditions the general principle can be presented deceptively simply: since individual preferences form the fundamental criteria for comparing consumption streams, the correct social discount rate is the subjective rate of time preference. Assuming that distribution effects may be neglected, a public investment project should be adopted if and only if the consumption stream yielded by it has a higher present value, calculated using the rate of time preference, than the social value of the resources absorbed by it.

The problem with this rule is that it is difficult to measure unambiguously the social value of the resources employed unless there is no taxation, no uncertainty and no externalities. Further complications arise if the rate of time preference is not unique, as, for example, when there exists a progressive income tax.

In the absence of such factors, the application is straightforward enough. The market rate of interest measures both the rate of time preference of each individual in the economy and the rate of profit in each production programme. The present value, discounted at the rate of time preference, of the consumption stream yielded by a displaced private project is hence exactly equal to the market value of the resources employed. It is therefore necessary and sufficient that the present value of the consumption stream yielded by the government project be greater than its market cost. The unadjusted market rate of interest may thus, in this case, be taken as the social discount rate, given that it directly measures the rate of time preference.

Problems arise when the social value of the displaced private production programme is different from the market value of the resources employed, as is generally the case with taxation, and some of the issues discussed in the previous chapter return with a vengeance. Further complications arise when the effects of risk and uncertainty are taken into account. These will be discussed in turn.

6.2   The effects of taxation

A. INCOME TAX

In Section 5.2 it was shown that the imposition of an income tax would cause the market rate of interest to rise so that the rate after tax was approximately the same as previously. If production effects could be neglected, the approximation would be good. Taking into account the bias caused by an income tax towards techniques yielding relatively early consumption and excess lending, the post-tax rate could be expected to be somewhat lower than the original rate.

The introduction of income taxation does not affect the status of the rate of time preference, now equal to the post-tax rate of interest, as the ultimate criterion for evaluating changes in consumption streams, and hence as the appropriate choice for a social discount rate.

But it does mean that one has to be careful in assessing the social cost of a public sector project. In particular, one has to distinguish between the cases where the resources displaced from the private sector were formerly used exclusively for the production of consumption in the present time period or for a production programme which yielded a consumption stream over time; in traditional macroeconomic terms, whether the displacement of resources has resulted in a reduction of consumption or investment.

If the public sector project only displaces consumption in the present period, no difficulties are encountered. But a problem arises if it displaces a private investment project. Since the pre-tax rate of profit will be higher than the post-tax rate,[3] if the private project has a zero net value, after taking resource costs into account, when discounted at the pre-tax rate of profit, it will almost certainly have a positive present value when discounted at the rate of time preference, which is equal to the post-tax rate.[4]

In other words, the social value of the resources used in the displaced private project is greater than the nominal value of the taxation or public borrowing used to acquire them. In this case a present value greater than the market cost does not guarantee that the public sector project is desirable. It might well displace a private project with a still higher social value.

Faced with this problem, some authors have suggested that the social discount rate should be superseded by a concept of social opportunity cost, typically defined as the private pre-tax rate of profit. The justification for this is the fact that an optimal social allocation of resources requires equality between the private and public sector rates of profit. Time preference is banished from the analysis, albeit with misgivings.[5]

However, this alternative ignores the problems posed by the second best. As is well known, unless the government is willing to eliminate all the distortions in an economy, the criteria appropriate in an optimal resource allocation will not necessarily be reliable guides to improved efficiency.

---

[3] As has been argued in Section 5.2, there will be a discrepancy caused by the effective double taxation of reinvested savings (as implicitly defined by the tax authorities in their definition of income). It should not be thought that taxation in itself is sufficient to cause a discrepancy between the pre-tax and post-tax rates of profit: see the case of the expenditure tax.

[4] It is conceivable, but empirically unlikely, that a reduction in the discount rate might cause a fall in the present value.

[5] See notably Baumol (1968). For a discussion see Nichols (1969), Landauer (1969), Usher (1969) and Baumol (1969), and the contributions of James and Ramsey already cited. For an earlier attempt to define social opportunity cost, see Marglin (1963b).

In this case, unless the government is willing to undertake investment on such a scale as to eliminate the distortions introduced by the income tax, there is no reason to suppose that the adoption of the private sector rate of profit for the public sector will lead to an improvement in social welfare. Indeed there are several good reasons why it should not.

In the first place, in altering the criterion in an attempt to cover the case where private investment is displaced, one has undermined its validity in the case where current consumption is displaced. Suppose that the present value of the public project is just negative when discounted at the private pre-tax rate of profit. If instead the rate of time preference (as measured by the post-tax rate of profit) were used as the discount rate, its present value would almost certainly be positive. Hence if one could be sure that the project displaced only current consumption (in which case there would be no need to adjust the value of the resources used), it should be accepted. But according to the social opportunity cost criterion it would be rejected.

Second, the social opportunity cost criterion is not necessarily valid even when private investment is displaced.

Suppose that the present values of the private and public projects under consideration have profiles as shown in Figure 6.1. The private project has rate of return r_p, the private (pre-tax) rate of profit. The public project has a slightly lower rate of return, r_g, and according to the social opportunity cost criterion it should be rejected. But if the profiles cross, as they do in the figure,[6] it is possible that the public project will have the higher present value

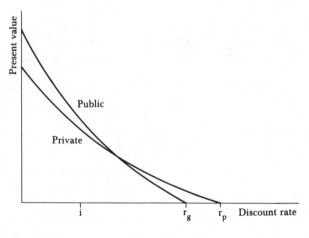

Figure 6.1

---

[6] This is likely to happen if the benefits of the public project are spread further into the future than those of the private project.

when discounted at the rate of time preference, measured by the post-tax rate of interest, i. If this is the case, the public project should in fact be preferred to the private one.

Ideally, of course, both should be accepted, and current consumption should be reduced instead. But the distortion caused by the income tax removes any incentive for the private sector to undertake such a substitution.

There is in fact no easy solution to the problem. At one extreme, if the public sector project affects only current consumption, the market will measure the true value of the resource costs involved. At the other, with the project financed exclusively by releasing resources from infinitely long-lived private investment projects, the cost should be multiplied by a factor of r_g/i to measure its true social value. The benefits yielded by the public sector project, dicounted at i, would have to be greater than this adjusted cost if the project is to be accepted.

To evaluate the efficiency of a public sector project, the authorities thus have to know in advance the extent to which the income tax is paid by giving up resources which would otherwise have been used by private projects, and it would have to know exactly which private projects would be abandoned.

Sandmo and Drèze (1971) assume that the government has knowledge of the utility functions of all individuals and of the production possibility frontiers of all firms, and they are then able to derive an efficient social discount rate which is a weighted average of pre-tax and post-tax interest rates, the weights being the partial derivatives of investment and compensated consumption with respect to the pre-tax interest rate.[7]

Without such knowledge, the choice of the correct social valuation to place on the cost of the public project would appear to be mostly a matter of intuition, within the limits imposed by the consumption-investment extremes. Perhaps as important a factor as any would be the effect of the project on private sector expectations.

Progressive income taxation causes an insuperable problem in as much as it gives rise to a dispersion in the rate of time preference. The rich will adjust to post-tax rates of interest which are lower than those of the poor, and therefore they will have lower rates of time preference. Use of the rate of time preference of the former will lead to the selection of projects which, in the eyes of the latter, unduly favour deferred consumption at the expense of current consumption. Use of the rate of the latter leads to projects which unduly favour current consumption, from the point of view of the former. The choice of the social discount rate thus acquires a political dimension, a

---

[7] For similar conclusions see Diamond (1968) and (within a highly aggregated model) Harberger (1972).

corollary of the more overtly political decision to institute progressive income taxation in the first place.

B. CORPORATION TAX

The argument that the social discount rate should be equated with the rate of time preference is not affected by the introduction of corporate taxation. But, as has been shown in Section 5.3, a corporation tax (for example, of the imputation type) is likely to exacerbate the departure from pareto-optimality by increasing the divergence between the rate of time preference of individuals and the pre-tax rate of profit, and hence the divergence between the technological rates of transformation in the private and public sectors. It therefore becomes all the more necessary to determine what proportion of the taxation financing a public project is paid by reducing private investment, and to estimate the true social value of this proportion.

C. EXPENDITURE TAXATION

An expenditure tax, of course, avoids these problems. For even if it is progressive, the triple equality between the rate of time preference of each individual, the rate of profit in private production and the market rate of interest continues to hold, and it should simply be extended to embrace the social discount rate as well.

6.3 Risk and uncertainty

It is a commonplace that a firm will undertake a risky investment project only if it yields an unusually high rate of profit. The difference between profit and the risk-free rate is known as the risk premium, and it is reflected in the rate of interest that the firm would have to pay if it had to borrow in order to finance the project (unless the firm is able and willing to insure against the contingencies in question, in which case it is reflected in the insurance premium).

It is traditionally argued that, other things being equal, the social discount rate should be equal to the risk-free market rate of interest and should not include a risk premium, even when inherently risky projects are being considered. The main reason is that society as a whole can carry its own insurance in a way that individuals and firms cannot. Whereas an individual or firm may be significantly affected by the outcome of a single investment project, for society as a whole the law of large numbers operates to smother the effects of chance, provided that none of the projects is on a mammoth scale. If a single project were of significant size, marginal analysis would not be appropriate in any case.

There are, however, two further points to consider. First, although one might decide not to add a risk premium to the market rate of interest in order to obtain the social discount rate, one should take into account the fact that the market rate of interest itself has already been affected by risk and uncertainty. As Baumol (1968) points out, the market rate of interest will prove, *ex post*, to have been too high if individuals and firms are risk-averse. For they will be induced to choose production programmes which favour earlier rather than later consumption, and this may be expected to cause an upward bias in the rate of interest. This in turn implies that, by way of compensation, the social discount rate should be set somewhat below the market rate of interest.

The second point concerns the difference between the social and private valuations of specific risky private projects displaced by public projects. It is of course an issue that has already been raised, though for different reasons, in the section on taxation. For a marginal, risky, private investment project, the present value of the benefits will be equal to the costs if the discount rate includes the risk premium considered appropriate by the private entrepreneur. It follows that from the point of view of society as a whole, which has no need to include a risk premium when discounting, the value of the benefits will almost certainly exceed those of the costs. In other words, the social value of the resources employed exceeds the nominal value.

The implications are parallel to those in the case of taxation. To evaluate a public project correctly, one should identify which (if any) private projects are displaced and treat the cost of the resources absorbed from them as the present value of their benefits (pre-tax, if there is taxation) discounted at the simple market rate of interest (post-tax, if there is taxation). If any adjustment be made to the latter, it should not be an upward one to allow for the riskiness of the public project, but a downward one to allow for the general upward bias described in the first point.

6.4   Interdependence

For the purposes of the present analysis, personal interdependence can be classified into two main categories: interdependence of utility, where the preference ordering of individual A is affected by the utility of individual B, and behavioural interdependence where it is affected by the actual consumption pattern of individual B. Strictly speaking, the first category may be considered to be a special subcategory of the second, but it is convenient to attempt to maintain the distinction because the former is likely to stimulate collective action via the public sector.

Neither has been investigated in the exposition of the Fisherian model. The first has been analyzed in detail by Sen (1967) within the framework of what he terms the isolation paradox (Sen, 1961), the possible willingness of individuals to undertake jointly an action that they would not be prepared to undertake separately. It may be subclassified into intragenerational and inter-generational interdependence. The former is traditionally taken into account by the schemes for progressive taxation and relief for the very poor that prevail in most countries, and there would not appear to be any reason to suppose that it should influence public investment criteria. But the latter, which has been discussed at length by Marglin (1963a), raises rather different issues.

Marglin argues that, if it were the policy of society as a whole to take into account the welfare of unborn generations, the market rate of interest would be an inappropriate guide to the social discount rate, in as much as it is determined by the preference orderings of individuals actually in existence. The public sector should be willing to undertake projects which favour deferred consumption to an extent which could not be justified by simple reference to the market rate of interest, in other words, it should be prepared to employ a discount rate which is lower.

Before evaluating this position, it should be noted that even in the narrow-est version of the Fisherian model, where each individual is absolutely selfish and his intertemporal preference ordering is based solely on his personal consumption, one generation will bequeath a substantial inheri-tance to the next, taking society as a whole.

For although each individual may leave a negligible estate, he will build up a stock of assets during his lifetime, either for direct use in production as a peasant producer, or at one remove from production as a shareholder in a firm, or in the form of bonds or other lending in the loans market. And since individual lifetimes overlap each other, the aggregate stock of capital goods per capita will be of the same order of magnitude as the average stock over an individual's lifetime. The difference between the two will depend upon changes in technology, changes in tastes, and demographic factors. But broadly speaking, even in this model one may expect the aggregate capital stock to be substantial and growing.[8]

Keeping this in mind, Marglin's position is vulnerable on at least two grounds. First, the welfare of future generations is already taken into account privately to some extent in most market economies. As has previously been noted, it may be argued that it is more realistic to conduct Fisherian analysis in terms of households rather than individuals, and from the household, with its finite life, it is but a short step to the indefinite continuity of the family. And one expression of this continuity is the transmission of wealth from one generation to the next. From a theoretical point of view, this implicitly means that the intertemporal preference ordering of the household extends

---

[8] For this reason Marglin's use of a model in which one generation replaces the previous one at a single moment in time is misleading. For an extended discussion of this point, see Lind (1964).

beyond the lifetime of the present head or decision-maker. But this does not involve any alteration in principle to the model, for such an extension will automatically be taken into account in the determination of the lending/borrowing plans of the household and hence in the determination of the market rate of interest. A society in which families place importance on the accumulation of capital goods for the benefit of their descendants may be expected *ipso facto* to have a relatively low market rate of interest, other things being equal. If the social discount rate is to be set lower than the market rate of interest, it must be argued that private accumulation for inheritance is not enough, or perhaps that its distribution is socially undesirable and that such fiscal or other measures that might be used to ameliorate it are impracticable or inefficient.

A second point (raised by Tullock, 1964) concerns the general principle of intergenerational equity. Judging by the current rate of technical progress, one may expect the next generation to enjoy a higher, much higher, standard of living, even after making allowance for the abuse of the environment and the side-effects of the growth of the population. The use of a low social discount rate would thus be tantamount to the poor subsidizing the rich, hard to justify under any circumstances.[9] As Addison (1714) wrote, 'most people are of the humour of an old fellow of a college, who, when he was pressed by the Society to come into something that might redound to the good of their successors, grew very peevish; "We are always doing", says he, "something for posterity, but I would fain see posterity do something for us."'[10]

A further issue, discussed by Mishan (1971), concerns the political accountability of the public sector. Unless the government has been elected on a platform of building for the future, it may be argued that it should act strictly in the interest of the existing electorate, and hence that adjustment of the social discount rate should not even be deliberated.

One final, less narrowly economic, consideration. If society as a whole derives satisfaction from the thought of leaving behind monuments to itself in the form of public works, then at last one has a case for lowering the social discount rate. But this is an argument which should be treated with some circumspection, for much of our present heritage was conceived and executed simply in the interest of those responsible for it, and the fact that subsequent generations have benefited was a minor or negligible factor.

Behavioural interdependence is altogether a different matter and one might argue that, as a first approximation, it may be neglected. For although, following Duesenberry (1949), such interdependence might increase the rate

---

[9] Nevertheless Sen (1967) has presented a case. But his model, like that of Marglin, assumes non-overlapping generations. For a critique, see Lecomber (1977).

[10] Quoted by Koopmans (1967).

of saving of those with the highest incomes, it would also reduce the rate of those with the lowest, and while there is no reason to suppose that the two tendencies exactly offset each other, there is likewise no obvious reason to suppose a significant net effect on aggregate saving and the market rate of interest.

But this argument presupposes that the average rate of saving is unaffected by interdependence. If, however, interdependence is a major factor, the norm or average rate of saving may very well be determined by chance and historical factors, self-perpetuating once it has been established. The Fisherian model, based as it is on self-interest, breaks down, and the market rate of interest ceases to be a useful guide to time preference. Indeed, under these conditions it is difficult to attach a meaning to time preference.

An intermediate, and perhaps more realistic, position would be to suppose that the conventional (independent preferences) approach offers an adequate guide to long-run behaviour at average income levels, but that interdependence may be responsible for significant lags in short-run adjustment. An example can be found in the wartime financing of defence expenditure via the voluntary purchase of Victory Bonds or War Loan Stock, with patriotic fervour providing a stimulus to compensate for any insufficiency in normal market demand.

6.5 Conclusions

Enough has been said to show that even in the rarified world of the Fisherian model the determination of public investment criteria is a complex matter. First, there is the problem of the correct social valuation of the resources absorbed by public investment. Second, there is the question of whether the discount rate should be set lower than the post-tax market rate of interest, to offset the upward bias caused by the effects of risk, or to take account of intergenerational interdependence, or both.

But third, and almost certainly most important of all, there is the question of whether the post-tax market rate of interest remains a reasonable guide to time preference when one departs from the Fisherian model and looks at what happens in practice. This is one of the issues that will be discussed in the next two chapters. The implications for public investment criteria will be reviewed in Chapter 12.

7
Critique of Fisher

7.1 Introduction

Chapter 4 took the Fisherian analysis of Chapter 3 and elaborated on it with the aim of making it more relevant to a modern economy and of investigating the significance and limitations of such concepts as aggregate capital and the wage rate/rate of interest frontier. The development was entirely technical. It is now time to face up to reality and to assess how plausible the model remains when its simplifying assumptions are relaxed.

This is a much more demanding task, both because one can no longer employ the analytical framework as a compass, and because, in the present context, the degree to which it enjoys empirical support is bound to be a matter of contention right down the line.

As its critics tirelessly point out, the Fisherian model depends upon the assumptions of perfect foresight, profit maximization by firms, and the existence of intertemporal preference orderings for individuals. It ignores uncertainty in all its forms, monetary phenomena, short-run dynamics, market imperfections, institutional rigidities and the fact that neither individuals nor firms can be portrayed, at least in narrowly economic terms, as ceaselessly striving to maximize subject to constraint. So how is it possible that the majority of the profession both recognizes these problems and yet continues to pay tribute to the Fisher-based neoclassical model?

The present chapter and the next attempt to answer this question and to judge how much support there is for the neoclassical position. Chapter 8 looks in detail at the issue which is arguably the most critical of all – whether there is any justification for the Fisherian focus on the loans market and substance to its parable of the equilibration of saving and investment.

The present chapter will first examine other aspects of the Fisherian model which attract criticism.

7.2   Relaxing the assumption of perfect foresight

The assumption of perfect foresight is without doubt the single most unrealistic feature of the Fisherian model and many of the other criticisms stem from it. Taken literally, it presupposes that each individual and firm either (i) knows all future prices, including interest rates, obtaining in the economy, or (ii) knows the intertemporal preference orderings of all individuals and the technical production possibilities of all firms, again from the present time until kingdom come, and that as a result of applying the principle of constrained maximization it is able to predict the relevant future prices for itself.

Alternative (i) underlies the foregoing description of the Fisherian model, but the actual mechanics by which prices are determined have not been considered. Implicitly, price determination in such a model would require a Walrasian *tatonnement* process: the intentions of individual agents are initially formulated tentatively and the consequent behaviour of the economy (and, in particular, of prices) determined; the latter provides a feedback for the individual plans, which are accordingly adjusted, and the behaviour of the economy predicted again; this iterative process continues until full consistency is achieved.

Despite the existence of a few future markets for some basic commodities, this is mere fantasy. But alternative (ii) is no more plausible. Neither is the necessary information available, nor could any individual or firm possibly begin to process it, even if it were.

One approach to the problem of relaxing the assumption has been an attempt to extend the existing general equilibrium framework by means of contingency markets to take account of the effects of risk. Another has been to modify the framework itself, introducing the notion of temporary equilibrium. A third has been to ignore the problem entirely on the ground that the macroeconomic effects of risk and uncertainty are not all that important in practice. Each of these will be considered in turn.

A. CONTINGENCY MARKETS

The origins of this approach are to be found in Arrow (1953), Allais (1953) and Debreu (1959), and it is described in some detail by Hirshleifer (1970).[1] For a guide to more recent contributions, see Guesnerie and Montbrial (1974).

---

[1] Hirshleifer also describes the asset portfolio approach which might be loosely described as its hedonistic equivalent. For its origins see Markowitz (1952, 1959), Roy (1952) and Tobin (1958, 1965).

In general terms, the approach replaces the assumption of perfect foresight with the assumption that there are a finite number of alternative events which may occur in the future. Individuals and firms possess subjective estimates of the probability of each event and they enter into contracts which are conditional on the occurrence of a specific event. The formal description of the determination of general equilibrium then proceeds in much the same way as in the perfect foresight case, contingent claims replacing certain ones.

The problem with this approach is that for the most part it paints an utterly unrecognisable picture of trading in an economy. True, the existence of insurance and betting industries testifies to the feasibility of markets in contingent claims, but the limitations of the former indicate the chief difficulty: the cost of arranging such contracts grows rapidly with the complexity of possible outcomes. It is not fortuitous that insurance policies are confined to very simple sets of possible outcomes, for example, the occurrence or non-occurrence of an accident, for even here the costs are significant. It would be unthinkable for such contracts to be extended to cover the success or failure of an individual career or industrial investment project. This elegant solution to the problem must therefore be discarded as unrealistic.

B. TEMPORARY EQUILIBRIUM

A second approach, which goes back as far as Hicks (1939), and has recently received renewed attention,[2] abandons the notion that individuals and firms co-ordinate their plans for the future at a single moment in time. Instead, temporary equilibrium is established with current markets and perhaps some future markets (for example, markets in financial assets) being cleared, and plans are revised at the beginning of each time period.

This modification of the general equilibrium framework provides a rationale for holding money as a store of value which is lacking in simpler versions, and thus potentially may yield a rigorous microtheoretical foundation for macroeconomic theory. But, promising though it may be, it is still in the experimental stage. It has not yet even been related to empirical data, and much less has there been any question of attempting to test it. Accordingly it could hardly be considered in itself as justification for adhering to the Fisherian or any other version of neoclassical capital theory.

C. THE CIRCULAR FLOW

A third approach is simply to assert that the assumption of perfect foresight is convenient for expounding Fisherian theory but that in practice it gives

---

[2] See Arrow and Hahn (1971) for an exposition, and Weintraub (1977) for a brief survey of the literature.

a highly misleading impression of both the information required and the difficulty involved in collecting it.

Taking the latter first, this view follows Schumpeter (1911) who, invoking Wieser's principle of continuity, characterizes the economy as a circular flow which acts as a computing machine with a built-in flywheel. The current structure of the economy, in particular current prices, enduring habits and existing long-term contracts and commitments, provides a good first approximation to its future structure.

Prediction thus generally requires the forecasting of marginal changes, a task of much smaller magnitude than the Walrasian forecasting *ab ovo* described in Chapters 3 and 4. And furthermore, if the abundant empirical literature on adaptive expectations, and, after Muth (1961), the growing one on rational expectations, have anything to contribute, this task will be assisted by the judicious exploitation of recent history.

Of course, forecasts based on such information are likely to be progressively more inaccurate the further one looks ahead, but, according to this view, it does not matter. For it may be argued that the current behaviour of individuals and firms, and hence the basic workings of the model, are likewise increasingly insensitive to future events the further one looks ahead, and so the impact of forecasting errors is correspondingly reduced.

To illustrate this point, the two-sector model used as a numerical example in Section 4.5 follows exactly the same trajectory if its thirty-year time horizon is replaced by a rolling horizon of four years, even if no value is attached to the terminal stocks of machines. And if as little as half the equilibrium value is attached to the stock, the rolling planning horizon can be reduced to two years without affecting the results.

A weaker version of the circular flow approach is to admit that uncertainty is important but to suppose, as Keynes (1937) suggested, that individuals act as if it were not.[3] This view accepts that expectations will be unfulfilled, but supposes that in the long run the model is unbiased.[4]

Probably the failure of neoclassical economists to become excited over the issue of perfect foresight may largely be attributed to this third position,[5] coupled with a belief that temporary equilibrium theory, rational conjectural

---

[3] 'How do we manage ... to behave in a manner which saves our faces as rational, economic men? ... (1) We assume that the present is a much more serviceable guide to the future than a candid examination of past experience would show it to have been hitherto ... (2) We assume that the *existing* state of opinion as expressed in prices and the character of existing output is based on a *correct* summing up of future prospects ... (3) ... we endeavour to conform with the behavior of the majority.' (p. 214)

[4] Of course for some economic activities this view may be untenable, as Keynes proceeded to argue with respect to the money market.

[5] This position is of course ardently contested in some quarters, notably by Shackle (1972, 1973, 1974).

general equilibrium theory or some similar development will ultimately provide respectable intellectual support. Indeed, reverting to a distinction made in Section 1.3, the third position and the newer versions of general equilibrium theory may be regarded as informal and formal approaches to the problem which are effectively complementary, the formal being a pragmatic makeshift which for the time being is standing in for the latter.

Non-neoclassical theorists of course also have to face the problem of uncertainty, and it may be worth observing that some of them, notably Kaldor (1959, 1961; Kaldor and Mirrless, 1962), have adopted a position similar to *c*. Others have attempted to sidestep the issue by limiting their analysis to the comparison of steady states. Robinson, for example, employs models which assume 'tranquillity', this being defined as a condition in which expectations are constant, held with certainty, and fulfilled, with the intention separating long-run from short-run influences (1956, p. 66). The difficulty with this approach lies in seeing the relevance of such analysis to the real world. If the authors' acknowledgement of the artificiality of such models is taken at face value, there is little reason to suppose that their properties are of any interest in practice. If the models are supposed to be realistic after all, it is at the cost of introducing assumptions stronger than those employed in general equilibrium analysis.

7.3 Monetary influences

In the Fisherian model, as in most pre-Keynesian theory, the rate of interest and the rate of profit are almost interchangeable terms. In believing that they are co-determined by real factors in the economy, Fisher was a direct inheritor of the quantity theory of money which may be traced back to Cantillon and Hume and beyond. Indeed in his own contribution, the *Purchasing Power of Money* (1911), he declares himself as having the 'satisfaction of finding myself for once a conservative rather than a radical in economic theory', and he hardly acknowledges the existence of money in the *Theory of Interest*.

However, with increasing importance being attached to the development of a unified theoretical framework, the neoclassical economist is now under obligation at least to sketch the relationship between his capital theory and his monetary theory.

The simplest approach to take is to revert to a loose form of the classical dichotomy, the Fisherian model providing an explanation of the long-run supply and demand for financial assets, and the Keynesian model (or the Friedman model, in the case of the new quantity theorists), possibly supplemented by the Markowitz–Tobin portfolio model, providing an explanation of the distribution of holdings between real balances and other assets. Although this position lacks theoretical rigour, it probably represents the thinking of the majority of neoclassical economists, now that the Patinkin attempt to integrate money directly into a general equilibrium framework has come to be regarded as unrealistically mechanistic.

Whether the two bodies of theory do in fact mesh together satisfactorily is another matter. First, one should note that Keynes's marginal efficiency of capital schedule preserves the link between the rate of profit and the rate of interest. True, he went to great lengths to emphasize the instability of the schedule, but this reflected more a belief in the instability of expectations than lack of confidence in the mechanism as such. It is also true that he was sceptical about the possibility of stimulating private investment with monetary policy, but this was because he thought that the (long-term) rate of interest was insensitive to monetary policy, not because, as has sometimes been asserted, he thought that investment was insensitive to the rate of interest.

In the short run, monetary factors are dominant. If there is any overriding mechanism, it is the liquidity preference function, and the location of this is determined by its own previous behaviour. It sets the rate of interest, and this in turn determines the volume of investment, the price of investment goods relative to consumption goods, and the rate of profit.

But in the present context it is the long run that matters and here the situation is less clear. There is no need to emphasize that there is very little discussion of the long run in Keynes's own writings or in subsequent commentary, and his model is badly equipped to investigate it. However, the available evidence in the General Theory, and the Treatise on Money before it, suggests that Keynes was quite conventional in this respect. At any rate there are no obvious incompatibilities between his short-run model and the Fisherian long-run model. This is a point that will be treated in greater detail in the discussion of saving and investment in Chapter 8.

In principle, of course, monetary factors could make themselves felt even in the long run if a liquidity trap or rigid wages were responsible for sustained involuntary unemployment. But in practice governments may be assumed to counteract such influence in their efforts to secure full employment.

7.4   Labour and wages

The Fisherian model has frequently been criticized for the very limited attention it pays to the determination of employment and wages.[6] Such criticism is usually rooted in the notion that the wage rate is the counterpart of the rate of profit and that there exists a trade-off between capital and labour which should not be ignored in any comprehensive treatment of either. This view, the legacy of the aggregate neoclassical approach, has been sustained by misunderstanding of the role of the so-called factor price frontier,

---

[6] See, for example, Nuti (1971).

and is no doubt reinforced by the short-run trade-off between profits and wages in national income.

But as soon as it is accepted that the objective of Fisherian theory is to explain the rate of interest, that its focus is the loans market, and that it is only secondarily and indirectly concerned with the markets for capital goods and labour, this criticism loses its force. Labour is neglected, not by oversight, but because it is not a central issue.

The contributions of the aggregate neoclassical approach and the factor price frontier to the false parallel between the wage rate and the rate of profit have been discussed in Chapters 2 and 4. The short-run national income trade-off, influential though it may be in this respect, is no less misleading. For the fact that the share of profits in national income is, *ex post*, the residual, and gains or loses at the expense of the share of wages, can have no bearing on *ex ante* Fisherian theory.

If there is an *ex ante* relationship between profits and wages, it is given by the intertemporal Euler equation which connects the present value of the stream of aggregate consumption to the present values of the streams of wages and rentals accruing to individual capital goods. But even this does not define a trade-off as such. For the main impact of a change in the rate of interest (and, even in a comparative dynamics exercise, this cannot occur autonomously) is likely to be on the value of capital goods and perhaps also on choice of technique, and, unless one adopts a highly oversimplified model, there is no reason to suppose a systematic effect on the wage rate.

Two approaches to the determination of employment and wages have been sketched in Chapter 4: one in which labour is effectively regarded as a 'discommodity', appearing as one element in each individual's preference ordering, and whose supply in determined in the same way as the consumption of commodities proper; another in which the supply of labour by each individual is regarded as institutionally determined.

At least three issues need to be considered: the question of which, if either, of the two approaches may be taken as a starting point for a more realistic treatment; whether neoclassical theory may be reconciled with the Keynesian analysis of involuntary unemployment; and whether neoclassical theory has been supported or undermined by recent empirical investigations of labour markets.

The first of these is difficult to evaluate even in general terms. It is conventional to begin by pointing out the irrelevance in a modern world of the Jevonian notion of each individual supplying labour up to the point where the increasing marginal disutility of working is equal to the decreasing marginal utility of the commodities bought with the income derived. For much of the labour force, the length of the standard working week is predetermined institutionally and contractually, and therefore cannot be chosen by the individual. But it would be equally wrong to accept the second approach uncritically. Marginal adjustments are clearly within the discretion of the self-employed, and also to some extent of those nominally employed on a standard working week but offered overtime. Some further scope for long-run adjustment, at least in the intensity of work supplied if not its duration, may be afforded by choice of occupation.

From the point of view of the Fisherian model, it does not greatly matter whether the first approach, or the second, or a mixture of the two is adopted. In the first case, employment and wages depend solely on preference orderings and technical production possibilities; in the second and third, institutional constraints will also play a hand, but the validity of wage equation (4.4) will not thereby be affected.

The second of the issues listed is but one aspect of the more general question of whether neoclassical analysis and Keynesian macrotheory are mutually compatible. The Fisherian model is predicated on the traditional neoclassical compromise where general equilibrium theory and Keynesian macrotheory are regarded as complementary, the former pertaining to the long run and the latter filling the gap in the short run. As was noted in Chapter 1, this distinction is slowly breaking down with the recent neoclassical efforts to provide a general equilibrium microfoundation for macrotheory. But it would appear safe to say that, even if this task is brought to fruition, it will have more impact on employment theory than on wage theory and that the conventional neoclassical teaching with regard to the latter is unlikely to be greatly disturbed.

Finally, one must consider the extent to which the neoclassical model is consistent with the empirical evidence. In the Fisherian model described above, labour is treated with such generality (each individual supplying a unique type) that the theory is untestable. For econometric testing, either labour must be classified into a finite number of categories or a finite list of attributes of labour must be identified. The former method, pioneered by Bowles (1970), suffers from the defect that the classification criterion – usually occupation or education – is inevitably somewhat arbitrary. The latter, in which each individual is supposed to possess various quantities of different characteristics (possibly with scope for substitution), has not even been modelled in a theoretically satisfactory manner. The limit of progress in this direction has been the disaggregation of labour into raw labour and human capital and the investigation of production relationships under very strong aggregation assumptions (for example, see Fallon and Layard, 1975). One is thus left facing a number of isolated studies, or groups of studies, which may or may not constitute evidence one way or the other. The most that can be said is that such studies do not actually contradict long-run neoclassical analysis.

7.5 Imperfect competition

A common complaint about neoclassical theory is that it usually adopts a competitive model as a first approximation and then fails to investigate the consequences of relaxing this assumption.

In the present context, however, it would not appear to be necessary to devote much attention to imperfect competition. First, one may observe that the most important market in the present analysis is the market for financial assets, and this is highly competitive in most advanced economies.

Second, turning to commodity markets, one should emphasize the distinction between the share of profits and the rate of profit. If an entrepreneur is able to use market power to earn profits above the competitive level, this will in the first instance be reflected in the value of his assets, rather than in profitability as such. In the simplest case, where monopoly results from the ownership of a patent, the market value of the firm as a whole will exceed the value of its physical assets by the discounted value of the quasi-rents attributable to the patent. Of course the rate of profit on the book value of his assets will be abnormally high, but such a calculation would fail to take account of the fact that part of his profits are attributable to the exploitation of the monopoly *per se*.

While imperfect competition in commodity markets cannot affect the rate of profit directly, it could in principle affect it indirectly by altering income distribution and hence borrowing and lending. But in the absence of evidence to the contrary there is no reason to suppose that such a feedback would be significant.

7.6 Other problems

The foregoing sections do not by any means exhaust the list of criticisms, justified or unjustified, that are made concerning the Fisherian model. Some others have been discussed in previous chapters, notably the problem of interdependence of individual preference orderings considered in Section 6.4, but a number of important issues remain. Before proceeding further it will be convenient to survey the state of the empirical literature relevant to the Fisherian model, and this is the task of the next chapter.

8
The equilibration of saving and investment in the short and long run

8.1 Introduction

In the basic Fisherian model there can be no formal analytical distinction between the short and the long run. The actions of all individuals and firms are planned for all future time periods simultaneously and the long run is necessarily consistent with the short periods that comprise it.

But when it is recognized that disequilibria may be significant in the short run, the relationship is less clear. As has been suggested in Section 7.2, the Fisherian position is to suppose that one could define an equilibrium time path that the economy would follow if perfect foresight and maximizing behaviour prevailed and to assume that the economy broadly follows such a trend, disequilibrium behaviour being relatively unimportant in the long run.

This view appears to have been adopted, implicitly at least, by the majority of neoclassical economists as an unselfconscious act of faith. Typically the fluctuations are regarded as the province of Keynesian analysis, thus neatly reconciling Keynes and Fisher. But why should one rule out the possibility that the fluctuations may obscure the trend, or reduce it to secondary importance? In the limit, one could argue that the trend might be absolutely irrelevant in the short run, and since the long run is nothing but a succession of short runs, absolutely irrelevant in the long run as well.

It would be profitless to pursue this point at a purely abstract level. In putting it into practical terms many different issues could be raised, and obviously the identification of the most important is a matter of subjective judgement. But one issue stands out as critical: the question of how the loans market is cleared.

To contrast the Fisherian and Keynesian approaches to this issue, the loans market in this context should be interpreted as the market for financial assets in general, and one should note that the net acquisition of financial assets by any agent is identically equal to the difference between his saving and investment.

In the Fisherian model, the market for financial assets is the arena in which intertemporal activities are coordinated and it is directly cleared by the interest rate.[1] In the Keynesian model, with its focus on the saving/investment half of the identity, the main equilibrating mechanism is the level of effective demand, the rate of interest being accorded a secondary or even negligible role. To what extent do these bodies of theory in fact mesh together?

This question is the subject of the present chapter and it will be approached in two stages. First, Section 8.2 outlines the reconciliation of the Fisherian parable with simple Keynesian theory that appears to underlie conventional neoclassical thinking. Then Section 8.3 looks at the empirical literature on different aspects of saving and investment behaviour and attempts to assess the degree to which it supports the Fisherian model. Section 8.4 summarizes the implications of this assessment.

8.2   First approach to a Fisher/Keynes reconciliation

A. CONSUMPTION AND SAVING

Even in the original form proposed by Keynes, the consumption function could be viewed as an extension of the Fisherian model. In the Modigliani-Ando-Brumberg life cycle theory, and also in its near-relative, the Friedman permanent income hypothesis, the link becomes explicit[2] and direct, with a substantial improvement in explanatory power.

The relationship between Fisherian theory and these versions of the consumption function may be illustrated with the simple two-period model (Figure 8.1). Consider the behaviour of an individual whose income stream for the two years, $\{\bar{Y}_1, \bar{Y}_2\}$, is represented by the point $\bar{A}$. The individual may modify his raw income stream by trading in the loans market, the market line $\bar{P}\bar{Q}$ having slope $-(1+i)$ where i is the market rate of interest. The optimal consumption stream $\{\bar{C}_1, \bar{C}_2\}$ is represented by the point $\bar{B}$.

Now suppose that the income in year 1 is increased by a small amount to Y_1. The new income stream $\{Y_1, \bar{Y}_2\}$ is represented by the point A, the new market line by PQ, and the new optimal consumption stream $\{C_1, C_2\}$

---

[1] Of course when one considers the heterogeneity of financial assets in terms of term to maturity and security, one should speak of a pattern of interest rates.

[2] Modigliani (1975, p. 2); Friedman (1957, p. 9).

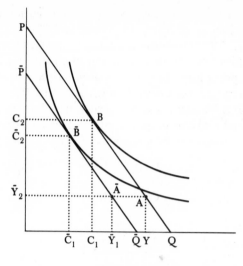

Figure 8.1

by the point B. Provided that the curvature of the intertemporal indifference curves does not alter appreciably in the relevant range, one may obtain a linear relationship between the change in consumption in each year and the change in income:

$$(C_1 - \bar{C}_1) = b_1(Y_1 - \bar{Y}_1) \qquad (8.1)$$

Writing $(\bar{C}_1 - b_1 \bar{Y}_1)$ as a, (8.1) may be rearranged as

$$C_1 = a + b_1 Y_1 \qquad (8.2)$$

and one has the consumption function as formulated by Keynes.

The consumption function may thus be-regarded as a perturbation feedback rule. In control theory, once one has found the optimal solution for a set of choice variables subject to a set of exogenous constraints, it is often relatively easy to find neighbouring optimal solutions when the constraints, or given parameters, are slightly altered.[3] In the present case it is the role of Fisherian theory to determine the optimal consumption stream from scratch. Keynesian theory then shows how this solution should be adjusted if income alters, the relevant Fisherian factors being encapsulated in the coefficient b_1, making their presence felt only in the long run. Keynes devoted two chapters of the *General Theory* to the determinants of the marginal propensity to consume and his discussion, particularly the reference to the

---

[3] See, for example, Bryson and Ho (1969).

role of the rate of preference, may be regarded as an informal elaboration on the Fisherian treatment described in Section 3.4.[4]

In fact Figure 8.1 illustrates more than the Keynesian consumption function. It implies that the determination of C_1 and C_2 may be regarded as a two-stage procedure. The first stage consists in evaluating the discounted value of the income stream, that is, the wealth, W, and this determines the location of PQ. The second stage consists of finding the optimal point on PQ, that is, the optimal consumption pattern over time that can be financed with this wealth. In other words, one should write

$$C_1 = C_1(W) \tag{8.3}$$

and

$$C_2 = C_2(W) \tag{8.4}$$

where

$$W = Y_1 + \frac{Y_2}{1+i} \tag{8.5}$$

for any given level of the interest rate. If one is willing to assume that the intertemporal indifference curves of the individual are homothetic, (8.3) and (8.4) may be rewritten

$$C_1 = k_1 W \tag{8.6}$$

and

$$C_2 = k_2 W \tag{8.7}$$

where k_1 and k_2 are independent of W.

Generalizing to a model with many time periods, one has the result that a change in income in any year will affect consumption only through its effect on wealth, and that in general its effect will be distributed over consumption in every year and not just be confined to the year in which it occurs.

This is of course the point of departure of both the life-cycle theory (Modigliani and Brumberg, 1954; Ando and Modigliani, 1963) and the permanent income hypothesis (Friedman, 1957). Thus even in this simplistic form the Fisherian model can claim to be, and indeed is accepted as, the foundation for much of current thinking on aggregate consumption theory. Discussion of the problems encountered by these approaches in practice will be deferred until Section 8.3 A, where the econometric performance of these and some leading non-Fisherian approaches will be evaluated.

---

[4] Thus one might regard as somewhat harsh Johnson's (1969) assertion that 'the assumption that saving is a constant proportion of income ... is an assumption of a naiveté amounting to deliberate stupidity ... which originated with Keynes' failure to reinforce the concept of the propensity to consume with any rational utility-maximizing rationale.'

B. INVESTMENT

On the investment side, the easiest way to link Fisherian and Keynesian theory is to equate the constructs of the rate of return and the marginal efficiency of capital, following the lead of Keynes himself in the *General Theory* (pp. 140–1): 'Although he does not call it the "marginal efficiency of capital", Professor Irving Fisher has given in his *Theory of Interest* (1930) a definition of what he calls "the rate of return over cost" which is identical with my definition ... Professor Fisher uses his "rate of return over cost" in the same sense and for precisely the same purpose as I employ "the marginal efficiency of capital".'

This is something of an overstatement, for in fact there are significant differences between the two concepts. In the first place, as Ramsey (1970) has argued, the marginal efficiency of capital is an equilibrium concept, if only in the short run. Its counterpart in the Fisherian model is therefore more properly the rate of profit (as defined in Section 3.5). The rate of return corresponds more closely to the marginal efficiency of a capital asset, as defined by Keynes in his build-up to the concept of the marginal efficiency of capital in general (pp. 135–6). Second, the rate of return is a more general concept, being employed in the comparison of any two courses of action, whereas the marginal efficiency of capital is restricted to the comparison of an investment project with the alternative of doing nothing. As Alchian (1955) has pointed out, when two mutually exclusive projects are being compared, use of the marginal efficiency may encourage the choice of the wrong project.

This is illustrated in Figure 8.2, which shows the present discounted value

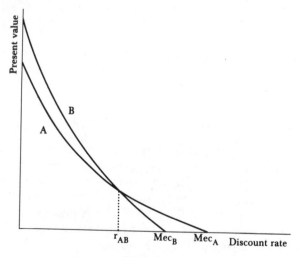

Figure 8.2

of two mutually exclusive investment projects, A and B, as functions of the discount rate. Formally one might describe as C the option of undertaking neither project, its present discounted value being given by the horizontal axis. The marginal efficiency, or internal rate of return, as it is now usually called, of A is given by the intersection of its present value function with the horizontal axis, the point labelled mec_A. Likewise that of B is given by mec_B. The fact that mec_A is greater than mec_B might be taken as an indication that A is to be preferred to B. But this will not necessarily be the case if the present value functions of A and B intersect, as they do in the diagram. The discount rate at which they intersect, r_{AB}, is by definition the Fisherian rate of return on adopting A instead of B, and, as was discussed in Section 3.6, the correct decision is to choose B if the interest rate is lower than r_{AB}, and to choose A if it is higher. This issue is fully discussed by Hirshleifer (1958, 1970). As was noted in Section 3.8, the validity of the rate of return itself depends upon the assumption that the rate of interest is constant.

But these remarks should not be allowed to obscure the essential similarity of the Fisherian and Keynesian views of investment determination. Both the rate of return and the marginal efficiency of capital are effectively tools in the search for the efficient production programme, and at a pragmatic level the two approaches do not differ.

Indeed the Keynesian model may be seen as an attempt to bring to the surface the Fisherian approach to capital formation and place it on an operational footing. The elimination of capital and investment from the Fisherian model is necessary for the theoretical rigour of its analysis of the determination of the rate of profit, but it means that one is left without any explicit guidance to the determination of investment in quantitative terms. At the cost of some theoretical rigour, the Keynesian model supplies a mechanism which at least in principle could yield quantitative predictions. The fact that Keynes regarded the marginal efficiency of capital schedule as susceptible to shifting is in no way inconsistent with this conclusion, for the emphasis on the importance of the state of expectations in his model is entirely in keeping with the Fisherian tradition.

C. THE EQUILIBRATION OF SAVING AND INVESTMENT

In the peasant-producer model of Chapter 3, production and consumption plans were coordinated by the clearing of the loans market, there being no special reason for attempting to distinguish borrowers from lenders as a class. Individual borrowing-lending schedules were combined to form a single aggregate schedule, and the market rate of interest was determined by the requirement that the excess demand for loans be zero.

Although the introduction of firms in Chapter 4 did not alter the analysis in principle, for heuristic purposes it is useful to construct separate

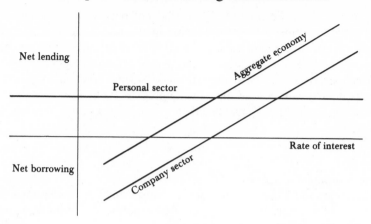

Figure 8.3

borrowing-lending schedules for the personal and company sectors, as illustrated in Figure 8.3. The aggregate schedule, formed by combining these two schedules, determines the market rate of interest as before. (Strictly speaking, only in the case of a two-period model could one construct a diagram as simple as Figure 8.3. In multiperiod analysis one would need a separate dimension for borrowing in each year and another for the rate of interest in each year.)

It should be noted that the borrowing-lending schedule should be interpreted as referring to the net acquisition of financial assets for the sector in question, rather than to either saving or investment directly. The relationship will be investigated in detail in the next section, the main differences, apart from the effects of the inclusion of unincorporated business in the personal sector, being the diversion of part of personal-sector saving into housing, and the financing of much of company-sector investment by retained profits.

Neglecting these differences, the equilibration of saving and investment in the Fisherian model may now be linked up with that in the Keynesian model, following the discussion in Subsections A and B. From the consumption function (8.3) one obtains a personal sector savings function

$$S = S(i, W) \qquad (8.8)$$

taking account of the fact that, at least in principle, the consumption of any individual is related to the rate of interest as well as to his lifetime wealth. And on the investment side one has

$$I = I(i) \qquad (8.9)$$

Hence one obtains the relationship

$$I(i) = S(i, W) \qquad (8.10)$$

As was noted in Section 3.6, Fisher did not believe that savings would necessarily be stimulated by an increase in the rate of interest (for which reason the personal sector savings function in Figure 8.3 has been drawn horizontally). Likewise Keynes (1936, pp. 93–4) was sceptical. Thus for practical purposes i may be dropped from the savings function. Furthermore, in full-employment equilibrium the aggregate flow of personal sector income represented by W may be taken as exogenous, and so (8.10) may be rewritten

$$I(i) = \bar{S} \qquad (8.11)$$

where $\bar{S}$ is the full-employment level of saving.

Next, one should take account of the absorption of private sector savings by the public sector. Writing I_g and S_g for public sector investment and saving, respectively, one has

$$I(i) = \bar{S} - (I_g - S_g) \qquad (8.12)$$

Thus in both cases one reaches the conclusion that, in full-employment equilibrium, the rate of interest is determined by the requirement that it should bring investment into line with that part of private sector savings not absorbed by the public sector.

If there is any difference between the approaches, it is over the role of fiscal policy in maintaining full employment in the long run. In the Fisherian model it is assumed that adjustments in the interest rate will suffice to secure full employment in the long run, without the intervention of fiscal policy. In the Keynesian model the position is less clear, since very little is said about the long run. However, in a brief sortie beyond his usual confines, Keynes states his belief that investment opportunities are gradually being exhausted:

> I should guess that a properly run community equipped with modern technical resources, of which the population is not increasing rapidly, ought to be able to bring down the marginal efficiency of capital in equilibrium approximately to zero within a single generation; so that we should attain the conditions of a quasi-stationary community where change and progress would result only from changes in technique, taste, population and institutions ... (1936, pp. 220–1)

and he makes clear his opinion that these factors are likely to be of secondary importance. Thus, even if there were a long-run tendency in his model towards full employment, Keynes felt that it would eventually be frustrated and that compensatory fiscal policy would be required.

Support for this interpretation is provided by Keynes himself in the *General Theory* (pp. 378–9):

... if our central controls succeed in establishing an aggregate volume of output corresponding to full employment as nearly as is practicable, the classical theory comes into its own from this point onwards... [and] ... there is no objection to be raised against the classical analysis of the manner in which private self-interest will determine what in particular is produced, in what proportions the factors of production will be combined to produce it, and how the value of the final product will be distributed between them.

This view of course is generally overlooked in the usual Keynes-versus-the-Classics analysis that occupied so much of the macroeconomic literature in the years following the *General Theory* (for example Metzler, 1951). There Keynesian theory is held to yield a monetary theory of the rate of interest, in contrast to the real theory of the Classics. But the difference is more apparent than real, for such analysis typically turns out to be discussing the nature of short-run equilibrium, all too often comparing the Keynesian short-run model with a 'classical' long-run model of unidentified parentage.[5]

8.3 Saving and investment in practice

The foregoing parable would appear to underlie much of neoclassical thinking on the determinants of saving and investment. Certainly it reflects the view propagated in teaching, the one arena (apart from forecasting models which are invariably short-term) where they are treated systematically. But, needless to say, it gives a totally inadequate picture of the complexity of both saving and investment, it fails to give due recognition to the way both are affected by uncertainty, and it gives a misleadingly sanguine impression of the degree of empirical understanding of the processes involved.

The complexity is partially illustrated by the sectoral disaggregation shown in Table 8.1. The table is based on the first of the financial accounts in the Blue Book (Central Statistical Office, 1971, 1977) and shows the average figures and standard deviations for the period 1961–70 at constant 1970 prices. The figures are intended merely to give a feel for the magnitudes and variability of the respective quantities, and the period in question may be considered to be reasonably representative in that it was a time of relative stability, antedating the oil crisis and the recent acceleration in inflation.

It may immediately be seen that the notion that personal sector saving and company sector investment dominate aggregate saving and investment, respectively, is erroneous on both counts, the former accounting for just

---

[5] For broader comment on the absorption of Keynes's ideas into neoclassical theory the *locus classicus* is Leijonhufvud (1968). Coddington (1976) is a further notable contribution.

Table 8.1   Sectoral disaggregation of saving and investment in the United Kingdom, 1961–70 (average figures and standard deviations, £ million, at 1970 prices)

	personal sector	*company sector*	*public corpora- tions*	*central govern- ment*	*local authori- ties*	*public sector*	*total*
Saving	2571 (301)	3649 (410)	769 (138)	1518 (1080)	400 (74)	2687 (1226)	8907 (1722)
[Saving net of stock appreciation and additions to tax reserves]	2415 (254)	3085 (301)	752 (131)	1518 (1080)	400 (74)	2670 (1204)	8171 (1318)
Capital transfers	− 259 (76)	182 (216)	32 (29)	− 42 (227)	86 (33)	76 (169)	0 (0)
Gross domestic fixed capital formation	1220 (153)	3216 (448)	1574 (216)	408 (98)	1520 (332)	3502 (622)	7939 (1145)
Increase in value of stocks	114 (46)	747 (330)	18 (39)	28 (12)	0 (0)	46 (44)	907 (386)
[Value of physical increase in stocks]	33 (15)	372 (168)	− 3 (42)	28 (12)	0 (0)	25 (43)	430 (181)
Net acquisition of financial assets	978 (208)	− 132 (348)	− 792 (190)	1040 (810)	− 1033 (233)	− 785 (735)	61 (571)
Overseas net acquisition of financial assets:	− 41 (39); residual: − 19 (280)						

Source: derived from Central Statistical Office (1971, 1977)

29 per cent of total saving, and the latter for 41 per cent of gross domestic fixed capital formation. Indeed in both cases the public sector is responsible for higher proportions.

Justification (or criticism) of the neoclassical story therefore requires an examination of the empirical literature on each of the significant cells in the table. Clearly it is far beyond the scope of the present enquiry to attempt a comprehensive review. Instead, the discussion in each case will be restricted to the basic issues of the consistency of the favoured model(s) with the Fisherian tradition and their degree of success in prediction.

There is unfortunately no well-established criterion of predictive success.

Indeed there has been remarkably little discussion of the principles that should underlie such a criterion (Granger and Newbold, 1973). Theil (1958, 1966) has argued that the criterion should be based on a loss function specific to the application in question, but congenial though such a notion may be to the economic mind, it has been difficult to implement operationally, and the criteria that have been adopted have been pragmatic and inevitably somewhat arbitrary in character.

In the present context, the most widely-used criterion of econometric success – sample period goodness of fit, as measured either by the R-squared coefficient or the standard error of the residual – must be regarded as of dubious value. As Mitchell (1927, pp. 266–7) and Friedman (1940, 1951) pointed out long ago, a good fit may owe as much to data-mining adjustments to a model as to the intrinsic validity of the model itself. All too often a model which has been highly tuned to fit the data from which its parameters are estimated turns out to be poor at predicting future behaviour. Mayer (1975), in a panoramic survey of studies that have evaluated two or more alternative econometric models explaining the behaviour of a given variable, concludes that the ranking by sample period goodness of fit explains only 16–25 per cent of the ranking in the post-sample (prediction) period, in the 99 cases considered.[6]

It is therefore preferable to employ a direct measure of predictive accuracy, and one of the most popular is the root-mean-square error, defined by

$$RMSE = \sqrt{\left\{\frac{1}{n}\Sigma(P_t - A_t)^2\right\}} \qquad (8.13)$$

where P_t and A_t are the predicted and actual levels of the statistic in question. Defining p_t and a_t to be the predicted and actual changes in the level (so that p_t is equal to $(P_t - A_{t-1})$ and a_t is equal to $(A_t - A_{t-1})$), the $RMSE$ may equivalently be written

$$RMSE = \sqrt{\left\{\frac{1}{n}\Sigma(p_t - a_t)^2\right\}} \qquad (8.14)$$

A closely-related statistic, also very popular, is the standardized root-mean-square error advocated by Theil (1966):

$$U = \sqrt{\left\{\frac{\frac{1}{n}\Sigma(p_t - a_t)^2}{\frac{1}{n}\Sigma a_t^2}\right\}} \qquad (8.15)$$

---

[6] For a further critique of the $\bar{R}^2$ criterion, see Dhrymes (1970).

where p_t and a_t are defined to be the proportional predicted and actual changes respectively. This has the advantages of taking into account the inherent variability of the statistic in question and of being unit free.

Another method of evaluating competing models is that proposed by Jorgenson, Hunter and Nadiri (1970), who fit them to one set of observations and test for structural change with a following set. They argue that a robust model is less likely to exhibit structural change than one which owes its goodness of fit to data mining. Their results are not reported here, first because they confined their evaluation to models of company investment, and second because their approach only indirectly evaluates the predictive accuracy of a model.

In what follows an effort will be made to assess predictive accuracy in an absolute sense. This is a difficult task and one that is seldom attempted, even by the model builders themselves. If an evaluation is made, it is usually that of relative accuracy, relative, that is, to the accuracy of competing models, econometricians understandably being more ready to point to the progress that has been achieved than to the distance that remains.

To provide some feeling for absolute accuracy, it is useful to be able to refer to the performance of economically-naive models, and three in particular will be mentioned in the discussion below. First, the super-naive model which always predicts no change, and hence has a Theil coefficient of unity. Second, the model in which the prediction is a moving average of a fixed number of past values of the same statistic. And third, the economically-naive but statistically-sophisticated optimal autoregressive schemes, of which the most highly developed is the integrated autoregressive moving average (ARIMA) model of Box and Jenkins (1970), where prediction is based on previous values with an optimal lag and differencing structure.[7]

In the present context, the third category, which of course includes the first two as arbitrary and suboptimal special cases, is perhaps the best yardstick. To perform well, an econometric model must have both a good economic specification and a good lag structure. Since the performance of an autoregressive model depends solely on its ability to model the lag structure, it can act as a control for the latter. It follows that a guide to the economic content of an econometric model is provided by the superiority of its performance over that of its autoregressive counterpart.

The discussion below will refer extensively to Ash and Smyth's (1973) use of the Theil coefficient to evaluate the major United Kingdom forecasts and to Cooper's (1972) use of the root-mean-square error to evaluate the leading quarterly econometric models for the U.S. The latter provides an

---

[7] For an economics-orientated text, see Nelson (1973).

autoregressive standard, but the former calculates the Theil coefficient only for the super-naive no-change model and for three and five year moving averages. However, even comparisons with the no-change model are frequently revealing. Reference will also be made to Nelson's (1972) comparison of the FRB-MIT-Penn quarterly forecasting model with an ARIMA model.

Two preliminary points with regard to these surveys are in order. First, one should make a distinction between forecasts which incorporate subjective adjustments and the raw predictions made by econometric models. A forecast is usually based on an econometric model, but the prediction provided by the latter usually serves only as a first approximation. The forecaster will typically modify the results to take advantage of information not utilized by the model, and is also likely to adapt either coefficients or estimates of exogenous variables if any part of the forecast conflicts with his *a priori* notion of what is reasonable. Such forecasts should therefore be more accurate than raw predictions and evaluations of them in general (and the Ash and Smyth evaluations, in particular) should be correspondingly flattering to the econometrician.

Second, turning to the unadjusted econometric models, the quality of their predictions will depend partly on the predictions of the variables treated as exogenous and partly on the modelling of the endogenous variables. It may be argued that comparisons of the performance of econometric models ought to focus on the latter, in which case it is desirable to hold the former constant. Cooper achieves this by simply setting the predictions of the exogenous variables equal to their true *ex post* values. Obviously, in eliminating a major source of error, he confers an advantage on the econometric model which is not shared by his autoregressive standard.

Finally, it should be stressed from the outset that the comments on predictive accuracy, which at times may read like a litany of despair, should not be regarded as belittlement of the achievements of econometricians, but as due recognition of the difficulty of the task that they face and the magnitude of the problems yet to be solved by them.

A. SAVING

i *Personal sector saving*

The consumption function is popularly regarded as the showpiece of applied economics, a key component of macroeconomic theory supported by an unparalleled econometric literature. It appears to be the general view that a broad theoretical consensus and a robust econometric specification have been established, and that current research is directed towards factors of secondary or topical importance.

But such complacency is unjustified. Although it is true that there seems to be broad agreement that the autoregressive structure, expressed in its most simple form as

$$C_t = a + bC_{t-1} + cY_t + u_t \qquad (8.16)$$

(where C_t is aggregate consumption in year t, Y_t is personal disposable income in year t, and u_t is a disturbance term) performs best, this would appear to be a consensus of expedience rather than of conviction. For, as is often the case, the autoregressive form is consistent with the opposite poles of adaptive expectations and partial adjustment, represented in this context by the Friedman (1957) permanent income approach and by the Brown (1952) habit-persistence model.[8] It may therefore equally well be interpreted as lending support either to the neoclassical approach or to one of its main rivals. Furthermore, exactly the same estimating equation, with the restriction $b + c = 1$, is used in the wealth-orientated models of Spiro (1962) and Ball and Drake (1964). The fact that all the more successful models reduce to a variant of it is indicative of the weakness of the current state of theory rather than a cause for satisfaction, for it is a form that is likely to perform reasonably well in any context, regardless of theoretical considerations, in the sense that it will yield a good fit to past observations.[9]

Whether it is capable of making accurate predictions is another matter. Ash and Smyth calculate the Theil coefficient for the semi-annual and annual Treasury forecasts, the quarterly, semi-annual and annual (both February and May) NIESR forecasts, and the OECD, London Business School and *Sunday Telegraph* semi-annual forecasts,[10] and find that only three have coefficients less than 0.5, which is hardly an ambitious target considering that the super-naive no-change model automatically has a coefficient of unity. The coefficient for the annual (May) NIESR forecast for the period 1963–71 is 0.34, which is not much better than that for the five-year moving average for the corresponding period, 0.41, despite being made five months into the year. Likewise, the coefficient for the annual Treasury forecast

---

[8] The equivalence of the two approaches in practice was observed long ago by Klein (1958) and conceded by Friedman and Becker (1958). As Wallis (1973) points out, the estimating equations for the two models differ only in the presence of a constant term in the former and in its absence in the latter – hardly the base for a powerful discriminatory test. Singh and Ullah (1976) note that the sampling properties of the estimators of the two models differ, but the very fact that they are contingent on the choice of model virtually precludes their use in a satisfactory test.

[9] Nevertheless, as Evans (1969) has demonstrated, estimates of such critical quantities as the short-run multiplier are remarkably sensitive to small changes in its specification. Using five related specifications of the function and the same body of time series data, he obtains estimates of the one-year marginal propensity to consume that range from 0.28 to 0.56, despite the fact that the long-run marginal propensity to consume is necessarily the same in each case.

Similar conclusions may be drawn from the more comprehensive comparative evaluation of several leading models by Davidson, Hendry, Srba and Yeo (1978).

[10] For brief descriptions of the London Business School, NIESR and Treasury models, together with a Box–Jenkins Study by Granger and Newbold, see Renton (1975).

(1951–71), 0.47, is not a great improvement on that of its five-year moving average counterpart, 0.63. Only the coefficient for the semi-annual *Sunday Telegraph* forecast (1967–71) for nondurables, 0.15, is impressive, but even this is somewhat suspect, for the forecast is made in current prices and hence the Theil coefficient appears to measure success in predicting inflation as much as, and perhaps more than, success in predicting the real change in the variable in question.

Cooper evaluates the Friend-Taubman, Fromm, Liu, Klein, OBE, Wharton-EFU and Goldfeld models, together with an autoregressive standard, by fitting them to the same 48 quarterly observations 1949–60 and calculating the mean-square prediction error over the 20 observations 1961–5. The autoregressive standard performs best for consumers' expenditure as a whole and better than four of the five models that predict nondurables and durables separately (a different model being best in each case). In his similar exercise, Nelson finds that the ARIMA model has less than half the mean-square prediction error of the FMP model for both nondurables and durables.

Perhaps the unprepossessing state of present aggregate consumption theory may be attributable in part to the narrowness of its scope. On the whole, attention has basically been directed towards the estimation of a single equation relationship between consumption and personal disposable income. The only common refinements are the separate treatment of consumer durables and the rest of consumption, and the division of the income variable into earnings, property income and pensions.

Such refinements, while a step in the right direction, are not enough. One issue that such a treatment neglects is the possible interrelationship between personal sector investment and saving. Personal sector investment mostly takes the form of private housing. Traditionally in the United Kingdom the tax advantages attending the purchase of a house for owner-occupation have been so great that the opportunities for such investment have certainly influenced saving behaviour. Individuals have undoubtedly been willing to save more when able to do so through the repayment of mortgages. At the same time, the rate of construction of private housing is linked to the availability of mortgages,[11] and this in turn in the United Kingdom is largely determined by the supply of deposits with building societies. One thus has a subsystem which is wholly ignored in conventional macroeconomic analysis.[12]

---

[11] See, for example, Bain (1970, p. 120).

[12] Similarly neglected is the subsystem of saving and investment in unincorporated businesses included in the personal sector. US survey data evaluated by Friend and Kravis (1957) indicate that, in the upswing of the cycle, entrepreneurs account for a disproportionate share of personal sector saving, and suggest that this saving is directly related to investment activity.

Another issue is the scope of the definition of consumption and income. The narrowest definition of income, take-home pay, appears to be becoming increasingly frequently the focal point in wage-bargaining, both between unions and employers, and between unions and government, and hence might be considered to be the relevant concept for the consumption function. Such a view implies that taxation is regarded as a total loss and that social security payments are equated with taxation.

However, part of government expenditure provides goods and services for the individual which would otherwise have been purchased by him directly, and thus may be perceived as a substitute for personal consumption. Arguably it should be included in both the consumption and the income concept in the consumption function. Similarly part of government expenditures may be perceived as a substitute for personal saving, and should therefore also be included in the income concept.

Indeed in a truly panglossian society, with companies and the public sector acting, and being perceived to act, optimally in the interest of individuals, there would be no advantage in disaggregation. With company and public saving perfect substitutes for personal saving, a simple consumption function on the lines of Section 8.2 would be sufficient to explain the aggregate amount.

The importance of the correct evaluation of government expenditure has been demonstrated by Bailey (1962), who shows that the perception of part of public expenditure as a substitute for consumption has a deflationary effect, lowering the direct multiplier to $b/(1 - b)$ and the balanced budget multiplier to zero, where b is the marginal propensity to consume. Conversely, the perception of part of public expenditure as a substitute for saving has an expansionary effect, raising the direct multiplier to $(1 + b)/(1 - b)$ and the balanced budget multiplier to $1/(1 - b)$.

It follows that a forecast of aggregate demand that fails to take account of the classification of government expenditure is likely to be misleading (unless the proportions perceived as substitutes for consumption and saving happen to form a neutral balance) if such perception is significant in scale. And, despite the above remark concerning the role of take-home pay in wage negotiation, this would appear to be the case, to judge by the efforts of the Trades Union Council to influence the scale and nature of public expenditure in incomes policy negotiations and by references to the concept of a social wage in Labour Party and trade union circles.

Although this may seem a fundamental point, it is one which only very recently has begun to receive serious attention. The long neglect of the Bailey contribution is all the more puzzling because the parallel issue of whether government debt instruments are perceived as net private assets already has a long history. Even now the literature on 'direct crowding out' is very limited (for a survey and a notable contribution, see Buiter, 1977).

Likewise the relationship between personal saving and company retentions received virtually no empirical attention until comparatively recently, despite the theoretical discussion in Keynes's *General Theory* and, even more explicitly, in Harrod (1948), and despite Denison's (1958) cautious finding (developed by David and Scadding, 1974) that their movements in the U.S. appeared to be offsetting. However, Holbrook and Stafford (1971) and Taylor (1971) found indirect evidence of a negative relationship between the two, and the results of Bhatia (1972), Feldstein (1973) and Feldstein and Fane (1973) suggest that the degree of substitution is high. But these experiments have not yet had significant influence on aggregate consumption theory and the topic still awaits a systematic and integrative treatment.

In view of these and other problems,[13] the limited success to date in forecasting aggregate consumption is only to be expected. Although much has been achieved to date, the modelling of consumers' expenditure remains an area where economists must be modest in their claims. As Taylor (1971) states 'It has always been a source of professional pride to me to be able to tell my undergraduate students in macro theory that economists know a lot about what makes consumers tick. However, in the light of experience of the past several years, I now state this proposition much more circumspectly, and perhaps should restrain myself altogether.'

Given the weakness of the short-term modelling of consumer behaviour, it hardly needs saying that the long-term determinants remain obscure, and that it is impossible to discriminate between the neoclassical and non-neoclassical approaches. It is true that there is little evidence that the interest rate has much influence (Suits, 1963; Bain, 1970),[14] as is supposed in some neoclassical models. But, as was pointed out in the previous section, it is possible for the substitution effect to be offset by the income effect, and hence one cannot regard this as a test of much significance.

ii Company sector saving

In the simpler expositions of Keynesian analysis, the role of company saving is often lost to sight, a shortcoming which to some extent may be traced back to the *General Theory* itself. For although Keynes notes the importance of company saving, he makes only a token effort to differentiate it formally from personal saving (Chapter 9), and none at all in his discussion of the multiplier.

---

[13] Even the extent to which private pension schemes are a substitute for other forms of personal saving is an open question. For conflicting views, see Cagan (1965), Katona (1965) and Munnell (1976).

[14] Nevertheless there do exist a few studies which detect an interest effect: Wright (1969a), Taylor (1971), Weber (1970, 1971) and Boskin (1978).

As can be seen from Table 8.1, the company sector was responsible for 41 per cent of aggregate saving in the United Kingdom in the period 1961–70, considerably more than the personal sector. It should be noted, however, that the definition employed in the table includes both stock appreciation (average figure 375) and additions to tax reserves (189). Eliminating these items to obtain a concept of company disposable saving, the proportion falls to 38 per cent, but still remains substantial.

Much of this is accounted for by the flow of depreciation provisions (1433), a semi-autonomous[15] by-product of the investment decision which will be considered in Subsection C.

The remainder, undistributed profits after additions to tax reserves, stock appreciation and depreciation (1535), the active decision variable in company saving, is one of the brighter areas in short-term forecasting. The standard approach is still the partial adjustment model proposed by Lintner (1953, 1956):

$$D_t - D_{t-1} = \alpha(\beta\Pi_t - D_{t-1}) \tag{8.17}$$

where D_t is the total amount of dividends paid by the company in year t, Π_t is its profits in year t, β is its target pay-out ratio, and α is an adjustment parameter, usually termed the reaction coefficient.

α is assumed to be less than unity for two reasons. First, if companies increased the dividend to the target level immediately on an increase in profits, they would run the risk of having to reduce it later if profits fell. And they are extremely reluctant to put themselves in a position where they would have to do this. A cut in the dividend is likely to reduce confidence in the company and make it more difficult and more expensive to obtain finance for expansion, and, perhaps even more worrying from the point of view of the board, leads to suspicion of poor management. Indeed such is the pressure to avoid cuts that when they do occur they are usually taken as indicating a major deterioration in the prospects of the company, and this information content may outweigh anything written in the annual report.[16]

The second reason is more positive. An increase in profits is likely to be accompanied by improved opportunities for investment. The lower the value of α, the further the actual payout ratio will lag behind the target ratio, and the easier it will be to obtain equity finance for investment with retained earnings rather than by the more troublesome and costly issue of new shares.

---

[15] When tax legislation permits accelerated depreciation, the projection of depreciation provisions naturally becomes a significant part of the investment decision.

[16] The information content of dividends appears to have been discussed first by Modigliani and Miller (1959). For a brief survey of the literature and an attempt at empirical evaluation, see Watts (1973). For a dividend model which focuses on information content and signalling, see King (1977).

Although attempts to estimate the adjustment process econometrically have met with considerable success (for a review, see Brittain (1966), Chapter 2), there has not yet emerged a consensus of opinion over the factors responsible for the parameters α and β. The latter, which is much the more important in the present context, does not appear to be inflexible in the long run, for as Brittain notes, the actual payout ratio (dividends divided by profits after taxes and depreciation) for all corporations in the United States fell from 71 per cent in 1929 to 36 per cent in 1947 and then rose again to 62 per cent in 1960.

Brittain argues that these changes can be partly accounted for by the liberalization of depreciation provisions and the rise in the level of personal income tax. The introduction of accelerated depreciation causes true profits to be understated when the rate of investment is rising, and hence the apparent payout ratio will overstate the true ratio. The rise in the level of income tax, coupled with relatively mild taxation of capital gains, was found by him to be a force in the opposite direction, inducing shareholders to save indirectly by investing in corporations with low payout ratios and causing the corporate sector as a whole to respond by reducing these ratios. Feldstein (1970, 1973), Feldstein and Flemming (1971), and Feldstein and Fane (1973) have also found evidence of this latter effect, despite the fact that, as has been argued in Section 5.3, a complete analysis shows that tax discrimination against dividends should not influence the payout ratio. However, it is not supported by the analysis of Briston and Tomkins (1970) of the introduction of the corporation tax in the United Kingdom.

Conspicuously absent from these empirical studies has been a discussion of what determines the normal value of the target payout ratio in the first place. In view of the rest of the literature, it would be natural to suppose (as suggested by Marris, 1972) that a firm would set its target payout ratio in such a way that its retained earnings might be expected to match the need for investment funds, at least in the medium run, and that the ratio would be gradually modified as investment exceeded or fell short of expectations with the passage of time. Table 8.1 supports this hypothesis for the United Kingdom, in as much as it shows that, although there have been substantial short-run discrepancies (as revealed by the high standard deviation of the net acquisition of financial assets[17]), company sector saving, supplemented by capital transfers, has almost exactly covered company sector investment for the period in question.[18]

---

[17] The ability of most firms to accommodate such discrepancies by drawing on their stock of financial assets or on short-term bank credit, or by postponing inessential expenditure, probably accounts for the findings of Kuh (1963) and Fama (1974) that company investment behaviour does not appear to affect company saving. Dhrymes and Kurz (1967), do find evidence of interaction, but their methodology is questioned by Fama.

[18] The relatively small role played by new equity in the UK has been demonstrated by Meeks and

iii Public sector saving

From Table 8.1 it may be seen that the public sector was responsible for 30 per cent of aggregate saving in the United Kingdom in the period 1961–70. Its role as one of the main policy instruments available to the government in the regulation of aggregate demand is reflected in its high degree of year-to-year variability, and its high standard deviation is not therefore in itself indicative of especial difficulty of prediction. Indeed, given its importance in the table, this would appear to be one of the quieter corners of most econometric models.

In the case of the two minor components, public corporations and local authorities, whose activities are narrowly circumscribed in nature and mostly subject to long-term policy, and whose saving is fairly stable, the task of the modeller is perhaps genuinely relatively simple. But the saving of central government, which bears the brunt of fiscal policy, especially in the short run (and which consequently makes the dominant contribution to the standard deviation of the public sector as a whole), is obviously a rather different matter.

In the short run, here more than anywhere else, the forecaster can and must take refuge in conditional predictions, writing revenue as a function of announced tax rates and estimating expenditure as the outcome of its own inertia and announced policy changes. But in the longer run this cell can contain little more than a blank.

B. CAPITAL TRANSFERS

The capital transfers shown in its second line are the most straightforwardly predictable elements of Table 8.1. The entry for the personal sector represents the (negative) balance between payments from the public sector, mainly in the form of grants for education and grants to farmers, and payments to the public sector in the form of estate duty and taxes on capital gains. That for the company sector has been significant only since central government started offering investment grants in 1966 (supplemented since 1972 by regional development grants). The high standard deviation of both the

---

Whittington (1976) in their study of quoted companies. They show that it accounted for 11.7 per cent of new funds in the period 1948–67 and 12 per cent in 1964–71. In the latter period only 4 per cent of new funds was raised by the issue of new shares for cash, the remaining 8 per cent representing share exchanges. The figure for 1948–64 is not disaggregated. Similarly, Goldsmith (1965, p. 247) estimates that new equity sold for cash accounted for only 5 per cent of new funds for non-financial corporations in the US, 1946–58. Anderson (1964) comes to similar conclusions. The very recent increase in the use of external finances reported in the Federal Reserve Bulletin (1975) proved to be a temporary phenomenon and was undoubtedly caused by the acceleration in inflation (Federal Reserve Bulletin, 1978).

company and central government figures is attributable to the introduction of this provision.

The net effect of capital transfers on the sector as a whole has been relatively small, and the individual components, which of course reflect intrasectoral transfers as well (notably central government grants to local authorities for roads), are likewise modest. But in this context it is worth observing that the latter do not include the writing-off of public corporation debt, effectively a transfer from central government, and in the period in question this occasionally involved substantial amounts: £432 million in 1963, £525 million in 1965, £1255 million in 1969 and £255 million in 1970.

C. FIXED INVESTMENT

i Personal sector investment

As Table 8.1 shows, the personal sector was responsible for 15 per cent of gross domestic capital formation in the United Kingdom in the period 1961–70. Perhaps more significant is the fact that it absorbs more than half of personal sector saving net of capital transfers, which further contradicts the simplistic notion that the role of the personal sector is the passive one of providing the savings required to finance the investment of the company sector. Admittedly, however, about 40 per cent of personal sector investment is undertaken by unincorporated businesses, and one could argue that behaviourally it would be desirable to aggregate this with the company sector proper.

The remaining 60 per cent of personal sector investment is mostly residential construction, and relatively little is known about its determinants. In the long run, population growth and income per capital are major factors, and so have been the gradual changes in the structure of the household, as the extended family has given way to the nuclear family, and the latter in turn has lost ground to single-person and other non-familial arrangements. But not enough is known to attempt even the most general quantitative predictions. In the short run the supply side must also be brought into the picture, and it appears to be the consensus that this is responsible for a countercyclical effect, residential construction being to some extent a residual claimant on productive resources. The demand side in the short run is complicated by the influence of both the cost of borrowing and the availability of mortgages from building societies, the dominant source of finance for this purpose in the UK[19]. The availability of mortgages is itself dependent, in the medium run at least, on the supply of deposits with the societies, and

---

[19] For a brief guide to recent studies of building society behaviour, see Hendry and Anderson (1977).

these are sensitive to the rate of interest offered by the societies relative to that offered by the banks, the other major repository of that part of personal sector savings kept in the form of liquid assets. Finally, as was noted in Subsection A.*i*, the propensity to save of the personal sector is likely to be a function of the total amount of mortgages outstanding.

One should further remember that these considerations apply to the demand for housing as a stock, new construction representing merely the margin. Of course the same problem arises when considering the demand for productive assets, but in the case of housing its durability is responsible for a relatively low ratio of annual investment to existing stock.

Although a large number of studies have attempted to unravel some aspects of what is clearly a complex set of relationships, the results are mainly qualitative in nature and controversial at that.[20]

ii Company sector investment

Of all the topics embraced by macroeconomic theory, the determination of company investment must be one that in recent decades has been treated with the greatest ingenuity, has given rise to most dissent, and has made least tangible progress. Some econometric models relate investment to the rate of change of sales, some to the rate of change of profits, some consider the flow of internal funds to be influential, others attach importance to the price of capital goods and the cost of funds, and further variety is afforded by differing treatments of uncertainty and the role of expectations.

But although individual models may differ sharply, it is impossible to construct a satisfactory classification of different approaches. Indeed, Jorgenson (1967, p. 137) argues that virtually all econometric work on investment behaviour has been based on the Fiherian approach and that the differences are pragmatic rather than theoretical.

Most explicitly neoclassical has been the work of Jorgenson himself (Jorgenson, 1963, 1965, 1967; Jorgenson and Stephenson, 1967; Jorgenson and Siebert, 1968b). Assuming that the objective of the firm is to maximize its net worth, and assuming a Cobb–Douglas production function, Jorgenson derives its desired capital stock as a function of the level of output, the price of capital goods relative to that of output, and the rate of interest. Employing rational distributed lags (Jorgenson, 1966), he in turn derives the rate of investment as a function of current and past changes in the desired capital stock. Replacement investment is determined separately assuming exponential depreciation of the existing capital stock.

Because the desired capital stock is proportional to output, investment

---

[20] For surveys of the UK and US literature on housing and mortgage markets, see Whitehead (1974) and Hadjimatheou (1976).

is effectively determined by current and past changes in output, and as Kuh (1963) points out, the Jorgenson model may alternatively be regarded as belonging to the family of Chenery–Goodwin capital-stock adjustment models (Chenery, 1952; Goodwin, 1948) which may be regarded as a natural development of the accelerator model whose origins may be traced to Aftalion (1909, 1913, 1927), Bickerdike (1914) and Clark (1917). Jorgenson would reverse the direction of affiliation (Jorgenson, 1971), but, *pace* his remarks about the advantages of a theoretical framework for empirical research (Jorgenson, 1967) there would seem to be no compelling reason to do so. Indeed it would appear that they and the similar models relating investment to changes in profits (for discussions see Meyer and Kuh, 1959; Eisner, 1960, 1967; Brown, Solow, Ando and Kareken, 1963; Thurow, 1969) have largely been developed *ad hoc*.

The changes in profits models admit directly (and hence the changes in sales models, indirectly) of a radically different interpretation: that investment is influenced by the flow of internal funds. In principle the investment decision should be independent of the financing decision (Modigliani and Miller, 1958), but many writers believe that uncertainty and imperfections in the capital market which affect both the firm's ability and willingness to borrow,[21] make this position untenable. The work of Dhrymes and Kurz, who regard the investment and divided behaviour of the firm as co-determined, has been mentioned in Section 8.3 A.*ii* but one should also note the interdependence hypothesized by the accelerator-residual funds model of Meyer and Kuh (1955, 1957) and Meyer and Glauber (1964).

According to the bifurcation model, as it is sometimes known, investment is determined by an accelerator mechanism in the upswing of the cycle, but in the downswing the flow of internal funds (retained profits plus depreciation provisions) becomes the dominant factor. In the downswing, the rate of investment may be expected to drop substantially if the usual criteria were maintained, and the firm could, if it chose, temporarily increase its dividends. But according to the Lintner dividend model discussed in Section 8.3 A.*ii*, it will be reluctant to do so, either because it fears having to cut its dividend later if conditions deteriorate further or because it will have to resort to relatively more expensive external funds to finance investment if conditions improve. Instead, the firm allows retained earnings to rise and absorbs the surplus by relaxing its normal investment criteria.[22] Since demand is static

---

[21] For early discussions, see Keynes's analysis of borrowers' risk and lenders' risk in the *General Theory*, and Kalecki (1937c).

[22] Support for this hypothesis is provided by the study of quoted industrial companies in the US, 1949–59, by Baumol, Heim, Malkiel and Quandt (1970). They estimate that the rate of return on retained earnings was much lower than that on external funds. For discussion of their paper see Whittington (1972), who comes to similar conclusions for the UK, Friend and Husic (1973) and Baumol, Heim, Malkiel and Quandt (1973), and for a further development, Grabowski and Mueller (1975).

or falling, such investment is likely to be primarily designed to cut variable costs and improve efficiency rather than to increase capacity.[23]

Some critics of the approach have argued that the flow of internal funds may affect the timing of investment but not its rate in the long run. Others point out that profits, and hence the supply of internal funds, are also likely to vary over the cycle so that the supposed surplus might not exist at all or be so small that it could be absorbed by building up the firm's cushion of financial assets or by bringing forward maintenance expenditure.

If profits and investment demand are synchronized (the consequences of which are discussed in detail by Kuh and Meyer, 1963), one reaches a position similar to the earlier one of Duesenberry (1958). Duesenberry also supposes that the cost of external funds is greater than that of internal funds, and that within the former new equity is more expensive than borrowing,[24] the differences being ascribed primarily to the effects of taxation. He further argues that, while the cost of internal funds and of new equity are relatively constant, the cost of borrowing rises fairly steeply with the scale of borrowing, and that the cost of funds schedule should have the shape shown in Figure 8.4. Thus if the investment demand schedule is elastic, as he reckons is typically the case, it is likely to intersect the cost of funds schedule in the segment where the firm is increasing its borrowing.

The Duesenberry model may of course be regarded as a straightforward development of Keynes's analysis of the determination of the rate of investment in the *General Theory*, which in turn may be regarded as one way of making the Fisherian approach operational, as has been argued in Section 8.2.

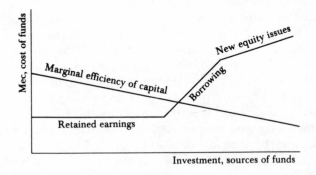

Figure 8.4

---

[23] For a development of this argument and some empirical evidence to support it, see Feldstein and Foot (1971).
[24] An hypothesis corroborated by Baumol, Heim, Malkiel and Quandt (1970) who find that the rate of return on new equity is higher than that on borrowing.

Thus, by a series of short steps, this brief excursion into investment theory has returned to its starting point. And the more one explores the literature (for surveys, see Meyer and Kuh, 1957; Eisner and Strotz, 1963; Jorgenson, 1971), the smaller the gaps become and the more difficult it is to discriminate either conceptually or empirically between the different models. As Kuh (1971, p. xx) states: 'The influence of static competitive neo-classical theory on investment by now has been clarified. Yet in a world of imperfect competition and pervasive uncertainty, the matter is so complex that presently we are unable to accept any one theory of investment strictly derived from standard neo-classical considerations on the basis of empirical evidence'[25] And Thurow (1969) predicts pessimistically that 'there is very little chance that the real world will ever generate data which are orthogonal enough to estimate the partial effects of the different factors which influence investment without making assumptions about the character of the economy's production function and the cost of capital.'

It is therefore not surprising that the predictive ability of forecasting models in this sphere has been unimpressive. Ash and Smyth calculate a Theil coefficient of just over unity for the NIESR quarterly forecasts of private investment (1965–70), which is worse than the naive model where the predicted amount is equal to the actual amount in the previous period. The Treasury half-yearly forecast, evaluated for the period 1969–71, has the even higher coefficient of 1.23. The London Business School (private nondwellings investment, 1968–71) and the *Sunday Telegraph* (private investment, 1967–71) half-yearly forecasts have better coefficients, 0.66 and 0.49 respectively, but they are still high. Private investment is not disaggregated from gross domestic fixed capital formation in the calculation of the Theil coefficient for the NIESR half-yearly and annual forecasts, the OECD half-yearly forecast or the Treasury annual forecast, so the coefficient for gross domestic fixed capital formation must act as a proxy. The NIESR and OECD half-yearly forecasts (both calculated for 1967–71) both have coefficients over unity. The NIESR and Treasury annual forecasts (both calculated for 1963–71) are 0·64 and 0·63. These last figures are particularly unprepossessing when it is remembered that the annual forecasts are made several months into the year in question and that much of the investment expenditure for the remainder of the year is by that time firmly committed.

One topic, of especial importance in the present context, will serve to underline the extent of present ignorance. The recent theoretical literature on the theory of the firm has called into question the Marshallian notion that a firm is managed with the singleminded objective of maximizing

---

[25] Similar agnosticism is expressed by Elliott (1973) at the conclusion of his critique of Jorgenson and Siebert. For a theoretical discussion of the influence of uncertainty on investment, see Nickell (1977).

its net worth and argues instead that firms have a strong tendency to seek growth for its own sake. It has long been recognized that in the modern corporation, which is responsible for the greater part of industrial output in the United Kingdom, the United States and similar economies, shareholders rarely exert effective control, at least in the short run, and managers are therefore to some extent free to pursue their own interests (Florence, 1933; Berle and Means, 1933; Gordon, 1945). According to the new theory (Marris, 1964; Baumol, 1967), these are biased in the direction of favouring growth, if need be at the expense of profitability, for two reasons. In the first place, growth is likely to improve the prestige and salaries of top management, since these are typically related to the size of the firm. Second, it is likely to ensure job security. The single statistic that receives most attention in the annual report of a company is the absolute level of profits, and as Keynes (*General Theory*, Chapter 9) points out, shareholders (and perhaps equally important, the financial press) are likely to be satisfied if profits are increasing, without discriminating between increases attributable to improved efficiency and increases attributable to new investment. Some companies do publish rate of return figures as an annex to their annual accounts, but usually such calculations employ historic cost (book value) estimates of capital and in any case they seldom attract comment. Besides protecting management from criticism, it should also be noted that increasing the amount of capital employed is likely to improve job security by reducing the chances of take-over or bankruptcy.

This view is illustrated in Figure 8.5. The curve PQ represents the trade-off between net worth and growth as a firm increases its rate of investment. While this is not important, the curve rises initially on the assumption that there exist some attractive investment opportunities that will increase the

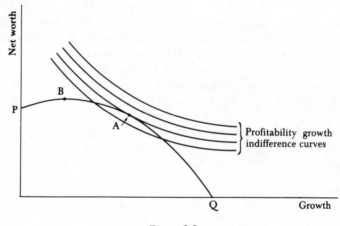

Figure 8.5

net worth of the firm if undertaken. At B, where the rate of return on investment is equal to the opportunity cost of funds, net worth is maximized. Beyond this point, growth can be increased only at the expense of undertaking progressively less attractive investment projects, and net worth falls. It is assumed that one can construct indifference curves for management showing the subjective trade-off between profitability and growth, these reflecting their special interests rather than those of shareholders. The optimal investment strategy, according to the new view, is that giving rise to the point A. In Marshallian theory, of course, the indifference curves would be horizontal lines and the point B would be chosen.

The new view has become sufficiently established that it has come to be regarded as orthodoxy. Indeed it is probably fair to say that, without departing from the principle of maximization subject to constraint, the meaning of the term neoclassical with regard to the behaviour of the firm has altered in this direction, the idea of there being a single agent, the Marshallian manager-proprietor, with a single maximand, profits, giving way to a two-level model which takes account of the separation of ownership and control and which describes the interaction of two distinct maximizing processes.

Nevertheless, there has been virtually no contact between this literature and recent econometric studies of investment behaviour. The latter have been quite silent about the extent to which profits are sacrificed for growth, or even whether such a sacrifice takes place at all.[26] Indeed the Jorgenson model excludes such a possibility in taking the Marshallian framework as its starting point. The accelerator and bifurcation models are neutral in this respect. The latter incorporate a tendency towards excess investment in the downswing of the cycle, but this hardly constitutes a systematic bias of the kind just described.

iii Public sector investment

For the prediction of public sector investment, as for that of public sector saving, the forecaster is dependent on the published programmes of the relevant policy-making bodies. In the long run this is absolutely the case, but in the short run the long gestation of most public sector investment projects, and consequent lag between commitment and disbursement, effectively render much of such expenditure autonomous and might correspondingly be expected to reduce the difficulty of forecasting.

In practice even the short-run forecasting of public sector investment

---

[26] Those studies which assert that the supply of retained earnings may affect investment could be regarded as consistent with the new view. But even within the old framework one would anticipate such an effect since taxation causes the cost of retained earnings to be lower than that of external funds.

appears to be highly inaccurate, at least in the United Kingdom. The Treasury forecasts are presumably based on better and more up-to-date information than the rest, and yet Ash and Smyth calculate the remarkably poor Theil coefficient of 1.10 for the half-yearly forecast for the admittedly short period 1969–71. The *Sunday Telegraph* figure is 0.90 for the period 1967–71, but it enjoys the advantage of being calculated in current prices, which appears to impart a downward bias to the Theil coefficient. The NIESR quarterly forecast of public investment in dwellings and other public investment have coefficients of 1.03 and 1.07, respectively, for the period 1965–70. One must conclude that in this context it is hard to improve upon the naive model of predicting no change.

D. INCREASE IN THE VALUE OF STOCKS

This item, confined mostly to businesses, that is, the company sector and unincorporated businesses included in the personal sector, may largely be ignored in the present analysis. Although stockbuilding (and the running down of stocks) is one of the most important elements in the trade cycle and its volatility creates especial problems in short-run forecasting,[27] in the long run its variations cancel out and its amplitude is relatively small compared with that of fixed investment. From Table 8.1 it may be seen that the average annual value of the physical increase in stocks for the private sector in the United Kingdom for the period 1961–70 was £183 million, while fixed investment came to £4436 million. For the public sector the ratio was even smaller.

It therefore follows that little harm can be done by assuming that stockbuilding follows the same trend as fixed investment and by treating it as a minor adjunct of the latter.

E. NET ACQUISITION OF FINANCIAL ASSETS AND FLOW OF FUNDS ANALYSIS

Table 8.1 shows that, in the United Kingdom in the 1960s, the personal sector surplus financed the public sector deficit on capital account, with the company sector almost financing itself and the foreign trade balance being negligible.

For the most part, the sectoral net acquisition of financial assets has played a passive role in the major short-term forecasting models, the constraint that the aggregate net acquisitions of financial assets must be equal to zero

---

[27] Ash and Smyth calculate Theil coefficients of around unity for most of the forecasting models surveyed by them.

being relegated to the status of a trivial corollary of the constraint that aggregate saving be equal to aggregate investment.

Even in theoretical models the only common improvement is the division of financial assets into money and bonds, permitting the *ad hoc* equations determining interest rates to be replaced by relations based on the clearing of the financial markets.

This is in spite of the fact that, since the seminal contributions of Copeland (1947, 1952), it has been recognized that there is considerable scope for more detailed attention to financial flows and that flow of funds analysis could in principle lead to an improvement in modelling in general and in the understanding of the equilibration of saving and investment in particular.

The main problem with flow of funds analysis is that, while it is relatively easy to obtain reasonably satisfactory estimates of changes in holdings of financial assets disaggregated by sector and type of asset, it is much more difficult to identify which changes are active, in the sense of being the imme-diate outcome of particular behaviour patterns, and which are passive, in the sense of merely being accommodating. In some instances individual intersectoral flows might shed more light on behaviour, but even when they can be isolated, which is usually only the case for instruments specific to two sectors, the same problem is liable to remain. And direct crowding out, where a change in one flow causes an offsetting change in another (not necessarily between the same sectors) is likely to be responsible for additional complexities (Stiglitz, 1974).

Further, for certain forms of analysis of financial behaviour, notably the asset portfolio analysis developed by Markowitz, Tobin and others,[28] it is essential to have stock data in the form of sectoral balance sheets in addition to the flow data, and these are comparatively hard to construct.

Nevertheless the potential benefits of such analysis have inspired a number of ingenious attempts to overcome the difficulties, ranging from the sub-jective matrix-adjustment method of the Bank of England (Central Statistical Office, 1968) to the formal fixed-coefficients approach developed by Stone (1966). These are reviewed at length in Cohen (1972) and Bain (1973). But it would appear that no approach has yet succeeded in specifying a sufficient number of behavioural equations to make the financial sector determinate without introducing unpalatably strong assumptions.

To date, the main contribution of flow of funds analysis has been the impetus it has given to the systematic collection and organization of financial data, data which hitherto have been used to improve existing analytical techniques rather than as the base for a new one. As Bain states in his con-cluding section, 'the reader may have been struck by the lack of any common theoretical core running through this survey ... no theory has been developed

---

[28] For references, see Section 7.2.A.

which stands comparison with the Keynesian model of income generation, emphasising short-run income and spending flows rather than long-run equilibrium situations', and Cohen makes similar remarks.

This is not to say that the future does not hold promise. The origins of flow of funds analysis are comparatively recent and the collection of comprehensive data much more recent still. The literature is growing fast and it is much too early to say what the ultimate contribution of flow of funds analysis may be.

8.4   Conclusions

In the previous section it has been argued that, despite the best efforts of those engaged in empirical research in the field, the various components of the savings-investment relationship cannot yet be predicted with sufficient accuracy to allow one much faith in any theory of the equilibration of savings and investment, short or long run.

Of course it must be borne in mind that in any case there are limits to the power of empirical research in this respect. On the one hand, one cannot claim validity for a theory even when it yields good predictions. The most that one can assert is that it has led to the formulation of a good model, there always being the risk that a good model may be formulated for the wrong behavioural reasons. Conversely, poor predictions do not enable one to reject a theory out of hand, for there is always the possibility that the theory is correct as far as it goes and that it merely needs supplementation.

In this context one cannot ignore the frequently-expressed view (for example, Friedman, 1953) that competitive pressures will enforce profit-maximizing behaviour on the part of firms. The survivor argument, as it is sometimes called, asserts that regardless of how managers describe their own behaviour, those who do not act as if they were profit-maximizers will make losses and eventually find themselves out of business. Naturally there may be lags, but in the long run one is entitled to assume that an approximation to profit maximization is the rule. As a corollary one may infer that labour is employed to the point where its marginal product is equal to the going wage and that investment is pushed to the point where the rate of profit is equal to the opportunity cost of funds.

While this argument might have some weight for those enterprises which do not make use of fixed capital, or do so but finance it by borrowing, it has much less for those with fixed capital financed by equity holdings. For such enterprises, non-profit-maximizing behaviour is likely to be punished in the first instance by a substandard rate of return on equity. In a Marshallian world, where shareholders are also managers, this might induce entrepreneurs either to improve their performance or to shift their funds elsewhere, and the survivor argument would still hold. But where management and ownership are divorced, as is now typically the case, management can use its control over retained profits to secure additional funds indefinitely in spite of earning a substandard rate of return.

A second point, stressed by Kaldor (1966), is that the survivor argument assumes, if not perfect foresight, at least relatively stable trading conditions. But when one takes account of the effects of uncertainty, it is by no means obvious that the survivors are going to be those firms that attempt to marginalize in the approved textbook fashion rather than those that ride hunches.

Thus even if there were no other problems, one would not be able to accept this short-cut justification of the first part of the Fisherian triple equality between the rates of profit, interest and time preference.

Two further preliminary points should be made before discussing the implications of the empirical evidence reviewed in Section 8.3 for the Fisherian triple equality. First, one should not look for literal equality between the three rates, even in the long run. Taxation, particularly income and company taxation, may be expected to drive permanent wedges between the three rates, as has been argued in Chapter 5, and risk and imperfections in the capital market may account for further discrepancies.

Second, as has been shown in Section 8.3, a significant part of both aggregate saving and aggregate investment is undertaken by the public sector, and is formally outside the scope of the Fisherian model. Nevertheless, this should not be regarded as affecting the validity of the triple equality as such, for in principle it may be handled by adapting Figure 8.3 to include the net borrowing of the public sector, as shown in Figure 8.6.[29] It will in all likelihood affect the equilibrium level of the rate of interest, and hence probably lead to a misallocation of resources, but it will not necessarily affect the validity of the triple equality, as such, for the private sector.

In the absence of any direct measure of the rate of time preference, or any satisfactory indirect measure (see Section 3.9) it is obviously impossible to perform any test of its hypothesized equality (or rather, relationship, taking account of the effects of taxation, etc.) with the rate of interest. In principle, indirect evidence might be supplied by testing for substitution effects within the framework of either the life-cycle or the permanent income models outlined in Section 8.2. But two problems discussed in Section 8.3 arise. First, while both approaches are popular, there is by no means a consensus in favour of either, and indeed the explanation of aggregate consumption behaviour still leaves much to be desired. Second, possibly because the substitution effect of a change in the rate of interest may be neutralized by

---

[29] In the diagram the net borrowing of the public sector has been depicted as autonomous, but there is no reason why it should not be regarded as a function of the rate of interest if this were demonstrated empirically.

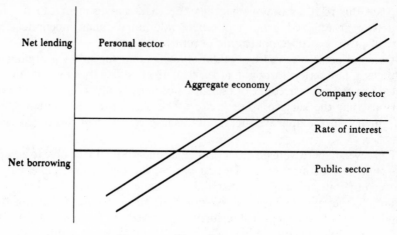

Figure 8.6

its income effect, empirical studies have almost unanimously failed to detect substitution effects in practice.[30] One must therefore conclude that the adoption of the (post-income-tax) rate of interest as an indicator of the rate of time preference of any individual, and as a corollary, of society in general, must be very largely a matter of faith.

Turning to the second half of the triple equality, it is evident that after due allowance for risk, there is at least an approximate correspondence between the rate of interest and the rate of profit, in as much as they are both of the same order of magnitude. But whether or not this correspondence has the properties hypothesized by the Fisherian model is another matter.

Since public sector investment may be regarded as autonomous and private sector investment in dwellings is governed by a special market for funds, it would appear that both may be neglected in the present discussion and that the margin should be sought within the company sector.

Of the different models that have been fitted to company sector net investment, it would appear that the Chenery-Goodwin-Koyck flexible accelerator performs best (Kuh, 1971; Jorgenson, Hunter and Nadiri, 1970; Jorgenson, 1971), but none of them performs well. To some extent this sad state of affairs may be attributed to the use of explanatory variables like sales and profits which, in the opinion of several authors (Gould, 1969; Fisher, 1971b; Gould and Waud, 1973) ought to be treated as endogenous. Quite apart from the biases thereby introduced, the use of endogenous

---

[30] It may be noted that in any case the substitution effects will be small in magnitude if there exists a high degree of complementarity between consumption in different years (see Section 3.6). For references to the few studies which conclude that a substitution effect exists, see p. 125n.

variables is likely to result in a model with poor predictive performance in spite of a high sample-period goodness of fit. Unfortunately there is little alternative in view of the difficulty in finding truly exogenous variables with substantial explanatory power.

Even if the predictive power of the flexible accelerator were good, it could still not be construed as validating a particular theoretical approach. For as has been argued in Section 8.3, changes in sales may be proxying for changes in the level of profits, which in turn may either be interpreted as affecting investment through changes in expected profits or through changes in the availability of internal finance. Discrimination is made all the more difficult by the high degree of multicolinearity between potential explanatory variables, which is greatly exacerbated by the need to estimate a complicated lag structure.[31]

In particular, the Chenery-Goodwin-Koyck model may be interpreted as lending support to Jorgenson's neoclassical approach to investment behaviour, and hence to Fisherian theory. But since the explanatory power of the price variables is relatively small compared with that of (appropriately lagged) changes in sales, it can equally well be interpreted as undermining the neoclassical approach. After all, the development of the accelerator was encouraged by the finding of a number of questionnaire studies that the interest rate is of minor or negligible importance in most investment decisions.

These questionnaire studies might be thought to have provided a direct and definitive clarification of the issue, at least in qualitative terms, but for a number of reasons their results are subject to doubt. Most of them were carried out at a time when interest rates were historically low; most assumed that the interest rate was the only determinant of the cost of capital and overlooked other factors; some could be faulted for using unrepresentative samples; perhaps most important of all, none could be said to have overcome the perennial problem of questionnaire studies, that *ex post* actions may differ significantly from *ex ante* intentions. For a critique of some of the best-known studies, including those that have had most impact of all, those reported in Wilson and Andrews (1951), see White (1956).

To sum up, it is hard to argue with the conclusions of Kuh (1971):

Valiant efforts to blend the theory of the firm with investment equations have not been overwhelmingly successful. Economists are left in the uncomfortable position of 'knowing' that neoclassical optimization models of firm behaviour 'must' contain important elements of truth while the data fail to reveal the influence of this central neoclassical ingredient unless aided by severe *a priori* restrictions.

---

[31] For a pessimistic critique of the modelling of lags in investment behaviour, see Nerlove (1972).

It follows that one must be similarly cautious about Fisherian theory as a whole. If the rate of interest is to equilibrate savings and investment, it must be shown to be a significant determinant for one or the other or both at the margin. But it has been argued earlier that one would not expect it to have much effect on savings at the margin even on theoretical grounds, and certainly very few empirical studies claim to have detected a significant influence. Now it appears that its effect on investment is putative at best, even in the long run.

One must therefore conclude that adherence to Fisherian theory can only be explained by the accumulation of diffuse experience. Indeed Fisher himself had no illusions on this score.[32] The next three chapters are addressed to the question of whether any of the leading alternative theories are any more compelling.

---

[32] 'It is impossible to present a verification of any theory of interest. The facts are too meagre, too conflicting and too intermixed to admit of clear analysis and precise interpretation' (1930, p. 372).

9

Non-neoclassical theories I
Kalecki

9.1 Introduction

The next three chapters discuss alternative non-neoclassical theories of the determination of the rate of profit. It would be impossible in such a short space to survey the field comprehensively. Instead, three theories which may be said to be representative will be looked at in some detail. First, Kalecki's, because it was the first to challenge the neoclassical doctrine and because it is finally achieving the recognition that it deserves. Second, the Kaldor-Robinson-Pasinetti model, which has exerted so much influence in Cambridge. And finally, the recent theory of Wood, because, in the belief of the present writer, its firm-theoretic model is the most promising of the current non-neoclassical approaches.

There is a great temptation to label these theories collectively as Cambridge, but this would suggest a degree of unity of thought that cannot be found and would diminish the originality of each of them severely. For this reason it is simplest to treat the leading figures individually.

Kalecki is chiefly remembered for three contributions to economic theory: his model of the trade cycle, his 'degree of monopoly' theory of pricing, and his independently developed Keynesian-style analysis of income determination. By comparison his fourth major contribution, the theory of the determination of profits first outlined in Polish in 1933 and in English and French in 1935,[1] has been greatly neglected. At one time it even appeared to

---

[1] A translation of the Polish version appears as Chapter 1 of Kalecki (1971). Kalecki (1935a) and (1935b) are also close translations, the former (originally presented at the 1933 Econometric Society meeting in Leyden) with the insertion of a detailed mathematical analysis of the trade cycle, the latter with the addition of a supplementary section discussing the behaviour of prices and production in the cycle.

be in danger of being forgotten entirely, in spite of the attention attracted by the later and similar models of Kaldor (1956), Robinson (1956) and Pasinetti (1962).

Partly this was Kalecki's own fault. By initially incorporating the model as a minor component in his analysis of the trade cycle, a topic of consuming interest at the time, he almost ensured that it would be overlooked.[2] Subsequent attempts to present the model in its own right (Kalecki, 1937a, 1942) seem to have made little impact. Thereafter, as preoccupation with trade cycles and imperfect competition lessened, Kalecki's name remained in the shadows. Recently the balance has been redressed to some extent, with the acceptance of part of his model as a key element of a textbook (Robinson and Eatwell, 1973), the publication of a full-length study (Feiwel, 1975a) and a festschrift (Kowalik, 1966), and the appearance of some shorter pieces (Kregel, 1971; Feiwel, 1975b; King and Regan, 1976; Asimakopulos, 1977).

9.2   Kalecki's theories of profits and relative shares

Although he never altered the main principles of his model, Kalecki tinkered with its details throughout his life, sometimes reversing his position completely. This complicates the expositor's task, and the following account is therefore to some extent chronological.

In his basic model Kalecki distinguishes just two income groups, capitalists and workers. Workers do not save and capitalists do not work, so the former receive all the wages, W, and the latter receive all the profits, Π. Capitalists' consumption, C_c, is a linear function of their income:

$$C_c = A + \lambda\Pi \tag{9.1}$$

where A is the fixed components of consumption and λ is a small constant. Total savings, S, thus given by

$$S = (1 - \lambda)\Pi - A \tag{9.2}$$

are equal to total investment, I. The latter is exogenous in the short run, being the lagged outcome of earlier decisions (an essential feature of all the versions of Kalecki's model of the trade cycle). Hence one may write

$$\Pi = \frac{A + I}{1 - \lambda} \tag{9.3}$$

The implications are obvious. The more that capitalists spend, either on consumption or investment, the greater will be their income. Thus one has

---

[2] For example, see Tinbergen (1935). This contains a brief description of Kalecki's model of the trade cycle, but no reference to his theory of savings and distribution.

Kalecki's version of the widow's cruse sketched but not developed by Keynes in his *Treatise on Money*.[3]

But how does this come about? In his first version Kalecki gives only the broadest indication. Suppose that investment increases. Employment, wages and profits in the investment goods sector rise, with secondary effects on the production of capitalists' and workers' consumer goods. The secondary effects in turn give rise to tertiary effects in the true multiplier fashion until the joint increase in output and profit margins (Kalecki argues that they rise and fall together) generates the increase in profits which provides the savings to match the new investment.

Missing from this explanation, of course, are quantitative details on the changes in wages, sectoral outputs and relative prices. Nor are any further details forthcoming in the restatement of the analysis in the second version of the trade cycle model (Kalecki, 1937b), except that the supply prices of investment goods rise with investment, but so do the prices of other goods as profit margins widen.

Kalecki next introduced the other main element of his theory of distribution – his make-up theory of pricing, based on the concept of the 'degree of monopoly' credited by him to Lerner (1934).

The theory went through various reformulations[4] and the final version will be outlined below.

The core feature of the theory is the model of oligopolistic pricing:

$$p = mu + n\bar{p} \qquad (9.4)$$

where p is the price set by a firm for its product, $\bar{p}$ is the average of the prices of competing firms, u is its unit prime cost (materials and labour), and m and n are constants. For the industry as a whole one has

$$\bar{p} = \frac{\bar{m}\bar{u}}{1 - \bar{n}} \qquad (9.5)$$

where $\bar{m}$, $\bar{n}$ and $\bar{u}$ are averages weighted by output. The higher the degree of monopoly, the higher is $\bar{m}/(1 - \bar{n})$ and so the mark-up, and *vice versa*. As an approximation, prime costs are assumed to be constant for each firm over

---

[3] Keynes (1930), Chapter 10. Possibly too much may have been made of the similarity between the widow's cruse analysis of Keynes and Kalecki, in view of the differences in the definitions and assumptions underlying the models. In any case it should be noted that there is no evidence to suggest that Keynes influenced Kalecki in this respect, for Kalecki does not appear to refer to the *Treatise* at any point in his writings. After the publication of the *General Theory* he went out of his way to recast his trade cycle model in Keynesian terminology, but nevertheless asserted the independent development of his model (Kalecki, 1942, p. 260n). Perhaps significant is the deletion of three references to Keynes in Kalecki (1937a) when that paper was reprinted otherwise almost unchanged as Chapter 4 of Kalecki (1971).

[4] See Kalecki (1938, 1939, 1943, 1954).

the relevant range of its output.[5] Hence, in the short run at least, prices can only be affected by changes in the degree of monopoly.

The mark-up theory of pricing has come in for a great deal of criticism. Perhaps the best-known onslaught is that of Kaldor (1956), who dismissed it as a tautology. In a sense it was, for Kalecki would have been pressed to predict the degree of monopoly in any industry. But this misses the point, which is that the degree of monopoly was to be regarded as stable, apart from foreseeable minor variations over the trade cycle[6], and hence could be used to predict changes in prices arising, say, from changes in prime costs. Suffice to say that, while he does not seem to have mounted a major counter-attack on his critics, Kalecki never altered his position; and that this part of his model has been adopted by Robinson and Eatwell (1973), along with his widow's cruse.[7]

With one further assumption the mark-up theory determines the relative share of wages. Writing k for $\bar{m}/(1 - \bar{n})$ for the economy as a whole, (9.5) states that k is equal to the ratio of aggregate turnover to aggregate prime costs. Turnover is equal to the sum of total income, Y, and the value of materials,[8] M; prime costs are equal to the sum of W and M. Hence

$$\frac{Y + M}{W + M} = k \tag{9.6}$$

and

$$w = \frac{1}{1 + (k - 1)(j + 1)} \tag{9.7}$$

where w is the share of wages and j is the ratio of the value of intermediate inputs to the wage bill.

Having determined the relative share of wages (which, as an empirical fact, 'shows great stability in a moderately long period'[9]) and the absolute amount of profits, one has an almost complete theory of distribution and, simultaneously, of the determination of income. But one problem remains.

---

[5] Kalecki first adopted this assumption in Kalecki (1938), and subsequently regarded Leontief (1941) as providing supporting evidence for it.

[6] Kalecki (1938, p. 109; 1939, p. 31). Note, however, that 'the degree of monopoly has undoubtedly a tendency to increase in the long run because of the progress of concentration.' (Kalecki, 1938, p, 109).

[7] Recently there has been a revival of interest in his degree of monopoly theory and an effort to develop its theoretical underpinnings and integrate it with the cost-push theory of Hall and Hitch (1939). See Eichner (1973) for an outline and original contribution, and Cowling and Waterson (1976) and Nickell and Metcalf (1978) for investigations of the relationship between monopoly profits and market concentration.

[8] Kalecki actually uses the term 'raw materials', but it is intended to cover semimanufactures in addition to what is usually meant by raw materials. To prevent M from being affected by vertical integration, production is measured at the plant level (Kalecki, 1939, p. 22).

[9] Kalecki (1939, p. 31) and frequently asserted elsewhere.

Kalecki

By wages has been understood the wages of manual labour, assumed to be variable with output and so part of prime costs. One still has to bring the salaries of overhead labour into the picture.

Kalecki was uncertain how to treat salaries and never settled on a definite line. In this first formal model of distribution, salaries are lumped together with profits in the larger category of non-wage-earners' income. The latter replaces profits in the consumption function (9.1), and the marginal propensity to consume now takes into account cycle-induced changes in its internal distribution among the component subgroups.[10] With the relative share of non-wage-earners' income implicit in (9.7) and its absolute share given by the equivalent of (9.3), total income may now be written as a simple function of aggregate investment.

However, in the very next chapter of Kalecki (1939) a different treatment is proposed. Initially salaries are effectively aggregated with wages, it being assumed that they move in proportion to one another and that there are no savings from either. Then, as a more reasonable assumption, salary recipients are divided into 'managers' and 'clerks', the former being aggregated with capitalists as in the first treatment, the latter continuing to be connected to the manual labour group.

Kalecki kept to this solution in Kalecki (1942) and (1943), but in Kalecki (1954), Chapter 2, he decided to take a more pragmatic approach. Asserting as before that the relative share of wages is constant over the cycle and that the share of salaries varies less than total income, and writing V for the total share of labour, he argues that one should expect to find a relationship of the form

$$\frac{V}{Y} = a + \frac{b}{Y} \tag{9.8}$$

where a and b are both positive constants, a lying between zero and unity. Regressing V/Y against $1/Y$ and a time trend for the United States 1929–41, he obtains a good and plausible fit.[11] Since V is equal to $(Y - \Pi)$, he then has Y as a function of Π.

The further link from Π to I is now weakened by workers' savings, S_w, which at last are taken into consideration. Kalecki does not attempt to specify a functional relationship for them, contenting himself instead with the observation that they are small compared with total savings and correla-

---

[10] Capitalists were disaggregated into rentiers, dividend recipients, small entrepreneurs and corporations. Also included were recipients of unemployment payments. In principle each subgroup had its own marginal propensity to consume, that of the last being unity.

[11] Kalecki (1954, p. 40): $V/Y = 0.425 + 7.07/Y + 0.0011t$, $R^2 = 0.85$. Repeating the regression with his data, one obtains a satisfactory Durbin–Watson statistic (1.73, 13 observations), but slightly different parameter estimates. Their t-statistics are 20.7, 8.1 and 2.1, respectively.

ted with them over the cycle (Kalecki, 1954, p. 56). Profits thus become a linear function of $(I - S_w)$, and so in turn is total income.

9.3 The short run

With the income-determination framework fully in place, one can put together a more careful and clearer picture of the theory of profits. First the short-run behaviour of relative prices. Kalecki's belief in the constancy of the real prime costs of finished products applied equally to investment goods and consumer goods. Hence he saw no reason for their relative prices to vary over the cycle, and produced supporting statistics (Kalecki, 1954, pp. 25–7). As for profit margins, he reversed his earlier position and came to argue that they would fall in the upswing and rise in the downswing. In the latter, for example, overheads (salaries) would absorb an increasing proportion of gross margins, the consequent pressure on profits providing 'a background for tacit agreements not to reduce prices in the same proportion as prime costs. As a result there is a tendency for the degree of monopoly to rise in the slump, a tendency which is reversed in the boom' (Kalecki, 1954, p. 18).

In spite of this he maintained that the ratio of prices to money wages stays constant over the cycle, in keeping with his belief in the constancy of the relative share of manual labour. This apparent inconsistency is resolved by the behaviour of raw materials, whose prices are asserted to fluctuate more violently over the cycle than those of finished goods and wages (Kalecki, 1938, p. 110; 1954, pp. 23–5).

Investment and consumption decisions are taken in real terms (Kalecki, 1954, p. 46). Since the former require some time for their execution, investment itself is exogenous in the short run, apart from unintended changes in inventories, which Kalecki thought it safe to neglect (Kalecki, 1942, p. 260). The consumption of workers is virtually equal to the whole of wages and salaries, the amount saved, S_w, being so small in relation to total savings that it is not worth troubling to investigate its variations. The composite consumption function for profits has already been described, likewise the share of labour relationship.

Consider again the effect of an increase in investment. As before, output, wages and profits increase in the investment goods sector,[12] in turn causing secondary and tertiary increases in the wage goods and capitalists' consumption goods sectors, the process halting only when the original investment

---

[12] In classifying all commodities as either investment goods, capitalists' consumption goods, wage goods or raw materials, and in dividing the economy into three sectors classified by type of final product, Kalecki neglects all intermediate production. One must suppose that it has been eliminated from the analysis, for example by means of an input-output table.

is matched by savings from the new profits (and, in the very short run, reductions in inventories). Unless output capacity should be approached, the prices of the different types of final product and the wages of manual labour should not change significantly. The general expansion will cause the degree of monopoly, and hence gross margins, in each sector to fall, but this will be balanced by a rise in the cost of raw materials. Although gross margins fall, net profit per unit does not follow suit since salaries rise more slowly than output (as is implicit in (9.8)).

In several instances Kalecki suggests that capitalists' consumption might more accurately be taken as a lagged function of profits (Kalecki, 1942, p. 260; 1954, p. 53). In this case in the short run an increase in investment will simply cause a secondary expansion of the wage-goods sector which will end when the additional profits from the latter are equal to the increase in wages in the investment goods sector, less the increase in workers' savings if any.

Where do the suppliers of raw materials fit into the model? Kalecki does not appear to elucidate at any point. But some raw materials presumably are imported, and Kalecki does give an account of how the closed economy described so far should be extended to cover foreign trade.[13]

Let the balance of trade be denoted B. Total savings must be equal to the sum of B and I, and so capitalists' savings are given by $(B + I - S_w)$. Hence from (9.2) one has[14]

$$\Pi - A - \lambda\Pi = B + I - S_w \qquad (9.9)$$

whence

$$\Pi = \frac{A + B + I - S_w}{1 - \lambda} \qquad (9.10)$$

A balance of payments surplus thus generates profits sufficient to provide the necessary savings, in exactly the same way as investment. Hence, Kalecki felt, Rosa Luxemburg was not far off the mark in her analysis of the economic motives for imperialism (Kalecki, 1939, p. 46; 1971, Chapter 13).

The same can be said of what he sometimes described as 'domestic exports' – the public sector deficit. Suppose for the moment that the government finances its expenditure by the issue of bonds to capitalists. Capitalists' savings must now cover the public sector deficit as well as investment and the balance of trade surplus. Thus an increase in the deficit, whether expended on investment goods or consumption goods, stimulates an expansion of the

---

[13] First in 1934 in a Polish paper translated as Kalecki (1971, Chapter 2), then in Kalecki (1939, Chapter 2).
[14] If the capitalists' consumption function is lagged, λ disappears from the denominator of (9.10) and A is increased by a term $\lambda\Pi_{-\theta}$, where θ is the length of the lag.

economy sufficient to increase profits by the same amount multiplied by the factor $1/1 - \lambda$.

If the government were to finance its deficit by taxing profits, capitalists' consumption would be given by

$$C_c = A + \lambda(\Pi - T) \tag{9.11}$$

where T is the amount of the taxation, assuming that capitalists relate their consumption to net income. The savings-investment relationship for the private sector becomes

$$\Pi - T - C_c = I - S_w \tag{9.12}$$

and so

$$\Pi = \frac{A + I - S_w}{1 - \lambda} + T \tag{9.13}$$

Gross profits are increased by exactly the amount of the tax, provided that S_w is unchanged, and the capitalists are unaffected. The net result is that output is stimulated, the wage cost accruing to the workers in the form of wage-goods and the profit element being appropriated by the government to pay for its expenditure.

By contrast, a tax on wages is not shifted at all. Apart from a minor effect via the level of S_w, such a tax cannot by itself influence the private sector savings-investment relationship and so cannot alter the level of profits. It follows that total output is likewise unaltered. The precise consequences of the tax would of course depend upon the application of the proceeds. For example, if it were used to increase unemployment benefits, the net effect would be a transfer of income from the employed to the unemployed. If it were used for investment, the increase in the output of that sector would be matched by an equal fall in the output of the wage-goods sector.

9.4   The trade cycle

Finally, for the purpose of investigating the long-term properties of Kalecki's model, it is necessary to sketch his trade cycle mechanism. The heart of it is his distinction between investment decisions and investment expenditures, these being separated by a time lag sufficient to make the latter effectively exogenous in the short run.

Kalecki's theory of investment decisions is not easily summarized, for he modified this component of his model almost continuously throughout his life, and it is by no means clear that it was approaching a final form. But one element that never varied was his assumption that investment decisions were an increasing function of the current *ex post* return on assets, that is, of the value of Π/K at the time in question.

According to his model, an increase in investment expenditure causes an immediate increase in the numerator of Π/K and hence in current investment decisions. After the time lag there is a corresponding increase in investment expenditure and a further rise in Π/K. This process repeats itself and generates in the short run a self-sustaining boom. But at the same time the denominator of Π/K is also increasing and eventually *ex post* profitability begins to fall. The boom ends, the process is put into reverse and the economy is propelled into a recession. Again it is the altering level of the capital stock that is ultimately responsible for the turning point: investment falls to below replacement needs, the capital stock falls, and eventually Π/K rises to the point where a new upswing begins.

Kalecki did not neglect monetary factors but came to the conclusion that they were empirically of secondary importance. He asserted that the short-term rate of interest rises in the upswing of the cycle and falls in the down-swing in line with the transactions demand for cash, but that the long-term rate is relatively stable. It is the latter which is relevant to investment decisions. Thus one can expect little feedback from this source over the cycle (Kalecki, 1954, p. 88).

9.5 Evaluation

A. THE PLAUSIBILITY OF THE MODEL

The distinctive feature of Kalecki's analysis is the critical role that profits play in the short-run equilibration of savings and investment. Obviously it is necessary to examine this equilibration process in the context of a modern economy.

First of all, the division of the private sector into capitalists and workers. In the former category Kalecki included rentiers, dividend recipients, and sometimes managers, in addition to incorporated and unincorporated businesses. Clearly even in principle it would be difficult to distinguish the first three categories from the other classes of individuals comprising the group of workers, and it would certainly be impracticable empirically.

For empirical purposes, at least, it is natural to reinterpret the two groups as the company and personal sectors respectively. This is the pragmatic solution suggested by Kaldor (1956), faced with a similar problem with his own model. It suffers from the defect that unincorporated businesses are included in the personal sector, whereas for Kalecki's analysis they should be aggregated with the company sector. But apart from this it does have the virtue that one may use data drawn directly from the national accounts.

It also has the advantage that there does exist considerable empirical support for the assumption of different savings behaviour for the two groups thus defined. As has been discussed in Section 8.3 A.*ii*, there appears to be a growing consensus among those engaged in research into the theory of the firm that dividend behaviour conforms to a partial adjustment model, which implies a short-run payout function equivalent to Kalecki's consumption function, λ being the short-run payout ratio.[15]

The problem with this interpretation is that the econometric evidence suggests that it is the long-run target payout ratio, not the short-run ratio, that is stable. In a period of expansion a firm will be under pressure to allow the latter to fall short of the former, to provide the finance for its increased investment, raising the absolute amount of dividends by the minimum necessary to keep shareholders satisfied. In a time of recession, with a relatively low level of investment, the short-run ratio may be permitted to catch up.

It may thus be argued that λ should be expected to be a decreasing function of I. To the extent that this is the case, the sensitivity of profits to changes in I will be diminished. In the limit, if firms manage to match increases in investment with increases in retained earnings, the level of profits is independent of the level of investment, and (9.10) becomes a simple identity.

One could go even further, for if one accepts the Meyer and Glauber bifurcation hypothesis, the level of investment in times of recession is determined by the level of retained earnings, and (9.10) should be stood on its head, rewritten with I as the dependent variable.

This is an empirical issue. Kalecki himself was much more concerned with econometrics than was usual among theorists of the time (for example, Keynes), but his technique was unsophisticated and in any case he never attempted to test (9.10) (or any variant of it) directly. Later advocates, for example Robinson and Eatwell (1973), have added nothing at all. Perhaps this is understandable, for it would require considerable ingenuity to discriminate between the Kalecki and the orthodox Keynesian models using time series data.

The leakage via λ is of course not the only ground for doubting that (9.10) determines profits. Neither the balance of trade, nor personal sector saving, nor indeed the effects of the activities of the public sector (not taken into account in the equation as it stands) may be considered to be exogenous, and so in principle one should construct a complete simultaneous equations model to investigate the relationship between profits and investment. The multiplier now depends not only on λ but also on the parameters of the other equations, and its stability is correspondingly more vulnerable than may appear at first sight, especially when the effects of expectations are taken into consideration.

---

[15] It should be noted that S_w now includes savings out of dividends in additions to savings out of wages, and that consequently the multiplier in (9.10) is somewhat lower than $1/(1 - \lambda)$. The multiplier will of course be lower still if there is a significant marginal propensity to save out of wages.

In consequence, even if one were to accept the structure of Kalecki's model as broadly correct, one may doubt the force of the causality relationship between investment and profits. The more sceptical one is about the stability of the parameters, the more difficult it is to distinguish the Kalecki model from traditional analysis.

B. THE SIGNIFICANCE OF THE MODEL

But leaving aside these misgivings, on the face of it Kalecki's model represents a clean break with the neoclassical approach. Profits are not determined by the marginal productivity of capital, either in an aggregate or in a micro sense. Instead they are the outcome of the equilibration of savings and investment, and effectively a function of the latter since investment expenditure is exogenous in the short run.

But to put Kalecki's model in perspective, one must look at the long run as well. In particular, one must take into account the feedback from profitability to investment decisions. In an early version (Kalecki, 1937c), this feedback was determined by a variant of Keynes's marginal efficiency of capital. The productivity aspect of the determinants of investment was later somewhat diluted, but it remained a basic element and indeed was essential to the trade cycle mechanism. Of course, owing to myopia on the part of entrepreneurs, *ex post* profitability is only coincidentally equal to *ex ante* profitability, but in the long run, along the trend, one may neglect differences between the two. In the long run, therefore, marginal productivity conditions underlie the analysis after all.

The widow's cruse is thus relegated to the position of a short-run distortion. And this is exactly the role that it plays in Keynes's *Treatise* version, where profits are explicitly defined to be windfalls, income accruing to entrepreneurs over and above the equilibrium return to capital, which is determined in the usual neoclassical way.

The problem of explaining the determinants of the cyclical discrepancy between *ex post* and *ex ante* profits arises in any neoclassical model. And so, far from being a threat to the neoclassical approach, Kalecki's model, like Keynes's before it, may be embraced by it as an attempt to shed light in a dark corner, to be judged on its empirical merits.

10
Non-neoclassical theories II
Kaldor and Pasinetti

10.1 Kaldor

As Solow once said in a Marshall lecture, hardly has one of Kaldor's models floated down to the ground before another is on its way.[1] However the model outlined in Kaldor (1956) has become a landmark, and even if Kaldor has since tentatively proposed a rather different approach (Kaldor, 1966) and at the time of writing appears to be thinking on yet different lines, no other theory has come near to dislodging it from its dominant position in the non-neoclassical pantheon.[2]

At first sight, at least, Kaldor's model seems to have much in common with Kalecki's, and Kalecki is included in the review of previous theories that forms the preamble to Kaldor's exposition of his own theory. But, as has already been mentioned, it is the degree-of-monopoly component of Kalecki's model that is singled out, and this is roundly abused. The profits-investment relationship, where the real parallel lies, receives brief acknowledgement in a footnote. Instead of Kalecki, Keynes is taken as Kaldor's source of inspiration. The model is presented as an extension of the Kahn–Keynes multiplier analysis and is dubbed by him neo-Keynesian, to the irritation of more orthodox Keynesians.

Like Kalecki, Kaldor follows the classical economists in assuming that the propensity to save out of profits is greater than that out of wages. Assuming

---

[1] See also Kaldor and Mirrlees (1962).

[2] An almost identical model was presented by Robinson (1956) (summarized in Robinson, 1975), who may therefore be credited as co-originator. But the indirect method of exposition and lack of development have caused her contribution to be relatively overlooked. For a comparison, see Kregel (1973, pp. 187–93). For a further early contribution, see Kahn (1959).

a closed economy, the private sector savings-investment relationship may be written

$$s_\pi \Pi + s_w W = I \tag{10.1}$$

supposing that for both income groups the marginal propensity to save is equal to the average propensity (the relaxation of this restriction, which is made for the sake of simplicity, would not cause any change of substance in the analysis: Kaldor, 1961). Since wages are the difference between aggregate income and profits, (10.1) may be rewritten

$$s_\pi \Pi - s_w (Y - \Pi) = I \tag{10.2}$$

and hence

$$\Pi = \frac{I}{s_\pi - s_w} - \frac{s_w}{s_\pi - s_w} Y \tag{10.3}$$

(10.3) is formally equivalent to Kalecki's (9.3), under the assumptions that savings out of wages are negligible ($s_w = 0$) and that consumption out of profits is a constant proportion of profits ($A = 0$ in (9.3)). And like Kalecki, Kaldor assumes that investment is exogenous, so that (10.3) may be regarded as a direct causality relationship if s_w is equal to zero.

If savings out of wages are not equal to zero, the causality is undermined by the second term on the right-hand side. But nevertheless one may derive a causality relationship for the share of profits in total income:

$$\frac{\Pi}{Y} = \frac{I/Y}{s_\pi - s_w} - \frac{s_w}{s_\pi - s_w} \tag{10.4}$$

The share of profits is thus determined by the proportion of income invested.

But the similarities between Kalecki and Kaldor end when one considers the time scales of their models. Kalecki's relationships are essentially short-run, and combine together to form a continuous, dynamic model. By contrast, Kaldor's model is intended to apply only when there is full employment, and thus may be regarded as yielding a set of relationships which characterize the trend formed by peaks of the trade cycle.

Accordingly Kaldor's model is completed with the simple condition

$$Y = \bar{Y} \tag{10.5}$$

where $\bar{Y}$ is full employment output. In (10.4), I/Y is the full employment proportion of income invested, and Π/Y is the corresponding full employment share of profits.

(10.4) may thus be interpreted as determining the price level relative to wages, given the size of the components of aggregate expenditure, supplementing the Keynesian short-run analysis where aggregate expenditure is determined with prices taken as given.

As in the Kalecki model, it is essential that investment expenditure be exogenous if the profits-investment causality relationship is to operate in the direction asserted. In Kalecki's model this is defensible on the ground that the relationship is short run and that investment expenditure depends upon decisions taken in the past. But in a long-run context this defence is inadmissible. Kaldor simply states his belief that investment, and hence I/Y, is determined by Keynes's 'animal spirits'.[3]

To see how the model works, suppose that the economy is in a situation of full employment equilibrium and consider the effects of an increase in investment expenditure.

The excess demand leads to an increase in the general price level and profit margins rise. Hence aggregate profits increase and aggregate real wages fall. Because the marginal propensity to save out of profits is greater than that out of wages, savings increase and consumption falls. The spate of inflation ceases when the increase in savings is sufficient to accommodate the increase in investment.

If the workers do not react, this is the end of the story. Investment has displaced consumption through a redistribution of income. If they do react, and succeed in obtaining higher money wages, the effect will simply be to sustain the state of excess demand. To the extent that they are successful in offsetting the effects of inflation, they make the inflation persist that much longer. Prices must eventually rise faster than wages if the excess demand is to be eliminated, and so in real terms the intervention of the workers can make no difference.

In both cases, therefore, the distribution of income will adjust so that the weighted average of the savings rates is equal to the proportion of total income invested. The real change in profits per unit change in investment is given by

$$\frac{d\Pi}{dI} = \frac{1}{s_\pi - s_w} \qquad (10.6)$$

Obviously, the narrower is the differential between the savings rates of the two groups, the greater is the necessary redistribution of income.

It should be noted that equilibrium is possible only if

$$s_\pi \geq \frac{I}{Y} \geq s_w \qquad (10.7)$$

---

[3] Both Kaldor and Robinson attach much importance to Keynes's (unacknowledged) adaptation of Galen's notion of animal spirits in the *General Theory*, playing down or even ignoring entirely the chapter developing his marginal efficiency of capital schedule. Of course neoclassical Keynesians, particularly those addicted to IS-LM analysis, tend to err in the opposite direction.

for otherwise no distribution of income can bring savings into line with investment. The requirement that I/Y be equal to the weighted average of the savings rates means that wages must be large compared with profits if I/Y lies relatively close to s_w, and the reverse if it lies relatively close to s_π.

At one extreme, if it happens that I/Y is equal to s_w, equilibrium requires that the whole of national income be distributed as wages. For if profits were positive, the average propensity to save would be greater than the proportion of income invested, and this would be incompatible with the assumption of full employment. There would be a downward pressure on prices which would persist until profit margins had been eliminated.

Conversely, at the other extreme, with I/Y equal to s_π, the whole of national income would have to be distributed as profits, for otherwise the average propensity to save would be lower than the proportion of income invested, and there would be chronic inflation.

Kaldor argues that in fact the wage share must be above some sociologically-determined minimum, and that the share of profits must be sufficient to guarantee that minimum rate of profit necessary to induce investment. These considerations have the effect of narrowing the limits of (10.7).

If full employment is sustained (or, alternatively, if one looks at the trend formed by trade cycle peaks), (10.4) provides a relationship between the share of profits and the rate of growth, and another between the rate of profit and the rate of growth. For

$$\frac{I}{Y} = \frac{I}{K} \cdot \frac{K}{Y} = \frac{\Delta K}{K} \cdot \frac{K}{Y} = gv \tag{10.8}$$

where g is the rate of growth and v is the capital-output ratio, and so (10.4) may be rewritten

$$\frac{\Pi}{Y} = \frac{gv - s_w}{s_\pi - s_w} \tag{10.9}$$

And since the rate of profit, ρ, is equal to Π/K, one has

$$\rho = \frac{\Pi}{K} = \frac{\Pi}{Y} \cdot \frac{Y}{K} = \frac{\Pi}{Y} \cdot \frac{1}{v} = \frac{g - s_w/v}{s_\pi - s_w} \tag{10.10}$$

The rate of profit thus depends upon the rate of growth, the savings rates, and the capital-output ratio. Kaldor assumes that the capital-output ratio may be regarded as an exogenous parameter, which implies that the rate of growth in question is the natural rate of growth, the rate of growth of the labour force plus labour-augmenting technical progress.

As in Kalecki's model, the rate of profit is not determined by the marginal productivity of capital in any sense. But whereas marginal productivity enters Kalecki's model in the long run by the back door, in Kaldor's model it wholly absent. Unless, of course, the capital-output ratio is responsive to the rate of profit, but this possibility has been excluded by assumption. Kaldor's model thus represents a much more radical break with the neoclassical tradition.

10.2   The effects of fiscal policy

Next, consider the effects of the activities of the public sector. Ignoring transfers, it will be assumed that the public sector is responsible for direct expenditure which is financed partly by the taxation of profits, T_π, partly by the taxation of wages, T_w, and partly by an increase in the issue of bonds, B.[4]

The private sector savings-investment relationship becomes

$$s_\pi(\Pi - T_\pi) + s_w(W - T_w) = I + B \tag{10.11}$$

Since wages are the difference between aggregate income and profits, this implies

$$(s_\pi - s_w)\Pi = I + B + s_\pi T_\pi + s_w T_w - s_w Y \tag{10.12}$$

$$\Pi = \frac{I + B + s_\pi T_\pi + s_w T_w}{s_\pi - s_w} - \frac{s_w}{s_\pi - s_w} Y \tag{10.13}$$

From (10.13) it may be seen that government expenditure financed by bonds has exactly the same effect on the distribution of income as does investment. Profits are increased by an amount $B/(s_\pi - s_w)$, that is by more, perhaps much more, than the value of the bonds. Profit-recipients may nominally be paying for the bonds, but it is the workers who are actually bearing the burden, possibly several times over.

Taxation of wages also increases the share of profits, unless there are no savings from wages. The incidence on wages is thus in general more than 100 per cent.

Taxation of profits increases gross profits by an amount

$$\frac{s_\pi}{s_\pi - s_w} T_\pi = T + \frac{s_w}{s_\pi - s_w} T_\pi \tag{10.14}$$

Such taxation is therefore completely shifted, indeed more than shifted if s_w is positive. It may be noted, in fact, that taxation of profits has exactly the same effect on post-tax profits as does taxation of wages.

As in the Kalecki model, in each of these cases it is the workers who pay. In general they overpay. As Kaldor points out, the only way to make profit-

---

[4] The fourth alternative, an increase in the supply of money, may be handled by treating money as non-interest-bearing bonds.

recipients bear part of the cost is to induce them to increase their savings rate; for example, by taxing dividends more highly than the retained earnings of companies.

As was mentioned in Chapter 5, Kaldor (1955) has been almost as enthusiastic an advocate of the expenditure tax as was Fisher. He mounted his case before he formulated his model of income distribution, and it is of interest to note that the latter offers support to his original commonsense arguments. It is obviously necessary to make some assumption concerning the extent to which the tax falls on consumption rather than savings and so the two extreme cases will be considered in turn.

First, suppose that the savings propensities s_π and s_w are unaffected by the expenditure tax, so that the initial incidence of the latter is on consumption. In this case (10.4), and so the pre-tax shares of profits and wages, are completely unaffected and the tax is not shifted at all.

Second, suppose that the marginal propensities to consume, $(1 - s_\pi)$ and $(1 - s_w)$, are not influenced by the tax and so the brunt of the latter is taken by the savings propensities. If the expenditure tax is imposed at a flat rate t, the effective savings propensities now become $1 - (1 + t)(1 - s_\pi)$ and $1 - (1 + t)(1 - s_w)$ for profits and wages, respectively, and (10.4) becomes

$$\frac{\Pi}{Y} = \frac{I/Y}{(1 + t)(s_\pi - s_w)} - \frac{s_w - t(1 - s_w)}{(1 + t)(s_\pi - s_w)} \tag{10.15}$$

Rearranging this as

$$\frac{\Pi}{Y} = \frac{1 - s_w}{s_\pi - s_w} - \frac{1 - I/Y}{(1 + t)(s_\pi - s_w)} \tag{10.16}$$

it may be seen that Π/Y is an increasing function of t, and hence in this case the expenditure tax will affect the wage share adversely.

Since the actual outcome may lie somewhere between these two extremes, the conclusion is that once again wages are affected more severely than profits. But the discrimination is less sharp than with the other forms of taxation and is the smaller, the greater the extent to which the savings decision takes precedence over the consumption decision.

10.3   Trade

The exposition in Kaldor (1956) is confined to a closed economy, but the analysis may readily be extended to take account of the effects of trade. Neglecting the public sector, the savings-investment relationship may be rewritten

$$s_\pi \Pi + s_w W = I + BT \tag{10.17}$$

where BT is the balance of trade. (10.4) now becomes

$$\frac{\Pi}{Y} + \frac{I/Y}{s_\pi - s_w} + \frac{BT/Y}{s_\pi - s_w} - \frac{s_w}{s_\pi - s_w} \tag{10.18}$$

A chronic trade surplus therefore promotes profitability. Like investment, it requires saving on the part of the economy, and this in turn requires a redistribution of income from wages to profits. By the same token, a trade deficit will have the opposite effect.

Returning to the analysis of the consequences of an increase in investment, it is obvious that in an open economy the inflationary effects may be partially or wholly offset by an increase in the trade deficit. To the extent that this is the case, redistribution of income from wages to profits will not take place.

If the Kaldor model were intended to apply to the short run, it would be severely undermined by this leakage. But since its proper context is the long run, where the balance of trade may be expected to be relatively insensitive to investment, the leakage is likely to be of less importance than in the Kalecki model.

10.4   Pasinetti

Pasinetti (1962) asserts that there is a slip in Kaldor's analysis and proposes a variant. Since workers save, they must accumulate capital or securities issued by capitalists, and hence will receive a part of total profits. This ought to be taken into account in the expression for their savings.

In fact there is no slip, for Kaldor defines his savings relationships in terms of type of income, rather than type of individual, and savings from profits accruing to individuals are simply a component of the larger category, savings from profits. But nevertheless Pasinetti's model is illuminating in its own right and it yields some striking results.

The savings relationships, as defined by Pasinetti, are

$$S_c = s_c \Pi_c \tag{10.19}$$

and

$$S_1 = s_1(W + \Pi_1) \tag{10.20}$$

where S_c is total savings of capitalists, s_c their savings rate, and Π_c the profits accruing to them, and S_1, s_1 and Π_1 are the corresponding terms for the workers.

Since

$$Y = W + \Pi_c + \Pi_1 \tag{10.21}$$

the aggregate savings-investment relationship may be written

$$s_c \Pi_c + s_1(Y - \Pi_c) = I \tag{10.22}$$

and so

$$\frac{\Pi_c}{Y} = \frac{I/Y}{s_c - s_1} - \frac{s_1}{s_c - s_1} \tag{10.23}$$

(10.23) is the counterpart to (10.4) in Kaldor's version. But here the aggregate savings-investment relationship determines only the share of profits accruing to capitalists, not the total share of profits.

An expression for the latter may be obtained if two additional assumptions are introduced: (a) supposing that the workers loan their savings to the capitalists, that the rate of interest is equal to the rate of profit,[5] giving

$$\frac{\Pi_1}{K_1} = \frac{\Pi_c}{K_c} = \frac{\Pi}{K} \tag{10.24}$$

where K_1 and K_c are workers' and capitalists' capital, respectively; and (b) that the economy is experiencing steady state growth, which implies that the capital stock of each group is proportional to its flow of savings:

$$\frac{K_1}{S_1} = \frac{K_c}{S_c} = \frac{K}{S} \tag{10.25}$$

(10.24) and (10.25) together imply

$$\frac{\Pi_1}{S_1} = \frac{\Pi_c}{S_c} = \frac{\Pi}{S} \tag{10.26}$$

In view of (10.19) and (10.20), and the fact that aggregate savings must be equal to aggregate investment, this may be rewritten

$$\frac{\Pi_1}{s_1(W + \Pi_1)} = \frac{1}{s_c} = \frac{\Pi}{I} \tag{10.27}$$

The second half of this equation yields an expression for total profits:

$$\Pi = \frac{I}{s_c} \tag{10.28}$$

and so for the rate of profit

$$\rho = \frac{g}{s_c} \tag{10.29}$$

since ρ is equal to Π/K and g is equal to I/K.

---

[5] In fact, as Laing (1969) points out and Pasinetti (1974) acknowledges, it is sufficient that the rate of interest be proportional to the rate of profit. See also Moore (1974).

Hence one has obtained the elegant Pasinetti result that the rate of profit is equal to the natural rate of growth divided by the capitalists' savings rate.

The result may appear paradoxical in that it involves s_c but not s_1. What is so special about capitalists that leads to this asymmetry? The answer is that they have only one source of income, profits, and that the relationship is a necessary condition for them to receive a constant, positive share of total income in a situation of steady state growth. For if the condition were not satisfied, so that

$$\frac{S}{\Pi} \neq s_c \qquad (10.30)$$

the ratio of aggregate savings to aggregate profits would be different from that of capitalists' savings to capitalists' profits. Since profits are assumed to be proportional to capital in each case, this implies that aggregate capital would be growing at a different rate from capitalists' capital, and hence that the capitalists' share of income in changing, contrary to assumption.

The workers' savings rate is nevertheless important for distribution, for, together with the capitalists' savings rate, it determines the way in which profits must be divided, and the share of total income that must go to wages, if steady state growth is to be possible.

10.5   Extensions of Kaldor and Pasinetti

A. TOBIN

In one of the wittiest, as well as one of the briefest, contributions to the literature, Tobin (1960) proposes a 'generalization' of Kaldor's model.

The essence of Kaldor's model is that there are two types of expenditure and two types of income, both of which have fixed expenditure proportions. The proportions of aggregate expenditure (consumption/investment) are also exogenous. Distribution is determined by the requirement that, for both types of expenditure, the weighted average of the income group proportions be equal to the aggregate proportion. For consumption and investment, respectively, these requirements are

$$(1 - s_\pi)\frac{\Pi}{Y} + (1 - s_w)\frac{W}{Y} = \frac{C}{Y} \qquad (10.31)$$

$$s_\pi \frac{\Pi}{Y} + s_w \frac{W}{Y} = \frac{I}{Y} \qquad (10.32)$$

and they determine Π and W (note that they are in fact equivalent to each other and to (10.4)).

Tobin suggests that Kaldor's specification was unnecessarily modest. Why not generalize it to n income groups (actors, bird-watchers, Conservative

peers,...) and n types of expenditure (aspirin, binoculars, cadillacs,...)? If one can maintain the same expenditure assumptions as before (fixed expenditure proportions for each group and in aggregate), one again obtains a set of linear equations which in general exactly determine the share of total income for each group. Again, the shares must be such as to make, for each type of expenditure, the weighted average of income group proportions equal to the aggregate proportion.

Tobin further observes that, in the original Kaldor model, if either income group became aware of the crucial role of savings propensities for distribution, it might be able to take advantage of it. Assuming that inequality (10.7) is satisfied, from equation (10.4) it can be seen that profit-recipients would be able to increase the share of profits if they were able to act, as a class, to reduce s_π. Likewise wage-recipients would benefit if they were able to increase s_w. In both cases the income group receives the whole of aggregate income if it makes its coefficients equal to the aggregate coefficients (as was shown in Section 10.1).

The same would apply in Tobin's model. If any individual group were sufficiently coordinated as to make its expenditure proportions equal to the aggregate proportions, it would be rewarded by receiving the whole of aggregate income.

Does the surrealism of the 'generalized' model reflect a weakness in the original model? To illustrate the points at issue, consider a small Tobin model with three types of income: profits, Π, non-manual wages, W_{nm}, manual wages, W_m, and two types of consumption good: necessities, C^1, and luxuries, C^2. Defining the savings and consumption coefficient subscripts appropriately, one has three relationships.

$$s_\pi \frac{\Pi}{Y} + s_{nm} \frac{W_{nm}}{Y} + s_m \frac{W_m}{Y} = \frac{I}{Y} \tag{10.33}$$

$$c_\pi^1 \frac{\Pi}{Y} + c_{\pi m}^1 \frac{W_{nm}}{Y} + c_m^1 \frac{W_m}{Y} = \frac{C^1}{Y} \tag{10.34}$$

and

$$c_\pi^2 \frac{\Pi}{Y} + c_{\pi m}^2 \frac{W_{nm}}{Y} + c_m^2 \frac{W_m}{Y} = \frac{C^2}{Y} \tag{10.35}$$

The first problem with this Tobin model is that, although I/Y may be exogenous, C^1/Y and C^2/Y cannot be, except under the most unrealistic assumptions. Indeed, (10.34) and (10.35) must be regarded as determining those proportions. Kaldor (1960) defends (10.33) from the same criticism on the Keynesian ground that investment decisions are independent of savings decisions.

There does, however, remain a second problem. Now that there are three income groups, (10.33) is insufficient by itself to explain the determination of relative shares. For example, given a situation of full employment disturbed by an increase in investment, the necessary extra savings could be generated by a shift in income from W_m to W_{nm}, or from W_{nm} to Π, or from W_m to Π, or a combination of these (assuming $s_\pi > s_{nm} > s_m$). And if there were more categories of income, the indeterminacy of their relative shares would be correspondingly greater.

There are two ways of overcoming this difficulty. The first is to assume that the components of the wage share bear stable ratios to one another. If this is the case, one may aggregate them and be able to assume a stable overall savings coefficient, thus returning to the original Kaldor formulation. The same applies to profits if they are disaggregated initially.

The second way out is simply to assert that savings out of profits are much greater than savings out of wages, and hence (10.33), and (10.4) before it, may be regarded as a direct relationship between investment and profits with the inclusion of a small disturbance term. The disturbance caused by changes in the aggregate propensity to save out of wages may blunt the invest-ment-profits relationship, but not significantly divert its thrust.

With regard to Tobin's suggestion that either income group could improve its share by collectively manipulating its average savings propensity, Kaldor is in complete agreement. But if collective action were possible, not only his model of distribution, but any other, including all neoclassical models, would be invalid.

B. SAMUELSON AND MODIGLIANI

In his original analysis, Pasinetti gives the impression that his steady state growth relationship (10.29), expressing the rate of profit as the ratio of the natural rate of growth and the capitalists' savings rate, was somehow confined to models of the Kaldor type. Samuelson and Modigliani (1966a) point out that this is by no means the case, for it could be applied to any framework that provides the features figuring in the basic Pasinetti assumptions. In particular, it could be applied to neoclassical models of the kind that Pasinetti was endeavouring to undermine, and with no little irony this is what they proceed to do.

Specifying a twice differentiable constant returns to scale production function governing output in a perfectly competitive one commodity economy, they investigate the dynamic properties and stability of the model, in addition to deriving the static steady state growth Pasinetti relationship. They also examine the consequences of weakening the relationship between rate of profit and the marginal product of capital, and of replacing the differentiable production function by one with fixed coefficients.

However, the part of their analysis that has attracted most attention is their suggestion that an alternative steady state configuration, overlooked by Pasinetti, is not only possible but empirically more plausible than the one investigated by him.

For the share of profits to be positive in Pasinetti's analysis, (10.23) requires that

$$s_1 < \frac{I}{Y} \qquad (10.36)$$

If s_1 were greater than I/Y, equilibrium would be impossible, for no distribution of income could bring savings into line with investment. If s_1 were equal to I/Y, the whole of aggregate income would be distributed to workers, either in the form of wages or profits. The rate of profit, and hence the exact division between wages and profits, is indeterminate. Capitalists as an income-receiving class cease to exist, and the aggregate savings-investment relationship simplifies to the Harrod–Domar condition for steady state growth:

$$s_1 Y = I \qquad (10.37)$$

or

$$s_1 = gv \qquad (10.38)$$

This may be regarded as a counterpart to (10.29), and Samuelson and Modigliani dub it the 'anti-Pasinetti' case. In the Pasinetti case, with I/Y greater than s_1, the ratio of the natural rate of growth to the capitalists' savings rate determines the rate of profit. In the anti-Pasinetti case, with I/Y equal to s_1, the ratio of the workers' savings rate to the natural rate of growth determines the capital-output ratio. A lucid diagrammatical treatment of the two cases, illustrated with reference to simple production functions, has been provided by Meade (1966), who in fact first noticed the anti-Pasinetti case (Meade, 1963).

Samuelson and Modigliani actually express the condition for the anti-Pasinetti case in the form

$$s_1 < s_c \frac{\Pi}{Y} \qquad (10.39)$$

(taking advantage of the fact that Π is equal to I/s_c in the Pasinetti case). They suggest that 0.20 and 0.25 would be 'econometrically reasonable' figures for s_c and Π/Y respectively for a mixed economy like the US or the UK, and hence that s_w could not be more than a modest 0.05, if the Pasinetti condition is to be satisfied. The figure of 0.20 for s_c might be thought of as the result of a dividend payout ratio of 2/3 for corporations and a propensity to consume out of dividends of 6/5.

However, it may immediately be noted, as Pasinetti (1966a) points out, that these 'econometrically reasonable' figures imply a very low capital-output ratio. Since

$$s_c \frac{\Pi}{Y} = \frac{I}{Y} = gv \qquad (10.40)$$

Samuelson and Modigliani's figures imply that

$$v = 0.05/g \qquad (10.41)$$

In other words, if the natural rate of growth were 3 per cent per year, a rate which mixed economies of the kind described have managed to attain over the past generation, the implicit capital-output ratio would be 1.67. And if the natural rate of growth were any higher, the implicit capital-output ratio would be lower still.

If the capital-output ratio were, say, 3, and the natural rate of growth 3 per cent per year, the condition would be that s_1 should be lower than 0.09, which is plausible enough.

Kaldor (1966) also questions the savings rates suggested by Samuelson and Modigliani. The relevant savings rate out of profits is the rate of gross savings out of gross profits (since savings and investment are both measured gross of depreciation provisions in the Pasinetti model). Kaldor asserts that this rate is 0.7 to 0.8 for the kind of economy under consideration. This in itself should ensure the validity of the Pasinetti condition, unless capitalists have a very pronounced tendency to overconsume out of dividend income.

In addition he points out that the rate of net acquisition of financial assets of the personal sector is a more appropriate measure of s_1 than the gross savings ratio, the difference being personal sector investment in dwellings, investment by unincorporated businesses, and purchases of consumer durables if included in gross savings. He reckons that s_1 thus defined, is likely to be very small indeed, say 0.02 or 0.01.

Further refinements which might affect the argument either way (for example, a consideration of the effects of taxation and government borrowing) could of course be introduced. But it is questionable whether any figures that might emerge could even in principle be relevant. For, as Samuelson and Modigliani (1966b) acknowledge, the relationship under consideration is one which involves steady state values of the quantities involved, and it is not at all clear that those derived from recent experience are acceptable approximations. The dispute therefore remains unresolved.

C. CHIANG

Kaldor assumes that savings behaviour should be related to source of income; Pasinetti, to type of recipient. Chiang (1973) observed that if one disaggregates both ways simultaneously, and attaches a different savings coefficient to each component, one obtains a more general model, of which the Kaldor and Pasinetti versions are special cases.[6] Writing $s_{\pi c}$, $s_{\pi l}$ and $s_{w l}$ for the savings

---

[6] For a parallel analysis, see Maneschi (1974).

coefficients, the first subscript referring to source of income, the second to type of recipient, the aggregate savings-investment relationship becomes

$$s_{\pi c}\Pi_c + s_{\pi l}\Pi_l + s_{wl}W = I \qquad (10.42)$$

Now if $s_{\pi c}$ is equal to $s_{\pi l}$, one has the Kaldor model, and if $s_{\pi l}$ is equal to s_{wl}, the Pasinetti model.

The Pasinetti steady state growth relationship

$$\rho = \frac{g}{s_{\pi c}} \qquad (10.43)$$

is unaffected on moving to the generalized model, provided that steady state growth is possible with the capitalists receiving a positive share. The condition for this (Chiang, p. 313) is

$$s_{\pi c} \geq \frac{I}{Y} > \frac{s_{\pi c}s_{wl}}{s_{\pi c} - s_{\pi l} + s_{wl}} \qquad (10.44)$$

assuming that the savings rates satisfy the inequality

$$s_{\pi c} > s_{\pi l} > s_{wl} \qquad (10.45)$$

If the first half of (10.44) were an equality, steady state growth would be possible only if the whole of aggregate income were absorbed by capitalists' profits. If the second half were an equality, capitalists' profits would be zero and one obtains a generalized version of the anti-Pasinetti case. The savings-investment relationship then reduces to

$$s_{\pi l}\Pi_l + s_{wl}W = I \qquad (10.46)$$

This is of course formally indistinguishable from the original Kaldor specification, and so one may apply the Kaldor results.

The similarity between the generalized anti-Pasinetti case and the Kaldor specification suggests that steady state growth with capitalists receiving a positive share is impossible in the latter. And this is indeed correct, unless there are no savings out of wages. For in Kaldor's model workers save the same proportion of their profits as do capitalists, and so their capital would grow at the same rate as that of capitalists if this were the only source of savings. But if in addition workers save out of wages, their capital stock must grow faster. Hence although capitalists' profits will grow in absolute terms, as a share of aggregate income they must decline asymptotically to zero.

If workers' savings from wages are equal to zero, then steady state growth with capitalists obtaining a stable positive share is possible. Their fraction of total profits will be proportional to their fraction of the total capital stock when the economy entered the steady state.

10.6 Evaluation

A. PASINETTI

In the case of the Pasinetti model, and in much of the discussion and elaboration of it and the Kaldor model, the steady state growth framework is explicitly adopted. But steady state growth is hardly of any direct interest in itself, and presumably the analysis is presented with the intention of acting as a guide to the relationships that will obtain in the long run. This suggestion is explicitly made by Pasinetti.[7]

But should the step from steady state growth to the long run be taken so lightly? For the Pasinetti result is essentially a *precondition* for the existence of a steady state growth with a constant share of profits going to capitalists, and is more a matter of logic than economics. If it is rewritten as

$$s_c = \frac{g}{r} \tag{10.47}$$

one has an alternative, but equivalent, interpretation: the condition for capitalists to maintain a constant share of total income is that their saving rate be equal to g/r.

If one departs from the context of steady state growth, the result collapses. If the share of profits is not constant, (10.27) loses its validity, and absolutely nothing can be said about the rate of profit.

As Morishima (1977) points out, Pasinetti nowhere discusses why the constant share condition should be added to the usual set of equilibrium conditions. Certainly it is not fulfilled in practice, for the long-run share of profits has been falling in the US, the UK and all similar economies (Kuznets, 1966, Chapter 4), and there is no indication that a lower limit is being approached. And as for the implicit suggestion that in practice the steady state may serve as a proxy for the long run, simulation experiments by Furono (1970) have indicated that the approach to Pasinetti equilibrium may take the best part of a millenium. One must therefore conclude that, despite the theoretical generality claimed for it, the Pasinetti result has absolutely no relevance at all.

There are other problems with the Pasinetti model, notably that of defining capitalists in a world where those individuals whose income is mainly derived from profits do not form a permanent and hereditary caste. But perhaps enough has already been said to dismiss the model from serious practical consideration. The discussion that follows will therefore focus on the original Kaldor formulation.

---

[7] Pasinetti (1966a) describes (10.29) as determining 'the long run equilibrium rate of profit' under the appropriate conditions. A similar statement is made in Pasinetti (1974), p. 144.

i The exogeneity of savings rates

Kaldor's analysis, like that of Kalecki, is based on the insight that the rate of saving out of profits is greater, much greater, than the rate of saving out of wages. This is an undeniable fact, and any serious analysis of the equilibration of savings and investment must take it into account.

But this should not lead one into assuming that these saving rates are stable, as is required for the working of the Kaldor model. Identifying profits with company sector earnings, and wages with personal sector earnings, as Kaldor suggests, and returning to (10.4),

$$\frac{\Pi}{Y} = \frac{I/Y}{s_\pi - s_w} - \frac{s_w}{s_\pi - s_w} \tag{10.4}$$

it can be seen that if firms coordinate their investment and saving plans, so that a change in the level of investment is accompanied by a change in the retention ratio, s_π, in the same direction, the effect on profits will be reduced.

Thus with an important difference, one of the problems arising with the Kalecki model recurs. The difference is that s_π should here be interpreted as the target, rather than the short-run, retention ratio, since the Kaldor model refers to the long run.

This is an advantage, since the empirical evidence indicates that the target ratio is relatively stable. But nevertheless, although it may be independent of cyclical fluctuations in investment expenditure, it is not necessarily independent of the investment trend, and it is the latter that counts in the context of Kaldor's model.

Indeed, as has been suggested in Chapter 8, there would appear to be considerable pressure on the average firm, and hence on the company sector as a whole, to adjust its target retention ratio so that internal funds are sufficient to finance investment expenditure in the long run. As in the Kalecki model, where a similar adjustment was argued on a short-run basis, this would weaken, or even eliminate entirely, the effect of investment on profits. Such empirical evidence as exists would appear to be inadequate to resolve this issue.

The stability of the personal sector savings rate is also important for the Kaldor model. For although it may be small compared with that for profits, variations in it have a much larger effect on aggregate savings, simply because the share of wages in national income is much greater than the share of profits. If the company sector were to rely on external funds to some extent, a relatively small increase in it would be needed.

Again, this issue cannot be resolved by an appeal to the empirical evidence.

As has been discussed in Chapter 8, the econometric literature on the consumption function has been more concerned with testing one theoretical approach against another than with providing a robust specification. Estimates of the short-run marginal propensity to consume vary widely between the different approaches, even when given the same data. It follows, *a fortiori*, that the long-run stability of the personal sector savings rate, like that of the corporate sector, is a matter for conjecture. Consequently the Kaldor model must be regarded as demanding a certain amount of faith, in this respect at least.

ii The exogeneity of investment

In Kalecki's short-run model the exogeneity of investment is assured by the lag between decisions and disbursement. In Kaldor's model this gap is immaterial, and one has to look at the empirical evidence more closely to assess his assertion that it is determined by animal spirits rather than by considerations of profitability.

Unfortunately, as has been observed in Section 8.3, the econometric literature on investment is in an even more indecisive state than that on consumption, and offers little guidance.

Even worse, it is entirely a matter of subjective judgement whether or not any given specification should be interpreted as reflecting the influence of profitability. For example, the accelerator approach does not formally include profitability as an explanatory variable. But it may be argued that changes in output, which are included, act as a proxy for it, since profits are procyclical. Likewise the Jorgenson regressions do not include profitability explicitly, but the assumption of profit-maximization is the starting point for his approach.

There is therefore no way of testing Kaldor's assumption, and its validity, like that of the assumption of exogenous savings rates, must remain a matter of opinion. But what is presumably the most informed opinion in this context, that of those developing the theory of the firm, would appear to be largely unfavourable to Kaldor. For although most allow that the role of profits is diluted in corporate decision-making by such considerations as growth and market power, they would not agree that it is completely replaced by them (although there are exceptions, notably Baumol (1958, 1962) and Wood (1975), as will be seen in the next chapter).

10.7 Conclusions

The Kaldor model, like that of Kalecki, has two strong points in its favour: its explicit treatment of the different roles played by the personal and company sectors in saving as well as investment, and its recognition of the importance of macroeconomic relationships, both of these being areas in which traditional neoclassical analysis tends to be very weak. And unlike the Kalecki model, it is a genuine alternative to the neoclassical model, in that it is entirely free from marginal analysis.

On the negative side of the balance sheet, there is the total lack of empirical support. Neither Kaldor nor anyone else has attempted to substantiate the model econometrically. However, one may well argue that such efforts would inevitably be futile. As has been discussed in Section 10.6, it is difficult to see how a rigorous test could be constructed, given existing data.

Unfortunately, even if there were major advances in the understanding of saving and investment, there would be virtually no hope of any significant developments in this direction. To test the model one must use time series data, given the insurmountable problems that would arise in an attempt to use intercountry comparisons. And by definition the only relevant observations would be those taken in years of full employment, perhaps one year in three. Given that one would surely require at least twenty observations to make any impression on the problem of multicollinearity, this implies that one would need a time series of about sixty years. Even if one were sanguine enough as to accept one year in two as being a year of full employment, one would need a time series of forty years.

Even if the Kaldor model were valid, one could hardly expect its parameters to remain constant over such a long period of time. It is therefore almost a foregone conclusion that econometric tests will be impotent. Favourable results could be questioned by critics of the model on the ground that they were attributable to the high degree of multicollinearity inherent in any macroeconomic model of this kind. Unfavourable results could be explained away by adherents to the model on the ground that its parameters are likely to shift from one generation to the next for sociological and institutional reasons.

A further problem concerns the specification of equilibrium for the model. Strictly speaking, the Kaldor equations apply only when all lags and leads have had time to work themselves out, aggregate supply and demand have been reconciled with one another, and relative prices are steady. It is true that Kaldor does informally sketch disequilibrium behaviour, but not in sufficient detail to warrant testing.

In practice, of course, equilibrium of this kind is never attained. Hence, even in years of full employment, the data are not necessarily appropriate for testing the model. And this naturally provides further scope for differences of interpretation between critics and adherents. Any test which undermined the Kaldor model could itself be undermined on the ground that it did not take account of the disequilibrium nature of the data, or that it did so in an inappropriate way.

Needless to say, similar remarks apply to all the major theories of distribution, neoclassical and non-neoclassical alike. And so, if one is prepared to ignore the prevailing weight of opinion concerning his assumptions, subscription to Kaldor's model is no more an act of faith than subscription to any of the others.

11
Non-neoclassical theories III
Wood

11.1 Introduction

The discussion of the post-Marshallian theory of the firm in Chapter 8 was limited to an assessment of its implications for the Fisherian model. Such is the usual reaction to this new body of literature when it impinges on other branches of economic theory – a passive reconsideration of the relevant assumptions which at most leads to more caution in the expression of conclusions. Apart from this, the post-Marshallian view of business behaviour has had remarkably little impact on the rest of economic theory and there have been minimal attempts at integration. Even its bearing on macroeconomic theory has hitherto been speculative rather than constructive.

Accordingly, the recent contribution of Wood (1975), a theory of distribution which takes it as a point of departure, is a positive and novel development.

In one sense Wood's model might be regarded as neoclassical, in that it shares the framework of maximization subject to constraint, but such a description would be misleading, for the importance that he attaches to the effects of uncertainty and ignorance about the future on capital markets and company financial policy leads him to reject the traditional neoclassical choice of maximand and specification of constraints.

Indeed superficially it might appear to belong to the Cambridge approach, in that it focuses on the strategic role of retained earnings in the financing of private investment and that it concludes, broadly speaking, that profits are determined by investment. But again such a label would not be apt, for its mechanism is very different from that of Kaldor and Robinson. In particular, its macroeconomic relationships depend upon a careful microeconomic modelling of the individual firm and are incomprehensible without it.

11.2   The micro relationships

The structure of the Wood model may be very briefly summarized: the firm strives to maximize its rate of growth of sales revenue subject to two constraints which relate growth to profitability. The first of these, termed by Wood the 'opportunity frontier', is largely a demand constraint, and the second, the 'finance frontier', takes account of the dominance of retained earnings in the financing of investment.

It should be emphasized from the outset that the analysis is intended to be medium-term. Wood visualizes firms as having a rolling planning horizon of, say, three to five years and determining their policies accordingly.

A. THE OPPORTUNITY FRONTIER

The opportunity frontier is probably the least controversial component of Wood's analysis. He argues that, for any given state of aggregate demand in the economy as a whole, there will be a trade-off between the profit margin of the firm, π, and the rate of growth of its sales revenue, g, as shown in Figure 11.1.

The curvature of the frontier reflects the discretionary power derived by the firm from imperfect competition in the market for its output and in the markets for non-financial factors of production. Movements along it are typically the result of non-price competition. Effectively, the firm may shift its demand curve by varying its selling expenditures, and hence is able to

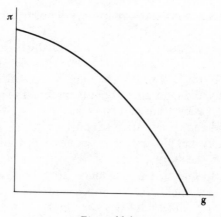

Figure 11.1

increase the rate of growth of its sales revenue if it is willing to accept a lower profit margin.[1]

B. THE FINANCE FRONTIER

Looking at the capital account of a firm, gross investment expenditure plus the increase in its holdings of financial assets must be equal to retained earnings plus the increase in long-term external finance. Wood argues that, in the medium run, (i) the increase in the holdings of financial assets must be at least equal to a proportion f, termed by him the target or minimum financial assets ratio, of gross investment; (ii) the increase in external finance can at most be equal to a proportion x, the target or maximum external finance ratio, of gross investment; and (iii) the proportion of profits retained, γ, the target gross retention ratio, may be considered to be exogenous. Hence the capital account imposes the constraint

$$I + fI \leq \gamma\Pi + xI \tag{11.1}$$

Before investigating the implications of (11.1) one should state Wood's reasons for assumptions (i)–(iii).

(i) The target financial assets ratio is determined by the need for the firm to increase its liquidity cushion as its scale of operations grows larger. Although the firm may be able to provide itself with sufficient funds, via retained earnings and external finance, to cover investment expenditure in the medium run, unforeseen contingencies may prevent it from doing so in the short run (for example, an unexpected fall in demand that leaves it with excess stocks and a reduced cash flow).

Wood assumes that the firm sets itself a target liquidity ratio, seeking to keep a certain balance between its stock of financial assets and its stock of physical assets. It follows that in the medium (and long) run the flow-increase in its holdings of financial assets should be proportional to its flow of investment in physical assets – in other words, that the target financial assets ratio should be constant. In the short run, of course, the actual ratio may fluctuate around the target ratio.

(ii) The target external finance ratio, x, is determined by several factors. First of all one must distinguish between external finance in the form of equity (rights issues) and that in the form of borrowing (principally debentures and continuously renewed bank loans).

The raising of new equity is on the whole exceptional, it generally being

---

[1] As Marris (1964) argues in places, it may be reasonable to suppose that for very low rates of growth, at least, there may be a positive relationship between growth and profitability. This would not affect Wood's model since only the downward-sloping part of the curve can act as a constraint.

thought that rights issues are disliked by shareholders, and recourse to it is usually occasioned by the appearance of especially attractive investment opportunities.

Borrowing is in principle limited by both supply and demand, but Wood argues that demand is the operative constraint. Clearly the greater the debt-equity ratio, the greater the chances of bankruptcy, and hence the greater the danger to the creditors of the firm, its shareholders and its employees alike. The first two classes can hedge their bets through diversification, but the third cannot, and Wood argues that it will be the managers of the firm who will apply a limit to the gearing ratio for fear of jeopardizing the safety of their own jobs.

The existence of a maximum gearing ratio implies that in the long run the increase in external finance cannot be more than a certain proportion of the increase in total assets, and hence investment in physical assets (assuming a stable liquidity ratio). Again, in the short run the proportion x may be influenced by transient factors.

(iii) The gross retention ratio, γ, is defined as the ratio of depreciation allowances plus retained earnings to gross trading profits. Given the level of profits, the key parameter determining retained earnings is the payout ratio, the proportion of net earnings distributed in the form of dividends. Wood argues that the medium-term target payout ratio depends upon management's perception of shareholders' attitudes to liquidity and certain sorts of risk, and tends moreover to be relatively stable over time. To some extent it may also be influenced by changes in corporate taxation.

Depreciation allowances depend of course on the medium-run rate of investment rather than on the level of profits. As Wood states, this implies that strictly speaking γ should be written as a function of both investment and profits, rather than as a simple constant, but this would not affect his model significantly.

Inequality (11.1) implies

$$\Pi \geq \frac{1+f-x}{\gamma} I \tag{11.2}$$

which determines the level of profits needed to finance a given level of investment. Writing K for the total physical assets of the firm and Y for its gross sales revenue, (11.2) may be rewritten

$$\frac{\Pi}{Y} \geq \frac{1+f-x}{\gamma} \cdot \frac{I}{K} \cdot \frac{K}{Y} \tag{11.3}$$

and hence

$$\pi \geq \frac{1+f-x}{\gamma} (g+\delta)v \tag{11.4}$$

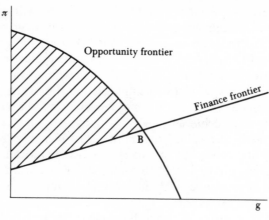

Figure 11.2

where v is the gross incremental capital-output ratio for the firm and δ is the depreciation rate for capital.

Figure 11.2 shows the finance frontier of the firm imposed upon its opportunity frontier. If the parameters in (11.4) were strictly exogenous, the finance frontier would be a straight line with a positive intercept proportional to δ. Since in fact they depend to some extent on g (and also, in the case of γ, on Π), the relationship will be correspondingly nonlinear.

Only those policies which lead to points in the shaded area of Figure 11.2 are feasible. Points lying under the finance frontier represent policies which do not generate enough internal finance to cover the investment required, and points outside the opportunity frontier are unattainable for lack of demand for the firm's product.

Following Baumol (1958, 1962), Wood argues that, in general, industrial and commercial companies attempt to maximize their rate of growth, and hence that the policy leading to the point B will be chosen. Profitability is subordinated and becomes a means rather than an end, affecting management's policy through its role in determining the opportunity and finance frontiers. Indeed the point B may be regarded as balancing the management's desire to keep profit margins as low as possible to generate growth of sales and its need to keep them high enough to finance its investment.

The formulation of the firm's (medium-term) investment programme is visualized by Wood as an iterative process. The firm starts by adopting a criterion rate of return, surveys its investment opportunities and provisionally accepts those with a rate of return higher than the critical level. This implies a certain growth rate for the firm, say g_1. Next, considering the market for its product, the firm estimates π_1, the maximum profit margin that it will be able to obtain with that rate of growth (the value of π corresponding to g_1

on the opportunity frontier). At the same time, it will estimate π_2, the minimum profit margin needed for financing that rate of growth (the value of π corresponding to g_1 on the finance frontier). If π_1 is greater than π_2, the firm can afford to grow faster, and it repeats the evaluation process using a lower criterion rate of return. If π_1 is less than π_2, the firm would be unable to finance all the investment contemplated and it must begin again with a higher criterion rate of return. When π_1 is equal to π_2, the maximum feasible growth rate is being achieved.

So far it has been assumed that v, the gross incremental capital-output ratio, is fixed. In the short run this may be the case, but within a medium-term framework it is more reasonable to suppose that the firm is able to choose from a range of techniques with differing capital intensities, and hence that the determination of v is part of the investment decision.[2]

The value of v obviously has a direct effect on the finance frontier. The more capital-intensive the technique, the steeper will be the slope of the finance frontier, and hence, other things being equal, the higher will be the required profit margin and the lower will be the maximum growth rate.

But at the same time the choice of technique is likely to affect the location of the opportunity frontier. Wood suggests that the more capital-intensive the technique, the lower will be the firm's operating costs and hence the further from the origin will be the opportunity frontier.

Taking both of these factors into account, the joint effect may be as shown in Figure 11.3. The lines of_1 and ff_1 represent the opportunity frontier and

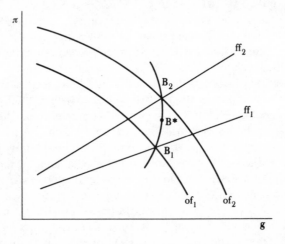

Figure 11.3

---

[2] Another aspect of the investment decision is the speed at which the firm chooses to replace obsolescent plant and equipment.

the finance frontier, respectively, for a low value of v, and the optimal policy is given by B_1; of$_2$ and ff$_2$ represent the lines for a higher value of v, and the optimal policy is given by B_2 in this case.

The point B may shift either to the left or to the right if the capital-intensity is increased. Wood argues that for very low values of v the maximum growth rate will increase with v, but beyond a certain point it will fall again, as shown by the heavy curve in the figure. The optimal choice of technique is then that which leads to the highest possible growth rate, that given by the point B*.

11.3 The macro model

The micro analysis is partial in as much as each firm must take as exogenous the general level of aggregate demand, and hence the location of its particular demand function. In aggregate this ceases to be the case and so at the macro level there can be no counterpart to the individual firm's opportunity frontier.

But such a counterpart would be unnecessary. For the existence of the individual opportunity frontier ensures that each firm will choose a policy where the financial constraint is binding, that is, represented by a point on the finance frontier rather than by one above it.

This implies that (11.1)–(11.4) may be written as equations rather than inequalities. There is no difficulty in aggregating the financial frontier across firms and one obtains

$$\Pi = \frac{1+f-x}{\gamma}I \tag{11.5}$$

and

$$\frac{\Pi}{Y} = \frac{1+f-x}{\gamma}(g+\delta)v \tag{11.6}$$

where Π, I and Y take on their usual aggregate meanings, the quantity $(1+f-x)/\gamma$ is the average of the corresponding quantities for the individual firms weighted by their investment expenditure, and v is the aggregate capital-output ratio.[3]

The aggregate relationship is termed by Wood the finance function since it shows the level of profits that will be generated by any given level of investment. The determination of the level of aggregate investment lies outside the scope of the model, but Wood suggests that, for example, one could

---

[3] Note that in (11.3) and (11.4) Y denotes the sales revenue of the firm, rather than the value added, and v is the capital-sales ratio. Here Y reverts to its usual definition of gross output net of intermediate inputs, and v is the corresponding capital-output ratio. v is the weighted average of the capital-output ratios of the individual firms multiplied by the proportion of total output produced by the company sector. Wood assumes that this proportion is fairly stable.

supply a multiplier-accelerator model managed by the government with fiscal policy.

To see how the model works, suppose that the economy is in equilibrium and that medium-term expectations concerning aggregate demand are improved as the result of a change in government policy. Each firm will believe that its opportunity frontier has shifted outwards and that as a consequence it can afford to grow faster than before. It increases its investment assuming that the improvement in demand will provide the additional profits needed to finance it. In terms of Figure 11.2, the point B shifts out along the finance frontier.

The prophecy of the increase in aggregate demand is thus self-fulfilling provided that the government takes appropriate fiscal measures to ensure that the average propensity to save rises to match the higher share of investment in total output, and the relationship between the increase in aggregate investment and the increase in aggregate profits is given by (11.5). Looking at the finance function in another way, (11.6) determines the share of profits that will be generated as the result of any particular rate of growth achieved by the economy. The role of the individual opportunity frontier is to determine the relative rates of growth of the individual firms.

Corporate taxation has much the same ultimate effect in this model as in the Kaldor model. Provided that the payout ratio remains stable, an increase in corporate taxation will lower the gross retention ratio and hence raise the level of gross profits. Internal finance must be the same as before if it is to cover its share of investment expenditure, and since depreciation provisions are unaffected this means that the increase in gross profits must be just sufficient to allow retained earnings to remain at their previous level. This in turn implies that total post-tax earnings are unaffected and thus that the increase in taxation is completely shifted.

Of course a change in corporation tax may be expressly designed to affect the payout ratio, for example by discriminating between dividends and retained earnings. If, say, taxation on the former is increased, companies may respond by reducing the payout ratio. To some extent this will offset the fall in γ and hence damp the rise in profits. The result is that post-tax profits will fall and the increase in taxation is only partially shifted.

11.4 Evaluation

The foregoing outline does not in any way do justice to the craft with which Wood constructs his model. The various flows which enter into the interplay between savings and investment are precisely identified and systematically related to the appropriate national income accounts. Feedbacks from one relationship to another are scrupulously pursued and their significance assessed. Above all, the macroeconomic analysis is carefully accompanied by a parallel microeconomic discussion which displays the works of the mechanism in action.

The logic of the model is impeccable, but it depends crucially on two basic sorts of behavioural assumptions: one about what firms maximize, the other about the constraints on them, the latter (or, at least, the distinctive ones among them) being Wood's assumptions about company financial behaviour – in particular, about the ways in which firms and shareholders react to the fact that the future is highly uncertain.

These assumptions, which are discussed mainly in Chapter 2 of his book, lie at the heart of his theory – his whole model flows from them – and they differ markedly from the orthodox assumptions. The usefulness or otherwise of his theory thus depends critically on whether or not they are correct, or at any rate more correct than the orthodox alternatives.

With regard to the objective of growth maximization attributed to the management of a firm, Wood cites virtually no empirical evidence. The most that can be said is that the evidence that is usually interpreted as supporting the conventional view (that management pursues some compromise between profitability and growth) is not actually inconsistent with his extreme position.

It may be worth noting that in principle the assumption is not absolutely essential to his model. Its role is to guarantee that the finance constraint is binding, and this would also be the case with the conventional view if the opportunity frontier were sufficiently elastic, that is, if the output and factor markets of the firm were sufficiently competitive. The greater the intensity of the competition, the smaller need be the relative weight attached to growth for the finance constraint to be binding.[4] Indeed in a very competitive market it would be binding even for a Marshallian profit-maximizing firm. But if Wood is right in believing (as he does) that imperfect competition is the rule, then he also needs to be right in thinking that the desire for growth is paramount.[5]

The degree of exogeneity of the target level of the gross retention ratio, γ, is bound to be a second area of contention. The issue at stake is not whether it is absolutely exogenous, but whether it is sufficiently exogenous for the level of profits to be sensitive to the level of investment. Any feedback to γ from either profits or investment is liable to reduce the elasticity of the former

---

[4] Note that the profitability-growth indifference curves conventionally attributed to management (see, for example, Williamson (1966)) cannot be directly superimposed on Figure 11.2 since the vertical axis in that diagram measures, not profitability, but the profit margin.

[5] A further point follows from the observation of Meeks and Whittington (1975) that much of the growth of large firms takes the form of the acquisition of other companies, usually by means of the exchange of shares. This raises the possibility that the opportunity frontier for such firms is backward-bending, with the maximum value of g reached before it cuts the finance frontier. For the lower the profit margin accepted by the firm in its quest for growth, the lower will be its share price, and the greater will be its difficulty in acquiring other companies.

with respect to the latter. The question is whether such feedbacks are so strong that the elasticity turns out to be negligible in practice.

One such feedback is built in from the start, for as Wood states, γ should be written as a function of both I and Π, in as much as it is the ratio of the sum of depreciation provisions and retained earnings to gross profits. But this might be regarded as a secondary matter, influencing the shape of the finance frontier without necessarily reducing the elasticity appreciably. More serious is the possibility, almost excluded by Wood, that γ might be responsive to the investment opportunities available to the firm.

In the short run one would not expect such a feedback, in view of the reluctance of firms to reduce the absolute money level of dividend payments. In the long run, however, the combined effects of growth and inflation make it possible to reduce the payout ratio without reducing the dividend level, and hence a change in g may be partially compensated by a change in γ. Indeed one could advance the extreme view that (11.4) should be rewritten

$$\gamma \geq (1 + f - x) \frac{(g + \delta)v}{\pi} \tag{11.7}$$

in which case the finance function (11.6) would unravel completely and the elasticity of profits with respect to investment would be zero. Whether firms do behave like this is another matter. The literature agrees that the payout ratio is relatively stable, but is remarkably silent concerning its long-run determinants.

These are not the only points at which one might take issue with Wood.[6] Indeed in a model described in such detail it would be surprising if they were. But they are both of critical importance for the validity of the investment-profits causality relationship.

11.5   Conclusion

To test Wood's model econometrically is just as difficult as testing other models and one cannot expect to discriminate decisively either in favour of it or against it. Nevertheless, in view of the virtual absence of empirical evidence in the specific potential areas of controversy just described, his model must be regarded as being in the experimental stage.

But there can be no doubt that the model offers a fresh and promising approach to the explanation of distribution. No theory can be taken seriously if it does not include a realistic account of company behaviour, and Wood may well be correct in his belief that such a model must be central.

---

[6] One might, for example, have doubts about the exogeneity of the external finance and financial assets ratios, especially the former, given Wood's own figure that a quarter of company investment is financed by external funds.

12

The present state of the controversy

12.1 Organizing principles

Perhaps the two greatest disappointments in the history of epistemology
have been the realization, first, that no hypothesis can be proved to be true,
and, second, that no hypothesis can be proved to be false (Popper, 1934;
Kuhn, 1962; Lakatos, 1970).[1] On this ground alone, therefore, one must
accept that an evaluation of the relative merits of the neoclassical and
Cambridge approaches to capital theory can amount to no more than a
subjective assessment of their relative plausibility.

Moreover this must be tentative even by modest standards of economics, given the restricted scope for econometric experiments of the kind
that are traditionally used to test economic theories, and the singular lack of
enthusiasm for empirical analysis on the part of the theorists. Since the relevant data, especially the macroeconomic data, may with a little ingenuity be
interpreted as fitting any of the theories described in this book, it follows that
much of the polemical writing that has enlivened the literature has thrown
more light on the commitment of the theorist than on his theory.

In the case of the neoclassical approach, where behaviour is treated as
being determined by maximization subject to constraint, the impossibility
of either proof or disproof is especially apparent, given the arbitrariness
in specifying what is being maximized by whom subject to which constraints.

---

[1] Curiously enough, epistemologists have almost invariably illustrated their discussions of what
is meant by scientific progress with examples drawn from the natural sciences, where in practice
the criteria are seldom in doubt, rather than the social sciences, where the issue is a guest at
every gathering. For a lucid introduction which should be required reading for all students of
economics, see Loasby (1971) Chapter 11.

But to suggest that, because in principle it is capable of explaining everything, it therefore explains nothing, is to misunderstand its role as an organizing framework in the development of economic thought. It should be regarded as a means of orientation, not a touchstone for absolute truth, and as such it remains remarkably fruitful, taking economics as a whole, to judge by the literature, and especially the empirical studies, to which it gives rise each year. Since this is as much as one has a right to expect, the extreme view that in its case 'a seductive exterior veils a hollow reality. For the accretion of assumptions necessary to sustain the theory has rendered it devoid of empirical significance' (Eatwell, 1977) simply indicates a lack of awareness of the limitations of the scientific method.

The dogmatic statement of Eichner and Kregel (1975) that the objective of neoclassical theory is 'to demonstrate the social optimality if the real world were to resemble the model' (whereas that of Cambridge theory is 'to explain the real world as observed empirically'), which expresses a feeling never far from the surface in the Cambridge writings, must therefore be regarded as naive. It takes the narrowest view of neoclassical theory and it ignores the results that it has achieved and its sustained capacity for evolution. In particular, in the present context, it ignores the informal approach to capital theory that has been treated at length in Chapters 3–8.

By contrast the Cambridge school[2] has no coherent organizing framework. This in itself is not a criticism, for coherence, like consistency, is not necessarily a scientific virtue.[3] The sceptic may reasonably take the view that the policy prescriptions of *ad hoc* models are likely to do less damage than those of dubious theoretical structures. But nevertheless it is hardly satisfactory to have as the main bond a common opposition to neoclassical theory. This negative factor may furnish a criterion for belonging, but it hardly offers any guidance to future development. And so there is every incentive to establish positive factors as well.

Eichner and Kregel assert that not only do such factors exist, but they actually form a paradigm as defined by Kuhn (1962). Their arguments are (i) that the Cambridge approach is concerned with growth, whereas the neo-classical approach is concerned with price theory; (ii) the Cambridge approach places the determination of income distribution and its effects at the core of its analysis, whereas the neoclassical approach treats it as a by-

---

[2] The Cambridge school of course represents only one non-neoclassical approach, and the foregoing remarks should not be taken as referring to others. In particular, they do not apply to the models of Kalecki and Wood, both of which in fact assume optimizing investment behaviour (in Kalecki's model, optimal from the point of view of the owner of the firm; in Wood's, from the point of view of its managers), and may therefore be regarded as having neoclassical affinities. A discussion of their positions will be deferred to Section 12.4.

[3] As Loasby (1976) points out, consistent plans are bound to be wrong in all respects if wrong at all, while inconsistent ones may be partially correct, and similarly insistence on coherence at all times may cramp the development of a theoretical approach.

product; (iii) the Cambridge approach embraces Keynesian demand analysis, whereas the neoclassical approach assumes that all markets are cleared; (iv) the Cambridge approach rests on Kaleckian micro theory, whereas the neoclassical approach assumes perfect markets, universal price-taking and U-shaped cost curves; (v) the Cambridge approach takes the future as uncertain, whereas the neoclassical approach assumes perfect foresight; and (vi) the two approaches have different purposes, as quoted above.

But even if the distinctions listed above were both valid and as sharp as Eichner and Kregel make out, they could hardly be said to constitute a paradigm as the term is usually understood. With the exception of (vi), which can hardly be taken seriously, they amount to a series of features which reflect either different interests or *ad hoc* assumptions and together could be described as defining at most a model.

As to the validity of their distinctions, the first (which echoes Robinson's (1956) complaint that 'economic analysis, serving for two centuries to win an understanding of the Nature and Causes of the Wealth of Nations, has been fobbed off with another bride – a Theory of Value') overlooks the recent neoclassical interest in growth theory (for surveys see Hahn and Matthews (1964) and Britto (1973)). Similarly the fifth neglects the growing neoclassical preoccupation with the problems of uncertainty, discussed in Section 7.2.

The third supposed distinction suggests that Eichner and Kregel have in mind a caricature of the neoclassical position. For the majority of neoclassicals have long accepted Keynesian theory and their main concern, now receiving attention, is that of assimilating it in a form more satisfactory than the prevalent IS-LM model. Indeed Keynes himself, with his subscription to the marginal productivity theory of the real wage and his marginal efficiency of capital theory of investment, could fairly be classified as a neoclassical thinker,[4] and there is no little irony in the adoption of the terms neo-Keynesian and post-Keynesian by some members of the Cambridge school. Even Robinson (1962) concedes that Keynes 'carried a good deal of Marshallian luggage with him'.[5] (Characteristically, she continues 'and never thoroughly unpacked it to throw out the clothes he could not wear', without giving the grounds for her implicit belief that he would have consented to being outfitted to her taste.[6])

As for the fourth distinction, the neoclassical approach assumes perfect competition only as a first approximation[7] and regards the shape of cost curves as an empirical matter.

---

[4] For an elaboration of this view, see Coddington (1976).

[5] See also Feiwel (1977).

[6] For further suggestions that Keynes failed to express what he really intended, see Robinson (1962, p. 78) and (1973a, p. 3) (cited by Coddington, 1976).

[7] For a discussion of the role of pure cases in the formulation of theoretical laws, see Nagel (1963). For a notable counterexample to Eichner and Kregel's assertion that neoclassical economists shrink from the analysis of imperfect competition, see Arrow and Hahn (1971, Chapter 6).

Only the second stands up to examination, and it can hardly shoulder the weight of a paradigm.

For completeness' sake one should mention in passing Sraffa's (1960) analysis of value, since it holds an honoured place in the Cambridge canon and is often cited as an alternative to the neoclassical model. To put it briefly, it investigates the way in which the prices of individual commodities depend upon the structure of inputs and outputs and the shares of wages and profits in total output. It avoids introducing neoclassical assumptions regarding the nature of production technology by assuming a steady state in which all inputs and outputs are fixed. To judge by the voluminous literature that it has spawned, this purity is evidently regarded as of almost gnostic significance by the Cambridge school. But since it is achieved at the price of assuming a completely static economy, it is difficult to see what practical relevance it might possibly have.[8] Not surprisingly, it has not been integrated with the rest of Cambridge theory, and although Nell (1967) argues that the Ricardian analysis that it exemplifies is an important distinguishing feature between the Cambridge and neoclassical approaches, this is not pursued by Eichner and Kregel. For a critique see Blaug (1974).

12.2   Differences in practice

Fortunately the gulf that separates the neoclassical and Cambridge approaches is generally much narrower in practice than it is in theory. Indeed adherents of the two approaches frequently find themselves in broad agreement when confronted with specific policy isues. For both approaches possess a high degree of flexibility and overlap to share more common ground than one might infer from the exchanges between them.

In the case of the neoclassical approach this flexibility is the result of the pragmatic adoption of *ad hoc* inductive models where its formal theory does not offer guidance. Much of neoclassical macroeconomics, in its present form, must be regarded as supplementary theory in this sense. Its existence may be counted both as a weakness and as a strength. As a weakness because it is evidence that there are limits to the heuristic power of the principle of maximization subject to constraint. As a strength because it permits the co-option of new material that may eventually either be integrated with the theory proper or be influential in modifying it, in either case contributing to

---

[8] As Robinson herself has said, 'an assumption of static over-all conditions is such a drastic departure from reality as to make it impossible to submit anything evolved within it to the test of verification and (it rules out) the discussion of most of the problems that are actually interesting...' (Robinson, 1956, opening paragraph of Preface). For a discussion of the irrelevance of Sraffa's analysis, see Burmeister (1975, 1977); Levine (1974, 1975, 1977); and Eatwell (1977).

its evolution. One of the objectives of this book has been to investigate the relationship between the supplementary and formal theory in the present context.

By the same token, the Cambridge approach, which as Eatwell (1977), taking a noticeably different view from Eichner and Kregel, puts it, 'consists of a union of theories', has even greater flexibility. Everything is permitted which is not specifically prohibited, that is, use of marginal analysis, and there is no reason why it should not also adopt those models used to supplement the neoclassical approach.

Besides this joint domain there is further common ground in which the two approaches stake out conflicting theoretical positions and yet reach the same empirical conclusions. The autoregressive aggregate consumption function discussed in Section 8.2 is an example, the explicitly neoclassical permanent income and life-cycle models of Friedman and Modigliani-Ando-Brumberg arriving at much the same specification as the relative income and habit formation models of Duesenberry and Brown. Thus in short-term demand management, adherents of the two approaches can work together without endlessly crossing swords over first principles.

Mercifully the possibility of agreeing to differ extends to much, perhaps the greater part, of policy-making in many fields. Capital theory, however, is an exception in this respect. In the short run there may not be appreciable scope for controversy, but in the long run the weakness of the empirical evidence has left theoretical speculation without a restraining hand, the implications of the two approaches are radically different, and the political issues are of strategic importance.

In particular, the significance of capital, the determination and significance of the rate of profit, taxation, and public investment criteria, remain bitterly contested topics. They will be reviewed in turn.

12.3 The significance of capital

Despite the fact that reswitching has finally driven home the lessons that should have been learnt long ago from Wicksell effects, the influence of the aggregate approach to capital theory lingers on. The idea that the rate of profit is an index of the scarcity of capital, with its implication that the latter may be treated as a factor of production, has had an especially powerful hold. Some neoclassical writers, notably Ferguson (1969) and Brems (1977), have refused to forsake it, faith making good its theoretical deficiencies. On the empirical side, countless econometric studies are published every year employing aggregate capital as an explanatory variable with no apparent qualms. Even the Cambridge writers display traces of ambivalence towards it, aggregate capital (or equivalently, the aggregate capital-output ratio) appearing in the analysis of Kaldor (1956, 1966), Pasinetti (1962, 1966a),

Robinson and Eatwell (1973) and Kregel (1973) talking about the 'degree of mechanization' when discussing choice of technique.

Traditionally, measures of aggregate capital served four functions. They could be used to classify techniques according to capital-intensity, they could be used to estimate the contribution of capital to growth, they could be used to explain the determination of the rate of interest, and they could be used as an argument in a production function. When the inadequacy of aggregate capital as an economic variable in theoretical analysis was at last understood, its use for any of these purposes ceased to be respectable. But, perhaps because it was long overdue, the neoclassical retreat has been unnecessarily precipitate.

For it was argued in Chapter 4 that, contrary to a widely-held supposition, the theoretical problems involved in the aggregation of capital are no different from those involved in the aggregation of output and labour, Wicksell effects notwithstanding. The main practical difference is that the capital aggregate is more dependent on, and therefore sensitive to, expectations than the other two. Hence if relative prices are sufficiently stable to allow one to treat output and labour as aggregates, it may be reasonable to treat capital in the same way. And while indices have their limitations, there is no point in exaggerating them.

In particular, turning to the first traditional use of aggregate capital, the fact that it is possible to construct examples where the ranking of two techniques by capital-output ratio (or capital-labour ratio) is reversed when one substitutes one set of relative prices and interest rates for another does not mean that it is never possible to construct such a ranking. As Sen (1974) has gently pointed out, it is hard to dispute the suggestion that moving earth by hands and baskets is less capital-intensive than using bulldozers, regardless of the set of relative prices and interest rates used for evaluation. Here at least one should not abandon commonsense simply because it is untidy.

The use of aggregate capital in growth accounting (Kendrick, 1961; Denison, 1962, 1967; Griliches and Jorgenson, 1966, 1967) should in principle lead to the same results and encounter the same problems as a disaggregated approach. The arbitrariness introduced by the path dependence of a Divisia index (Richter, 1966) will be the same in both cases.[9] The problem of evaluating the technical progress embodied in a new type of capital good will be the same in both cases (though in practice it is more likely to be glossed over at the aggregate level).[10] And the partial dependence of technical

---

[9] The estimates of growth due to capital, labour and technical progress will in general depend not only on the change in the state of the economy over the period in question but on the *way* in which this change has occurred. For a discussion, see Dougherty (1974).

[10] See Anderson (1961) and Gordon (1961) for discussion of the tendency towards a downward bias in indices of deflated capital stock. For a more general discussion see Fellner (1961).

progress on investment (Arrow, 1962) or growth of output (Kaldor and Mirrlees, 1962) will cloud both approaches equally. Aggregation as such is therefore not likely to be an issue when considering the value of conventional growth accounting (or, for that matter, the unconventional approach of Rymes (1971) and Peterson (1979).)

As for the third traditional use, the durability of the Clark–Knight notion that the rate of interest is determined by the marginal product of capital is illustrated by Friedman's (1971) suggestion that, since the aggregate capital stock of a country is large compared with annual net investment, its real yield (and hence the real rate of interest) is effectively fixed in the short/medium run, even if it is subject to 'very rapidly diminishing returns'. Similar examples abound in the neoclassical literature. Since it remains so deeply entrenched in conventional neoclassical thinking, it is of interest to consider whether a case may be made for it as a pragmatic approximation.

As a starting point, it has been shown in Chapter 4 that, even at switch points in examples of reswitching, the ratio of ΔY to ΔK will be equal to the rate of interest provided that relative prices are unaffected. It is therefore impossible to dismiss as meaningless the assertion that the marginal product of capital should be equal to the rate of interest in equilibrium.[11]

But as such the assertion is merely a consistency condition. For it to attain a more positive status one must introduce the strong assumption that the transformation frontiers of producers are linear and have the same slope in the relevant regions. As has been shown in Section 3.6, under this assumption productivity becomes the dominant factor and the rate of time preference adjusts to the rate of interest instead of codetermining it. Even then, Friedman's argument depends on expectations being stable, for in the absence of perfect foresight the transformation frontiers are merely estimates. In particular, the slope of the function is merely an estimate. It therefore follows that even in this model the rate of interest will be stable only if these estimates are stable.

Whether or not the transformation frontiers are linear is an empirical question, and in view of the fragile state of the econometric literature on investment behaviour it is one that will not be settled in the near future. In the meantime the more general Fisherian model is likely to remain the orthodox neoclassical approach.

Finally, there is no comfort in the Fisherian approach for those who use aggregate capital in production functions. Indeed the merit of the approach resides in the fact that it replaces the problematical Clarkian current flow analysis with a rigorous analysis of the supply and demand for consumption streams through time. And no encouragement is given by

---

[11] Robinson (1970b) takes the even more extreme position that 'the marginal product of capital in industry as a whole has no existence apart from the rate of profit'.

Solow's (1956) and F.M. Fisher's (1969) discussions of the difficulties of aggregating micro functions into a macro function or by F.M. Fisher's (1971a) experiments with a simulation model. Furthermore, the econometric problems are formidable, not the least of them being the difficulty of discriminating between a fit of a supposed technological relationship and a fit of the national accounting identity

$$Y = iK + wL \qquad (12.1)$$

the latter probably being responsible for many of the apparently good results obtained in early Cobb–Douglas function studies.

12.4   The determination and significance of the rate of profit

There can be no doubt that the simple Fisherian parable of peasant producers is too naive to carry much conviction in a modern economy. Even if one is sympathetic to the Fisherian proposition that the loans market lies at the heart of the analysis, it is obviously quite inadequate to suppose that the participants form a homogeneous group differentiated only by the timing of their consumption in relation to that of their receipts. The grouping of the participants into personal, company, public and overseas sectors must be recognized and incorporated into the model. In this respect the Cambridge models have been much more realistic.

The splitting of the private sector into personal and company sectors separates control of investment from ownership and so sets at one remove the delicate balancing between present and future consumption responsible for the triple equality of the rates of time preference, interest and profit. As has been discussed in Chapter 4, this would make no difference if firms could be counted on to act strictly in the interests of their shareholders and maximize the discounted value of the stream of profits. But the modern theory of the firm indicates that such an assumption cannot be maintained. As has been observed in Chapter 8, the inclination of management, especially of the larger corporations, to set store by growth for its own sake as well as profitability, and their apparent willingness to be content with a rate of return on investments financed by internal funds lower than that on those financed by external funds, imply a dispersion in the rate of profit and weaken its link with the rate of interest.

The link is further weakened by the effects of taxation, discussed at length in Chapter 5. Unless all taxation were replaced by an expenditure tax, or equivalently by a corporation tax with free depreciation, there would be a tendency for the pre-tax (and post-tax) rates of interest and profit to diverge from one another and from the rate of time preference.

The picture is made more complex still by the fact that a progressive income tax will cause a dispersion in the rate of time preference, if the

Fisherian analysis of intertemporal consumer behaviour is correct. But here also there are grounds for scepticism. The Fisherian model implies that individuals can and do make marginal decisions, that is, that they are not constrained by imperfections in the loans market, and that this introspective characterization of their behaviour is realistic. The first assumption is belied by the difficulty, indeed near impossibility, of borrowing to increase consumption,[12] and, for at least a generation, of lending at a positive real rate of interest. The second assumption is certainly undermined by habit formation in the short run which perhaps remains significant in the long run.

Thus, as was concluded in Chapter 8, it is hard to submit the Fisherian model to any kind of test that could either strengthen or weaken one's belief in its plausibility. And even those who are persuaded by it must allow that the forces of time preference and technology mesh together so unevenly in the loans market that they can determine at most a range for the long-run rate of interest, rather than a single value. The theory may thus be regarded, say, as explaining why one may expect the post-tax rate of interest to lie between zero per cent and 20 per cent per annum rather than between 20 per cent and 50 per cent.

Those neoclassicals who are not persuaded by the Fisherian model may well find that of Kalecki appealing, for contrary to the supposition of some of the Cambridge writers, it does not constitute a dramatic break with the orthodox neoclassical tradition. It is true that, in the short run, profits, and hence *ex post* profitability, are determined by the requirement that they should generate sufficient savings to match investment and thereby eliminate excess demand, rather than by direct market forces, that is, by Keynesian rather than by Walrasian adjustment. But this is also true of the neoclassical models in the short run. In the long run, investment is regulated by its profitability and the Kalecki model could thus almost be classified as belonging to the aggregate neoclassical approach. The main reservations would concern the determinants of the (long-run) rate of profit that calls forth the trend level of investment and the determinants of the savings coefficient for profits and wages. On both these scores Kalecki is silent and hence the model admits to interpretations ranging from watered-down Fisherian (some link between the savings rates and the equilibrium profitability being hypothesized) to Paretian, with savings being determined by sociological factors.

Likewise the Wood model embodies much that is attractive to the moderate neoclassical, especially its well-articulated recognition of the facts of life as reported by the literature on the behaviour of firms. But its conclu-

---

[12] There appears to be virtually no empirical evidence as to whether this constraint is important or not. Motley and Morley (1970) suggest that 'any divergence between actual and optional consumption is quite small', but their technique is questioned by Thurow (1970).

sions are critically dependent on the assumptions that growth is more important to management than profitability *per se*, and that retention ratios (and other aspects of company finance policy) are not appreciably influenced by *ex ante* profitability even in the long run. These assumptions form a watershed, rejection leaving one with a variation on the neoclassical theme, acceptance bringing one into the Cambridge world where the rate of growth is in some way exogenously given and the rate of profit is determined by the savings requirements dictated by it.

The latter description applies equally, of course, to the Kaldor model, although it reaches the same conclusion by a different route. Here investment and growth are not determined by the singleminded aggrandizement of corporations but by their animal spirits. Because this has the same effect of insulating investment from the influence of profitability, it leads to the same result.

To summarize, the different approaches to the determination of the rate of profit present a spectrum with the extremes held by the general equilibrium and Kaldorian approaches and the intermediate points by less clear-cut positions where doubts about the saving and investment assumptions are entertained and perhaps more consideration is given to institutional complexities.

It follows that the significance of the rate of profit presents a parallel spectrum. At the general equilibrium extreme it is simply another price, one which harmonizes production and consumption over time, and which can be tampered with only at the cost of relinquishing pareto-optimality.

In the more moderate neoclassical view, which acknowledges the loosening of the bonds between the rate of profit and the rate of time preference, and which takes account of the distortions introduced by the fiscal and monetary policies by the public sector, much of its normative significance evaporates. It may still be regarded in a broad sense as a price partly responsible for co-ordinating intertemporal activity, but considerations of pareto-optimality now lead to the unrewarding obscurities of the second-best.

In Kalecki's model the long-run trend level of the rate of profit can hardly be said to have any significance at all, in that it receives no more attention than a parameter. Even in his last paper on the business cycle, Kalecki (1968), one finds only a bare reference to the 'normal rate of profit' and no further explanation.

In the Kaldor and Wood models, the abdication of the rate of profit from its role as a price removes all traces of its normative significance and it becomes the mere by-product of the interaction between two exogenous factors, the rate of growth and savings behaviour. The government may intervene in its determination without giving grounds for complaint either by those saving or by those investing, which is only to be expected if neither group allows its behaviour to be influenced by it.

12.5 Taxation

The implications of the basic Fisherian model for taxation were spelled out in some detail in Chapter 5, the most important being that the expenditure tax (or, nearly equivalently, a corporation tax with free depreciation) would be the least damaging form it could take, since both income tax and corporation tax cause a bias against investment. It was noted, however, that the apparent double taxation of savings under an income tax that so exercised Fisher may be expected to be largely shifted by an approximately offsetting rise in the pre-tax rate of interest.

The criterion for such conclusions was the effect on pareto-optimality, and several fairly obvious points need to be made when one takes a more realistic look at an economy. First, in view of the remarks in the previous section, there is room for doubt as to whether pareto-optimality would be approximated even in the absence of taxation. Second, even if it were, there is a strong presumption that the welfare loss occasioned by taxation would not turn out to be disturbingly large if it could be measured within the Fisherian framework. Virtually all empirical comparative statics studies of welfare losses caused by market distortions have returned negligible estimates (Harberger, 1959). Third, the analysis in Chapter 5 neglects part of the welfare loss due to the effects of taxation on growth. The effects on growth due to the inhibiting of investment would be taken into account under the previous item, but the disincentive effects of taxation on pure entrepreneurship and innovation would not. The latter might well be substantial, in which case they should be a dominant consideration in the design of taxation. This, of course, is an area in welfare economics which remains frustratingly intractable.

Taking these points together, even if one accepts the neoclassical position, the theoretical case for the superiority of the expenditure tax is less compelling than Fisher made out in his long campaign for its adoption.

However, this happens to be one of the few areas in which major neo-classical and Cambridge writers find themselves in accord, with Kaldor (1955) also taking up the case for the expenditure tax. As was noted in Chapter 5, his reasons are pragmatic and intuitive, his treatise on the subject preceding the development of his analysis of income distribution. But, turning to the latter, one finds that it lends support to his objective of promoting equity.

In Section 10.2 it was shown that, according to the Kaldor model, a straight tax on profits will be more than completely shifted and that a straight tax on wages will have an incidence of more than 100 per cent. But an expenditure tax, if it does not affect the savings propensities associated with profits and wages, will leave the pre-tax shares of profits and wages unaltered. It therefore follows that a flat-rate expenditure tax will at least be neutral, and a progressive tax will remain progressive. If the expenditure tax does reduce the savings propensities, it will weigh more heavily on wages than on profits, but the discrimination is likely to be less severe than under the other forms of taxation.

As has been seen in Section 11.3, the Wood model of income distribution leads to much the same conclusions, for exactly the same underlying reason: net profits must be sufficient to finance investment, and hence, as a first approximation, a tax on profits must be entirely shifted, while a tax on wages will not be shifted at all (Wood, 1975, pp. 134-40). The incidence of an expenditure tax is not discussed, but his analysis suggests that one should assume that the rate of saving out of profits, being largely determined by the payout ratios of the corporations, will not be greatly affected, and hence, if one also believes that personal savings are likewise insensitive, being mostly contractual, the results of the first of the Kaldor cases obtain and the tax is not shifted.

It would therefore appear that, whatever one's persuasion on the subject of income distribution, the expenditure tax has much to be said for it. Its drawbacks are the need for a comprehensive accounting of income and wealth to the tax authorities, and the disruption caused by the transition from a conventional tax system. The former has already been developed in many countries, but the latter is forbidding. It is probably easier and less costly to engineer a political revolution than such a radical tax reform.[13]

12.6 Public investment criteria

In Chapter 6 it was shown that even if one adopts the neoclassical approach there can be no simple formula for evaluating public investment projects. The traditional assertion that one should select those projects with positive present value when discounted at the market rate of interest cannot be maintained when the effects of taxation and risk are taken into account.

Taxation causes problems because it drives a wedge between the pre-tax rate of profit, the intertemporal rate of exchange with nature, and the rate of time preference, assumed to be measured by the post-tax rate of interest. Consequently the market value of the resources employed will be a valid measure of the cost only in the extreme case where a project displaces the immediate production of consumption goods. If the project displaces private investment, the cost should be measured as the present value of the consumption stream that would have been yielded by it. Since, in general, public investment will displace a mixture of private consumption and investment, this implies that any evaluation must be *ad hoc* and is likely to be highly subjective.

Risk will aggravate the problem to the extent that it causes the *ex post*

---

[13] For a more optimistic assessment, see Kay and King (1978).

rate of profit in private production to be greater than the *ex ante* rate, thereby widening the gap between it and the rate of time preference.

Turning to the Cambridge side, it is disconcerting to find that public investment in a mixed economy has received negligible attention and that most of the guidance is negative. One certainty is that the market rate of interest, pre-tax or post-tax, is not a relevant factor, for the Cambridge theories of distribution preclude even the flawed neoclassical link between it and the rate of time preference. Indeed Cambridge writers appear to have little use for the concept of individual time preference, and less interest in its measurement, in spite of the fact that they allow contemporaneous prices their usual role. Dobb, in particular, asserts that 'individuals' choice over time are notoriously irrational' (1960, p. 18), attaching special importance to the problems of Veblan–Duesenberry interdependence and habit formation. In addition, he warns against the influence of Pigou's 'defect of the telescopic faculty' although, as has been shown in Section 3.3, this should be interpreted as referring to a bias in time preference rather than to time preference itself.

One would expect to glean some clues from the Cambridge writings on the planning of a socialist economy, but even here one is disappointed. In Robinson and Eatwell (1973), a premium is added to the 'labour cost of investible resources' (pp. 277–8), but its function is only to determine project selection, it being set in such a way as to ensure full employment.

Similarly Dobb, who accepts the principle of discounting even if he rejects the individualistic criterion of time preference, advocates the use of a 'minimum ratio of effectiveness' (1960, p. 27), but its role is that of ensuring efficiency in choice of technique, and it is determined by, rather than a determinant of, the aggregate rate of investment.

The remarks made in the neoclassical context concerning the impossibility of using a single discount rate to achieve efficiency apply equally to the Cambridge proposals. Thus the critical issue reduces, as might be anticipated, to the question of whether the State knows better than the individual. Although one may be aware of the operational difficulties of the neoclassical solution, above all the daunting task of collecting the information required by its complex evaluation procedure, and although one may be sympathetic to the Cambridge criticisms, the Cambridge approach appears to be reluctant to offer anything in its place.

12.7   Income distribution

Some of the heat may be taken out of the neoclassical/Cambridge controversy by the continuing fall in the share of profits in national income. According to Kuznets's estimates (1966, Table 4.2, Assumption 1), the share of gross profits in the United Kingdom declined from 46 per cent in

1860–9 to 25 per cent in 1954–60. A similar decline is recorded for France and, over a shorter period, the United States, Germany and Switzerland. The only exception to this pattern is Canada, for which only two observations (1926–9 and 1954–60) are available and the share is 19 per cent in both cases.

The decline is not easily explained by the Cambridge models, since the share of profits is determined by the share of investment, and this has, if anything, displayed a tendency to rise (Kuznets, 1966, Table 5.3). One would therefore have to ascribe it to shifts in parameters, one possible explanation being that the savings ratios have altered over time as the share of output supplied by incorporated businesses has risen and as personal savings have become increasingly contractual. The growth of the public sector may also be expected to have had a significant effect.

Presumably such changes are of a once-and-for-all nature and the Cambridge approach would predict that the share of profits will eventually stabilize. According to the neoclassical side, even this cannot be taken for granted. If the fall is the outcome of the effects of technical progress, as has been suggested in Dougherty (1974), it is conceivable that, although the absolute amount of profits will continue to grow, their share may decline asymptotically to zero.

In either case it is evident that functional income distribution is becoming less and less important as a factor in the determination of personal income distribution. As Tinbergen concludes, referring to the more developed countries, 'incomes after taxes contain only a small portion from capital and ... increasingly income-after-tax differences are due to differences in *human* capital' (1975, p. 149).

12.8   Conclusions

The question of what determine the rate of profit must remain open, and there is absolutely no point in pretending otherwise. It is an issue where, in Voltaire's words, 'doubt is not a very agreeable state, but certainty is a ridiculous one'.

The greatest weakness of the neoclassical model, as it appears in the textbooks, is its handling of the equilibration of savings and investment. As has been observed in Chapter 8, empirical research in this area remains patchy. A number of topics have received detailed attention in isolation, but only the crudest attempts have made at a comprehensive treatment. On the theoretical side, not until relatively recently have neoclassicals begun to do something about the inability of the traditional general equilibrium models to explain the limited empirical macro evidence that does exist. This may be rectified as a result of the concerted research now under way, but one must not expect too much. The fundamental problem is empirical ignorance, and at present this must limit the usefulness of theoretical refinement.[14]

Elaborate mathematical analysis of the existence of equilibrium and stability may assist in screening out specific models, but it can have no bearing on the approach as a whole. Plausible results cannot be taken as evidence of the validity of a model, and implausible ones only indicate that a particular formulation is unacceptable.

These remarks apply with equal force to the Cambridge approach. If possible, the neglect of empirical work is even worse, and it would appear that they expect to succeed in their besiegement of the established orthodoxy, not by undermining it with a slow and painful examination and interpretation of the data, but by blowing trumpets and hoping that the walls will crumble of their own accord. Not for nothing does Kregel find Kuhn's visionary language appealing. 'It is sometimes mentally impossible to conceive of both the old and the new at the same time. To see or understand one point of view may imply completely blotting out the other. This occurence Kuhn calls a "Gestalt shift".' (Kregel, 1973, p. 3). And if the Cambridge approach represents such a shift, one may dispense with the tiresome business of debating the issues piecemeal. Indeed there is no point in attempting to do so.

But, as has been argued in Section 12.3, one has to be exceptionally sympathetic to find much in the claim to have established a new paradigm, or even much that carries conviction in the individual Cambridge models.

Nevertheless, the approach may yet be developed and become more persuasive, either by those who have constructed the existing models or by other non-neoclassical writers with different points of view and new contributions. It could claim to be still in its infancy, for its history is relatively short compared with that of the neoclassical approach. Admittedly there has been little development of Kalecki's model, or of those of Kaldor and Pasinetti. But the Wood model, while perhaps less than compelling, in taking account of the literature of the theory of the firm has given a lead in a direction that may usefully be followed by neoclassicals and non-neoclassicals alike. So it may yet be too early to judge.

And even if the non-neoclassical models never gain the ascendancy, they will at least have served a purpose in stimulating the neoclassical approach to shake off its complacency and re-examine itself. As Jevons (1871, p. 266) said, 'a despotic calm is usually the triumph of error. In the republic of the sciences sedition and even anarchy are beneficial in the long run to the greatest happiness of the greatest number.'

---

[14] For forceful expressions of this view, see Phelps Brown (1972) and Worswick (1972).

Bibliography

ADDISON, J. (1714) in *The Spectator*, 8 August, 20.

AFTALION, A. (1909) 'La Réalité des Surproductions Générales: Deuxième Partie', *Revue d'Economie Politique*, 23 (2), 201–24.

——(1913) *Les Crises Periodiques de Surproduction*, Paris: Rivière

——(1927) 'The Theory of Economic Cycles Based on the Capitalist Technique of Production', *Review of Economics and Statistics*, 9(4), 165–70.

AKYUZ, Y. (1972) 'Income Distribution, Value of Capital, and Two Notions of the Wage-Profit Trade-Off', *Oxford Economic Papers*, 24(2), 156–65.

ALCHIAN, A. A. (1955) 'The Rate of Interest, Fisher's Rate of Return over Costs and Keynes' Internal Rate of Return', *American Economic Review*, 45(5), 938–43.

ALLAIS, M. (1953) 'L'Extension des Théories de L'Equilibre Economique Général et du Rendement Social au Cas du Risque' *Econometrica* 21(2), 269–90.

ANDERSON, P. S. (1961) 'The Apparent Decline in Capital-Output Ratios', *Quarterly Journal of Economics*, 75(4), 615–34.

ANDERSON, W. H. L. (1964) *Corporate Finance and Fixed Investment: An Econometric Study*, Boston: Harvard University Press.

ANDO, A., and F. MODIGLIANI (1963) 'The "Life Cycle" Hypothesis of Saving: Aggregate Implications and Tests', *American Economic Review*, 53(1), 55–84.

ARROW, K. J. (1953), 'Le Rôle des Valeurs Boursières pour la Répartition la Meilleure des Risques', in *Econométrie*. Paris: Centre Nationale de la Recherche Scientifique (translated in *Review of Economic Studies*, 31(2), 91–6).

——(1962) 'The Economic Implications of Learning by Doing', *Review of Economic Studies*, 29(3), 155–73.

——(1966) 'Discounting and Public Investment Criteria', in A. V. Kneese and S. C. Smith (eds), *Water Research*, Baltimore: Johns Hopkins Press.

——and F. H. HAHN (1971) *General Competitive Analysis*, Edinburgh: Oliver and Boyd.

ARTIS, M. J., E. KIERNAN and J. D. WHITELEY (1975) 'The Effects of Building Society Behaviour on Housing Investments', in Parkin and Nobay (1975).

ASH, J. C. K. (1975) 'Forecasting the Forecasters', *Bankers Magazine* 219 (April), 23–8.

——and D. J. SMYTH (1973) *Forecasting the United Kingdom Economy*, Farnborough: Saxon House.

ASIMAKOPOLOS, A. (1977) 'Profits and Investment: A Kaleckian Approach', in Harcourt (1977).

——and J. B. BURBRIDGE (1975) 'Corporate Taxation and the Optimal Investment Decisions of Firms', *Journal of Public Economics*, 4(3), 281–7.

BAILEY, M. J. (1957) 'Saving and the Rate of Interest', *Journal of Political Economy*, 65(4), 279–305.

——(1959a) 'Saving and the Rate of Interest: Reply', *Journal of Political Economy*, 67(1), 83–6.

——(1959b) 'Formal Criteria for Investment Decisions', *Journal of Political Economy*, 67(5), 476–88.

——(1962) *National Income and the Price Level*, New York: McGraw-Hill.

BAIN, A. D. (1970) *The Control of the Money Supply*, London: Penguin.

——(1973) 'Flow of Funds Analysis: A Survey', *Economic Journal*, 83(4), 1055–93.

——, C. L. DAY and A. L. WEARING (1975) *Company Financing in the United Kingdom*, London: Robertson.

BALL, R. J., and P. S. DRAKE (1964) 'The Relationship between Aggregate Consumption and Wealth', *International Economic Review* 5(1), 63–81.

BAUMOL, W. J. (1958) 'On the Theory of Oligopoly', *Economica*, 25(3), 187–198.

——(1962) 'On the Theory of Expansion of the Firm', *American Economic Review*, 52 (5), 1078–87.

——(1967) *Business Behavior, Value and Growth* (second edition), New York: Macmillan.

——(1968) 'On the Social Rate of Discount', *American Economic Review*, 58(4), 788–802.

——(1969) 'On the Social Rate of Discount: Comment on the Comments', *American Economic Review*, 59(5), 930.

——(1973) 'Efficiency of Corporate Investment: A Reply', *Review of Economics and Statistics*, 55(1), 128–31.

——, P. HEIM, B. G. MALKIEL and R. E. QUANDT (1970) 'Earnings Retention, New Capital and the Growth of the Firm', *Review of Economics and Statistics*, 52(4), 345–55.

BENTHAM, J. (1789) *An Introduction to the Principles of Morals and Legislation*, London: Payne.

BERLE, A. A., and G. C. MEANS (1933) *The Modern Corporation and Private Property*, New York: Macmillan.

BHADURI, A. (1966) 'The Concept of the Marginal Productivity of Capital and the Wicksell Effect', *Oxford Economic Papers*, 18(3), N. S., 284–8.

BHATIA, K. B. (1972) 'Capital Gains and the Aggregate Consumption Function', *American Economic Review*, 62(5), 866–79.

BICKERDIKE, C. F. (1914) 'A Non-Monetary Cause of Fluctuations in Employment', *Economic Journal*, 24(3), 357–70.

BLAUG, M. (1962) *Economic Theory in Retrospect*, Homewood, Illinois: Irwin.

——(1968) Second edition of Blaug (1962).

——(1974) *The Cambridge Revolution*, London: Institute of Economic Affairs (Hobart Paperback).

BLINDER, A. S., and R. M. SOLOW (1973) 'Analytical Foundations of Fiscal Policy', in A. S. Blinder *et al.*, *The Economics of Public Finance*, Washington: Brookings Institution.

BLISS, C. J. (1975) *Capital Theory and the Distribution of Income*, Oxford: North-Holland.

BÖHM-BAWERK, E. V. (1889) *Positive Theorie Des Kapitales* (translated as *Positive Theory of Capital*, London: Smart, 1891).

BOSKIN, M. J. (1978) 'Taxation, Saving, and the Rate of Interest', *Journal of Political Economy*, 86 (2pt2), S3–S27.

BOWLES, S. S. (1970) 'Aggregation of Labor Inputs in the Economics of Growth and Planning: Experiments with a Two-Level CES Function', *Journal of Political Economy*, 78(1), 68–81.

BOX, G. P., and G. M. JENKINS (1970) *Time Series Analysis*, San Francisco: Holden Day.

BREAK, G. F. (1974) 'The Incidence and Economic Effects of Taxation', in A. S. Blinder *et al.*, *The Economics of Public Finance*, Washington: Brookings Institution.

BREMS, H. (1977) 'Reality and Neoclassical Theory', *Journal of Economic Literature*, 15(1), 72–83.

BRISTON, R. J., and C. R. TOMKINS (1970) 'The Impact of the Introduction of Corporation Tax upon the Dividend Policies of United Kingdom Companies', *Economic Journal*, 80(3), 617–37.

BRITTAIN, J. A. (1966) *Corporate Dividend Policy*, Washington: Brookings Institution.

BRITTO, R. (1973) 'Some Recent Developments in the Theory of Economic Growth: An Interpretation', *Journal of Economic Literature*, 11(4), 1343–66.

BROMWICH, M. (1976) *The Economics of Capital Budgeting*, Harmondsworth: Penguin.

BROWN, M., K. SATO and P. ZAREMBKA (1976) *Essays in Modern Capital Theory*, Amsterdam: North-Holland.

BROWN, T. M. (1952) 'Habit Persistence and Lags in Consumer Behaviour', *Econometrica*, 20(3), 355–71.

BRUNO, M. (1967) 'Optimal Accumulation in Discrete Capital Models', in K. Shell (ed.), *Essays on the Theory of Optimal Economic Growth*, Cambridge, Massachusetts: M. I. T. Press.

——(1969) 'Fundamental Duality Relations in the Pure Theory of Capital and Growth', *Review of Economic Studies*, 36(1), 39–53.

BRYSON, A. E., and Y.-C. Ho (1969) *Applied Optimal Control*, Waltham, Massachusetts: Blaisdell.

BUCHANAN, J. M. (1959) 'Saving and the Rate of Interest: Comment', *Journal of Political Economy*, 67(1), 79–82.

BUITER, W. H. (1977) '"Crowding Out" and the Effectiveness of Fiscal Policy', *Journal of Public Economics*, 7(3), 309–28.

BURMEISTER, E. (1968) 'The Social Rate of Return in a Linear Model', *Weltwirtschaftliches Archiv*, 101(2), 255–71.

——(1975) 'A Comment on "This Age of Leontief . . . and Who?"', *Journal of Economic Literature*, 13(2), 454–7.

——(1977) 'The Irrelevance of Sraffa's Analysis without Constant Returns to Scale'. *Journal of Economic Literature*, 15(1), 68–70.

CAGAN, P. D. (1956) 'The Monetary Dynamics of Hyperinflation', in M. Friedman (ed.), *Studies in the Quantity Theory of Money*, Chicago: University of Chicago Press.

——(1965) *The Effect of Pension Plans on Aggregate Saving: Evidence from a Sample Survey*, National Bureau of Economic Research, Occasional Paper 95, New York: Columbia University Press.

CANNAN, E. (1897) 'What is Capital?', *Economic Journal*, 7(3), 278–84.

CENTRAL STATISTICAL OFFICE (1968) *Economic Trends*, February.

——(1971) *National Income and Expenditure*, London: HMSO.

——(1977) *National Income and Expenditure, 1966–1976*, London. HMSO.

CHAKRAVARTY, S., and A. S. MANNE (1968) 'Optimal Growth when the Instantaneous Utility Function Depends upon the Rate of Change in Consumption', *American Economic Review*, 58(5), 1351–3.

CHAMPERNOWNE, D. G. (1954) 'The Production Function and the Theory of Capital: A Comment', *Review of Economic Studies*, 21(2), 112–35

CHENERY, H. B. (1952) 'Overcapacity and the Acceleration Principle', *Econometrica*, 20(1), 1–28.

CHIANG, A. C. (1973) 'A Simple Generalization of the Kaldor-Pasinetti Theory of Profit Rate and Income Distribution', *Economica*, 40(3), 311–13.

CHRISTENSEN, L. R., and D. W. JORGENSON (1973) 'U.S. Income, Saving, and Wealth, 1929–1969', *Review of Income and Wealth*, 19(4), 329–62.

CLARK, J. B. (1891) 'Distribution as Determined by a Law of Rent', *Quarterly Journal of Economics*, 5(3), 289–318.

——(1899) *The Distribution of Wealth*, New York: Macmillan.

CLARK, J. M. (1917) 'Business Acceleration and the Law of Demand: A Technical Factor in Economic Cycles', *Journal of Political Economy*, 25(3), 217–35.

CLOWER, R. (1965) 'The Keynesian Counter-Revolution: A Theoretical Appraisal', in Hahn and Brechling (1965).

CODDINGTON, A. (1976) 'Keynesian Economics: The Search for First Principles', *Journal of Economic Literature*, 14(4), 1258–73.

COHEN, J. (1972) 'Copeland's Moneyflows after Twenty-Five Years: A Survey', *Journal of Economic Literature*, 10(1), 1–25

COMMISSION ON MONEY AND CREDIT (1963) *Impacts of Monetary Policy*, Englewood Cliffs, New Jersey: Prentice-Hall.

COOPER, R. L. (1972) 'The Predictive Performance of Quarterly Econometric Model of the United States', in Hickman (1972).

COPELAND, M. A. (1947) 'Tracing Money Flows through the United States Economy', *American Economic Review*, 37(2), 31–49.

——(1952) *A Study of Moneyflows in the United States*, New York: National Bureau of Economic Research.

COWLING, K., and M. WATERSON (1976) 'Price-Cost Margins and Market Structure', *Economica*, 43(3), 267–74.

DARBY, M. R. (1974) 'The Permanent Income Theory of Consumption—A Restatement', *Quarterly Journal of Economics*, 88(2), 228–50.

DAVID, P., and J. L. SCADDING (1974) 'Private Savings: Ultrarationality, Aggregation, and "Denison's Law"', *Journal of Political Economy*, 82(2ptl), 225–49.

DAVIDSON, J. E. H., D. F. HENDRY, F. SBRA and J. S. YEO (1978) 'Econometric Modelling of the Aggregate Time-Series Relationship between Consumers' Expenditure and

Income in the United Kingdom', *Economic Journal*, 88(4), 661–92.

DEBREU, G. (1959) *Theory of Value*, New York: Wiley.

DEMSETZ, H. (1974) 'Where is the New Industrial State?', *Economic Inquiry*, 12(1), 1–12.

DENISON, E. F. (1958) 'A Note on Private Saving', *Review of Economics and Statistics*, 40(3), 261–7.

——(1962) *The Sources of Economic Growth in the United States and the Alternatives before Us*, New York: Committee for Economic Development.

——(1967) *Why Growth Rates Differ*, Washington: Brookings Institution.

DEWEY, D. (1965) *Modern Capital Theory*, New York: Columbia University Press.

DHRYMES, P. J. (1970) 'On the Game of Maximizing $\bar{R}^2$', *Australian Economic Papers*, 9(2), 177–85.

——, and M. KURZ (1967) 'Investment, Dividend, and External Finance Behavior of Firms', in Ferber (1967).

DIAMOND, P. A. (1968) 'The Opportunity Costs of Public Investment: Comment', *Quarterly Journal of Economics*, 82(4), 682–8.

——(1970) 'Incidence of an Interest Income Tax', *Journal of Economic Theory*, 2(3), 211–24.

DOBB, M. (1960) *An Essay on Economic Growth and Planning*, London: Routledge and Kegan Paul.

DOUGHERTY, C. R. S. (1972) 'On the Rate of Return and the Rate of Profit', *Economic Journal*, 82(4), 1324–50.

——(1974) 'On the Secular Macroeconomic Consequences of Technical Progress', *Economic Journal*, 84(3), 543–65.

DREZE, J. H. (1974) 'Discount Rates and Public Investment: A Post-Scriptum', *Economica*, 41(1), 52–61.

DUESENBERRY, J. S. (1949) *Income, Saving, and the Theory of Consumer Behavior*, New York: Oxford University Press.

——(1958) *Business Cycles and Economic Growth*, New York: McGraw-Hill.

——, G. FROMM, L. R. KLEIN and E. KUH (1965) *The Brookings Quarterly Econometric Model of the United States*, Chicago: Rand McNally.

DURAND, D. (1959) 'The Cost of Capital, Corporation Finance, and the Theory of Investment: Comment', *American Economic Review*, 49(4), 639–55.

EATWELL, J. L. (1977) 'The Irrelevance of Returns to Scale in Sraffa's Analysis', *Journal of Economic Literature*. 15(1), 61–8.

ECKAUS, R. S., and K. S. PARIKH (1968) *Planning for Growth*, Cambridge, Massachusetts: M.I.T.

EICHNER, A. S. (1973) 'A Theory of the Determination of the Mark-up under Oligopoly', *Economic Journal*, 83(4), 1184–200.

——, and J. A. KREGEL (1975) 'An Essay on Post-Keynesian Theory: A New Paradigm in Economics', *Journal of Economic Literature*, 13(4), 1293–314.

EISNER, R. (1960) 'A Distributed Lag Investment Function', *Econometrica*, 28(1), 1–29.

——(1967) 'A Permanent Income Theory for Investment: Some Empirical Explorations', *American Economic Review*, 57(3), 363–90.

——and R. H. STROTZ (1963) 'Determinants of Business Investment', in Commission on Money and Credit (1963).

ELLIOTT, J. W. (1973) 'Theories of Corporate Investment Behavior Revisited', *American Economic Review*, 63(1), 195–207.

ERRITT, M. J., and J. C. D. ALEXANDER (1977) 'Ownership of Company Shares: A New Survey', *Economic Trends*, London: Central Statistical Office.

EVANS, M. K. (1969) *Macroeconomic Activity*, New York: Harper and Row.

FALLON, P. R., and P. R. G. LAYARD (1975) 'Capital-Skill Complementarity, Income Distribution, and Output Accounting', *Journal of Political Economy*, 83(2), 279–301.

FAMA, E. F. (1974) 'The Empirical Relationship between the Dividend and Investment Decisions by Firms', *American Economic Review*, 64(3), 304–18.

FEDERAL RESERVE BULLETIN (1975) 'Recent Developments in Corporate Finance', 61(8), 463–71.

——(1978) 'Recent Developments in Corporate Finance', 64(6), 431–40.

FEIWEL, G. R. (1975a) *The Intellectual Capital of Michal Kalecki*, Knoxville: University of Tennessee Press.

——(1975b) 'Kalecki and Keynes', *De Economist*, 123(2), 164–97.

——(1977) Review of S. Fujino, *A Neo-Keynesian Theory of Income, Prices and Economic Growth*, *Journal of Economic Literature*, 15(1), 88–90.

FELDSTEIN, M. S. (1970) 'Corporate Taxation and Dividend Behaviour', *Review of Economic Studies*, 37(1), 57–72.

——(1973) 'Tax Incentives, Corporate Saving, and Capital Accumulation in the United States', *Journal of Public Economics*, 2(2), 159–71.

——(1978) 'The Welfare Cost of Capital Income Taxation', *Journal of Political Economy*, 86 (2pt2), S29–S51.

——and G. FANE (1973) 'Taxes, Corporate Dividend Policy and Personal Savings: the British Postwar Experience', *Review of Economics and Statistics*, 55(4), 399–411.

——and J. S. FLEMMING (1971) 'Tax Policy, Corporate Saving and Investment Behaviour in Britain', *Review of Economic Studies*, 38(4), 415–34.

——and D. K. FOOT (1971) 'The Other Half of Gross Investment: Replacement and Modernization Expenditures', *Review of Economics and Statistics*, 53(1), 49–58.

——and S. C. TSIANG (1968) 'The Interest Rate, Taxation, and the Personal Savings Incentive', *Quarterly Journal of Economics*, 82(3), 419–34.

FELLNER, W. (1961) 'Appraisal of the Labour-Saving and Capital-Saving Character of Innovations', in Lutz and Hague (1961).

——*et al.* (1967) *Ten Economic Studies in the Tradition of Irving Fisher*, New York: Wiley.

FERBER, R. (ed.) (1967) *Determinants of Investment Behavior*, New York: National Bureau of Economic Research.

FERGUSON, C. E. (1969) *The Neoclassical Theory of Production and Distribution*, Cambridge: Cambridge University Press.

FISHER, F. M. (1969) 'The Existence of Aggregate Production Functions', *Econometrica*, 37(4), 553–77.

——(1971a) 'Aggregate Production Functions and the Explanation of Wages: A Simulation Experiment', *Review of Economics and Statistics*, 53(4), 305–25.

——(1971b) 'Discussion' in Fromm (1971).

FISHER, I. (1897) 'The Role of Capital in Economic Theory', *Economic Journal*, 7(4), 511–37.

——(1906) *The Nature of Capital and Income*, New York: Macmillan.

——(1907) *The Rate of Interest*, New York: Macmillan.

——(1911) *The Purchasing Power of Money*, New York: Macmillan.

——(1927) 'The Income Concept in the Light of Experience', *Die Wirtschaft Theorie Der Gegenwart*, 3, 22–45, (reprint in English, no publisher listed).

——(1930) *The Theory of Interest*, New York: Macmillan.

——(1937) 'Income in Theory and Income Taxation in Practice', *Econometrica*, 5(1), 1–55.

——and H. W. FISHER (1942) *Constructive Income Taxation*, New York: Harper.

FLEMMING, J. S. (1976) 'A Reappraisal of the Corporation Income Tax', *Journal of Public Economics*, 6(1,2), 163–9.

FLORENCE, P. S. (1933) *The Logic of Industrial Organization*, London: Kegan Paul, Trench, Trubner.

FRIEDMAN, M. (1940) 'Review' (of Tinbergen *Business Cycles in the United States of America, 1919–1932*, Vol. II), *American Economic Review*, 30(3), 657–60.

——(1951) 'Comment', in Universities—National Bureau Committee for Economic Research, *Conference on Business Cycles*, New York: National Bureau of Economic Research.

——(1953) 'The Methodology of Positive Economics', in *Essays in Positive Economics*, Chicago: University of Chicago Press.

——(1956) *Studies in the Quantity Theory of Money*, Chicago: University of Chicago Press.

——(1957) *A Theory of the Consumption Function*, Princeton: Princeton University Press.

——(1960) 'Comments' in I. Friend and R. Jones (eds), *Consumption and Saving*, vol. II, Philadelphia: University of Pennsylvania.

——(1963) 'Windfalls, the "Horizon", and Related Concepts in the Permanent-Income Hypothesis', in C. F. Christ *et al.*, *Measurement in Economics*, Stanford: Stanford University Press.

——(1971) *A Theoretical Framework for Monetary Analysis*, New York: National Bureau of Economic Research.

——and G. S. Becker (1958) 'Reply' (to Klein, 1958), *Journal of Political Economy*, 65(6), 545–9.

FRIEND, I. and F. HUSIC (1973) 'Efficiency of Corporate Investment', *Review of Economics and Statistics*, 55(1), 122–7.

——and I. B. KRAVIS (1957) 'Entrepreneurial Income, Saving and Investment', *American Economic Review*, 47(3), 269–301.

FROMM, G. (ed) (1971) *Tax Incentives and Capital Spending*, Brookings Institution, Amsterdam: North-Holland.

FURONO, Y. (1970) 'Convergence Time in the Samuelson-Modigliani Model', *Review of Economic Studies*, 27(2), 221–32.

GAREGNANI, P. (1970) 'Heterogeous Capital, the Production Function and the Theory of Distribution', *Review of Economic Studies*, 37(3), 407–36.

GEORGE, HENRY (1879) *Progress and Poverty*, London: Kegan Paul, Trench.

GOLDSMITH, R. W. (1965) *The Flow of Capital Funds in the Postwar Economy*, National Bureau of Economic Research, New York: Columbia University Press.

GOODWIN, R. M. (1948) 'Secular and Cyclical Aspects of the Multiplier and Accelerator', in L. A. Metzler *et al.*, *Income, Employment and Public Policy*, New York: Norton.

——(1961) 'The Optimal Growth Path for an Underdeveloped Economy', *Economic Journal*, 71(4), 756–74.

GORDON, R. A. (1945) *Business Leadership in the Large Corporation*, Washington: Brookings Institution.

——(1961) 'Differential Changes in the Prices of Consumers' and Capital Goods', *American Economic Review*, 51(5), 937–57.

GORMAN, W. M. (1968) 'Measuring the Quantities of Fixed Factors', in J. N. Wolfe (ed.) *Value, Capital and Growth*, Edinburgh: Edinburgh University Press.

GOULD, J. P. (1969) 'The Use of Endogenous Variables in Dynamic Models of Investment', *Quarterly Journal of Economics*, 83(4), 580–99.

——and R. N. WAUD (1973) 'The Neoclassical Model of Investment Behavior: Another View', *International Economic Review*, 14(1), 33–47.

GRABOWSKI, H. G., and D. C. MUELLER (1975) 'Life-Cycle Effects on Corporate Returns on Retentions', *Review of Economics and Statistics*, 57(4), 400–9.

GRANGER, C. W. J., and P. NEWBOLD (1973) 'Some Comments on the Evaluation of Economic Forecasts', *Applied Economics*, 5(1), 35–47.

——, ——(1974) 'Spurious Regressions in Economics'. *Journal of Econometrics*, 2(2), 111–20.

GREBLER, L., and S. J. MAISEL (1963) 'Determinants of Residential Construction: A Review of Present Knowledge', in Commission on Money and Credit (1963).

GREEN, H. A. J. (1964) *Aggregation in Economic Analysis: An Introductory Survey*, Princeton: Princeton University Press.

GRILICHES, Z., and D. W. JORGENSON (1966) 'Sources of Measured Productivity Change: Capital Input', *American Economic Review*, 56(2), 50–61.

GUESNERIE, R., and T. DE MONTBRIAL (1974) 'Allocation under Uncertainty: A Survey', in J. D. Drèze (ed.), *Allocation under Uncertainty: Equilibrium and Optimality*, International Economic Association, London: Macmillan.

GUILLEBAUD, C. W. (1935) 'Income Tax and the "Double Taxation" of Saving', *Economic Journal*, 45(3), 484–92.

HADJIMATHEOU, G. (1976) *Housing and Mortgage Markets*, Farnborough, Hampshire: Saxon House.

HAHN, F. H. (1965) "On Some Problems of Proving the Existence of an Equilibrium in a Monetary Economy', in Hahn and Brechling (1965).

——(1973) 'The Winter of Our Discontent', *Economica*, 40(3), 322–30.

——(1977) 'Keynesian Economics and General Equilibrium Theory: Reflections on Some Current Debates', in Harcourt (1977).

——and F. B. R. BRECHLING (eds) (1965) *The Theory of Interest Rates*, London: Macmillan.

——and R. C. MATTHEWS (1964) 'The Theory of Economic Growth: A Survey', *Economic Journal*, 74(4), 779–902.

HAITOVSKY, Y., G. TREYZ and V. SU (1974) *Forecasts with Quarterly Macroeconomic Models*, New York: National Bureau of Economic Research.

HALL, R. L., and C. J. HITCH (1939) 'Price Theory and Business Behaviour', *Oxford Economic Papers*, 2, 12–45.

HARBERGER, A. C. (1959) 'Using the Resources at Hand More Effectively', *American Economic Review*, 49(2), 134–46.

——(1962) 'The Incidence of the Corporation Income Tax', *Journal of Political Economy*, 70(3), 215–40.

——(1971) 'Discussion', in Fromm (1971).

——(1972) 'On Measuring the Social Opportunity Cost of Public Funds', in *Project Evaluation: Collected Papers*, London: Macmillan.

HARCOURT, G. C. (1972) *Some Cambridge Controversies in the Theory of Capital*, Cambridge University Press.

——(1975) 'The Cambridge Controversies: The Afterglow', in Parkin and Nobay (1975).

——(ed.) (1977) *The Microeconomic Foundations of Macroeconomics*, International Economic Association, London: Macmillan.

HARRIS, D. J. (1973) 'Capital, Distribution and the Aggregate Production Function', *American Economic Review*, 63(1), 100–13.

HARROD, H. R. F. (1948) *Towards a Dynamic Economics*, London: Macmillan.

HAYEK, F. A. (1935) 'The Maintenance of Capital', *Economica*, 2(3), 241–76.

——(1941a) *The Pure Theory of Capital*, London: Routledge and Kegan Paul.

——(1941b) 'Maintaining Capital Intact: A Reply', *Economica*, 8(3), 276–80.

HENDRY, D. F., and G. J. ANDERSON (1977), 'Testing Dynamic Specification in Small Simultaneous Systems: An Application to a Model of Building Society Behaviour in the United Kingdom', in M. D. Intriligator (ed.) *Frontiers of Quantitative Economics*, Amsterdam: North-Holland

HICKMAN, B. G. (ed.) (1972) *Econometric Models of Cyclical Behavior*, (editor), Studies in Income and Wealth No. 36, Conference on Research in Income and Wealth. New York: Columbia University Press.

HICKS, J. R. (1939) *Value and Capital*, Oxford: Oxford University Press.

——(1941) 'Maintaining Capital Intact: A Further Suggestion', *Economica*, 9(2), 174–79.

——(1961) 'The Measurement of Capital in Relation to the Measurement of Other Economic Aggregates', in Lutz and Hague (1961).

HIRSHLEIFER, J. (1958) 'On the Theory of Optimal Investment Decision', *Journal of Political Economy*, 66(4), 329–72.

——(1970) *Investment, Interest and Capital*, New Jersey: Prentice-Hall.

HOLBROOK, R. S. (1967) 'The Three-Year Horizon: An Analysis of the Evidence', *Journal of Political Economy*, 75(5), 750–4.

——and F. STAFFORD (1971) 'The Propensity to Consume Separate Types of Income: A Generalized Permanent Income Hypothesis', *Econometrica*, 39(1), 1–21.

HOMMA, M. (1977) 'A Comparative Static Analysis of Tax Incidence', *Journal of Public Economics*, 8(1), 53–65.

HOUTHAKKER, H. S. (1950) 'Revealed Preference and the Utility Function', *Economica*, 17(2), 159–74.

HUME, D. (1752) *Political Discourses*, Edinburgh: Fleming.

JAFFE, W. (1965) *Correspondence of Leon Walras and Related Papers*, Amsterdam: North-Holland.

JAMES, E. (1969) 'On the Social Rate of Discount: Comment', *American Economic Review*, 59(5), 912–16.

JEVONS, W. S. (1871) *The Theory of Political Economy*, London: Macmillan.

Bibliography 207

JOHNSON, H. G. (1967) 'Recent Developments in Monetary Theory', in *Essays in Monetary Economics*, London: Unwin.

——(1969) 'Inside Money, Outside Money, Income, Wealth, and Welfare in Monetary Theory', *Journal of Money, Credit, and Banking*,1(1), 30–45.

JOHNSON, W. E. (1913) 'The Pure Theory of Utility Curves', *Economic Journal*, 23(4), 483–513.

JORGENSON, D. W. (1963) 'Capital Theory and Investment Behavior', *American Economic Review*, 53(2), 247–59.

——(1965) 'Anticipations and Investment Behavior', in J. S. Duesenberry, G. Fromm, L. R. Klein and E. Kuh (1965).

——(1966) 'Rational Distributed Lag Functions', *Econometrica*,32(1), 135–49.

——(1967) 'The Theory of Investment Behavior', in Ferber (1967).

——(1971) 'Econometric Studies of Investment Behavior: A Survey', *Journal of Economic Literature*, 9(4), 1111–47.

——, J. HUNTER and M. I. NADIRI (1970) 'The Predictive Performance of Econometric Models of Quarterly Investment Behavior', *Econometrica*, 38(2), 213–24.

——and Z. GRILICHES (1967) 'The Explanation of Productivity Change', *Review of Economic Studies*, 34(3), 249–83.

—— and C. D. SIEBERT (1968a) 'A Comparison of Alternative Theories of Corporate Investment Behavior', *American Economic Review*, 58(4), 681–712.

——, ——(1968b) 'Optimal Capital Accumulation and Corporate Investment Behavior'. *Journal of Political Economy*, 76(6), 1123–51.

——and J. A. STEPHENSON (1967) 'The Time Structure of Investment Behavior in United States Manufacturing, 1947–1960', *Review of Economics and Statistics*, 49(1), 16–27.

KAHN, R. F. (1959) 'Exercises in the Analysis of Growth', *Oxford Economic Papers*, 11(2), 143–56.

KALDOR, N. (1955) *An Expenditure Tax*, London: Allen and Unwin.

——(1956) 'Alternative Theories of Distribution', *Review of Economic Studies*, 23(2), 83–100.

——(1959) 'Economic Growth and the Problem of Inflation', *Economica*, 26(3 and 4), 194–211 and 287–98.

——(1960) 'A Rejoinder to Mr Atsumi and Professor Tobin', *Review of Economic Studies*, 27(2), 121–23.

——(1961) 'Capital Accumulation and Economic Growth', in Lutz and Hague (1961).

——(1966) 'Marginal Productivity and the Macro-Economic Theories of Distribution', *Review of Economic Studies*, 33(4), 309–19.

——(1972) 'The Irrelevance of Equilibrium Economics', *Economic Journal*, 82(4), 1237–55.

——and J. A. MIRRLESS (1962) 'A New Model of Economic Growth', *Review of Economic Studies*, 29(3), 174–92.

KALECKI, M. (1933) *Proba Teorji Konjunktury*, Warsaw: Instytut Badania Konjunktur Gospodarczych i Cen (translated into English as Chapter 1 of Kalecki, 1971).

——(1935a) 'A Macrodynamic Theory of Business Cycles', *Econometrica*, 3(3), 327–44.

——(1935b) 'Essai d'une Théorie du Mouvement Cyclique des Affaires', *Revue d'Economie Politique*, 49(2), 285–305.

——(1937a) 'A Theory of Commodity, Income, and Capital Taxation', *Economic Journal*, 47(3), 444–50.

——(1937b) 'A Theory of the Business Cycle', *Review of Economic Studies*, 4(2), 77–97.

——(1937c) 'The Principle of Increasing Risk', *Economica*, 4(4), 440–7.

——(1938) 'The Determinants of Distribution of the National Income', *Econometrica*, 6(2), 97–112.

——(1939) *Essays in the Theory of Economic Fluctuations*, London: Allen and Unwin.

——(1942) 'A Theory of Profits', *Economic Journal*, 52(2–3), 258–67.

——(1943) *Studies in Economic Dynamics*, London: Allen and Unwin.

——(1954) *Theory of Economic Dynamics*, London: Allen and Unwin.

——(1968) 'Trend and Business Cycles Reconsidered', *Economic Journal*, 78(2), 263–76.

——(1971) *Selected Essays on the Dynamics of the Capitalist Economy*, Cambridge: Cambridge University Press.

KATONA, G. (1965) *Private Pensions and Individual Saving*, Institute for Social Research, Monograph No. 40, Ann Arbor: University of Michigan.

KAY, J. A. (1972) 'Social Discount Rates', *Journal of Public Economics*, 1(3,4), 359–78.

——and M. A. KING (1978) *The British Tax System*, Oxford: Oxford University Press.

KENDRICK, D., and L. TAYLOR (1970) 'Numerical Solution of Non-Linear Planning Models', *Econometrica*, 38(3), 453–67.

KENDRICK, J. W. (1961) *Productivity Trends in the United States*, Princeton: National Bureau of Economic Research.

KEYNES, J. M. (1924) 'Alfred Marshall, 1842–1924', *Economic Journal*, 34(3), 311–72.

——(1930) *Treatise on Money*, London: Macmillan.

——(1936) *The General Theory of Employment, Interest and Money*, London: Macmillan.

——(1937) 'The General Theory of Employment', *Quarterly Journal of Economics*, 51(2), 209–23.

KING, J., and P. REGAN (1976) *Relative Income Shares*, London: Macmillan.

KING, M. A. (1972) 'Corporate Taxation and Dividend Behaviour: A Further Comment', *Review of Economic Studies*, 29(2), 231–4.

——(1974) 'Dividend Behaviour and the Theory of the Firm', *Economica*, 41(1), 25–34.

——(1975a) 'The United Kingdom Profits Crisis: Myth or Reality?', *Economic Journal*, 85(1), 33–54.

——(1975b) 'Taxation, Corporate Financial Policy, and the Cost of Capital: A Comment', *Journal of Public Economics*, 4(3), 271–9.

——(1977) *Public Policy and the Corporation*, London: Chapman and Hall.

KLEIN, L. R. (1958) 'The Friedman-Becker Illusion', *Journal of Political Economy*, 65(6), 539–45.

KNIGHT, F. H. (1931) 'Professor Fisher's Interest Theory: A Case in Point', *Journal of Political Economy*, 39(2), 176–212.

——(1944) 'Diminishing Returns from Investment', *Journal of Political Economy*, 52(1), 26–47.

KNOX, A. D. (1952) 'The Acceleration Principle and the Theory of Investment: A Survey', *Economica*, 19(3), 269–97.

KOOPMANS, T. C. (1957) *Three Essays on the State of Economic Science*, New York: McGraw-Hill.

——(1967) 'Intertemporal Distribution and "Optimal" Aggregate Economic Growth', in Fellner *et al.* (1967).

KOWALIK, T. *et al.* (1966) *Problems of Economic Dynamics and Planning: Essays in Honour of Michal Kalecki*, Oxford: Pergamon.

KOYCK, L. M. (1954) *Distributed Lags and Investment Analysis*, Amsterdam: North-Holland.

KREGEL, J. A. (1971) *Rate of Profit, Distribution and Growth: Two Views*, London: Macmillan.

——(1973) *The Reconstruction of Political Economy*, London: Macmillan.

——(1976a) *Theory of Capital*, London: Macmillan.

——(1976b) 'Economic Methodology in the Face of Uncertainty', *Economic Journal*, 86(2), 209–25.

KRZYZANIAK, M. (1967) 'The Long-Run Burden of a General Tax on Profits in a Neoclassical World', *Public Finance*, 22(4), 472–91.

KUENNE, R. E. (1963) *The Theory of General Economic Equilibrium*, Princeton: Princeton University Press.

KUH, E. (1963) *Capital Stock Growth: A Microeconomic Approach*, Amsterdam: North-Holland.

——(1971) Second edition of Kuh (1963), Amsterdam: North-Holland.

——and J. R. MEYER (1963) 'Investment, Liquidity, and Monetary Policy', in Commission on Money and Credit (1963).

KUHN, T. S. (1962) *The Structure of Scientific Revolutions*, Chicago: University of Chicago.

KUZNETS, S. (1966) *Modern Economic Growth*, New Haven: Yale University Press.

LAING, N. F. (1969) 'Two Notes on Pasinetti's Theorem', *Economic Record*, 45(3), 373–85.

LAKATOS, I. (1970) 'Falsification and the Methodology of Scientific Research Programmes', in I. Lakatos and A. Musgrave (1970).

——and A. MUSGRAVE (eds) (1970) *Criticism and the Growth of Knowledge*, Proceedings in the International Colloquium in the Philosophy of Science, London, 1965, Volume 4, Cambridge: Cambridge University Press.

LANDAUER, C. (1969) 'On the Social Rate of Discount: Comment', *American Economic Review*, 59(5), 917–18.

LANDSBERGER, M. (1971) 'Consumer Discount Rate and the Horizon: New Evidence', *Journal of Political Economy*, 79(6), 1346–59.

LAUMAS, P. S. (1969) 'A Test of the Permanent Income Hypothesis', *Journal of Political Economy*, 77(5), 857–61.

LECOMBER, R. (1977) 'The Isolation Paradox', *Quarterly Journal of Economics*, 91(3), 495–504.

LEIGH, A. H. (1946) 'Von Thünen's Theory of Distribution and the Advent of Marginal Analysis', *Journal of Political Economy*, 54(6), 481–502.

LEIJONHUFVUD, A. (1968) *On Keynesian Economics and the Economics of Keynes*, New York: Oxford University Press.

LEONTIEF, W. (1941) *The Structure of American Economy, 1919–1929*, Cambridge, Massachusetts.

LERNER, A. P. (1934) 'The Concept of Monopoly and the Measurement of Monopoly

Power', *Review of Economic Studies*, 1(3), 157–75.

——(1944) *The Economics of Control*, New York: Macmillan.

LEVINE, A. L. (1974) 'This Age of Leontief . . . and Who? An Interpretation', *Journal of Economic Literature*, 12(3), 872–81.

——(1975) '"This Age of Leontief. . .and Who?" A Reply', *Journal of Economic Literature*, 13(2), 457–61.

——(1977) 'The Irrelevance of Returns to Scale in Sraffa's Analysis: A Comment', *Journal of Economic Literature*, 15(1), 70–2.

LIND, R. C. (1964) 'The Social Rate of Discount and the Optimal Rate of Investment: Further Comment', *Quarterly Journal of Economics*, 78(2), 336–45.

LINDAHL, E. (1933) 'The Concept of Income', in *Economic Essays in Honour of Gustav Cassel*, London: Allen and Unwin.

LINTNER, J. (1953) 'The Determinants of Corporate Saving', in W. W. Heller, F. M. (Boddy and C. L. Nelson (eds), *Savings in the Modern Economy*, Minneapolis: University of Minneapolis Press.

——(1956) 'Distribution of Incomes of Corporations among Dividends, Retained Earnings, and Taxes', *American Economic Review*, 46(2), 97–113.

LIVIATAN, N. (1965) 'Estimates of Distributed Lag Consumption Functions from Cross Section Data', *Review of Economics and Statistics*, 47(1), 44–53.

LOASBY, B. J. (1976) *Choice, Complexity and Ignorance*, Cambridge: Cambridge University Press.

LONGFIELD, M. (1834) *Lectures on Political Economy*, Dublin: Milliken.

LUTZ, F. A., and D. C. HAGUE (eds) (1961) *The Theory of Capital*, London: Macmillan.

MCLURE, C. E. (1975) 'General Equilibrium Incidence Analysis: The Harberger Model after Ten Years', *Journal of Public Economics*, 4(2), 125–61.

MALINVAUD, E. (1953) 'Capital Accumulation and Efficient Allocation of Resources', *Econometrica*, 21(2), 233–68.

MANESCHI, A. (1974) 'The Existence of a Two-Class Economy in the Kaldor and Pasinetti Models of Growth and Distribution', *Review of Economic Studies*, 41(1), 149–50.

MARGLIN, S. A. (1963a) 'The Social Rate of Discount and the Optimal Rate of Investment', *Quarterly Journal of Economics*, 77(1), 95–111.

——(1963b) 'The Opportunity Costs of Public Investment', *Quarterly Journal of Economics*, 77(2), 274–89.

MARKOWITZ, H. M. (1952) 'Portfolio Selection', *Journal of Finance*, 7(1), 77–91.

——(1959) *Portfolio Selection*, Cowles Foundation Monograph 16, New York: Wiley.

MARRIS, R. L. (1964) *The Economic Theory of Managerial Capitalism*, London: Macmillan.

——(1972) 'Why Economics Needs a Theory of the Firm', *Economic Journal*, 82(1) (Supplement), 321–52.

MAYER, T. (1975) 'Selecting Economic Hypotheses by Goodness of Fit', *Economic Journal*, 85(3), 877–83.

MEADE, J. E. (1963) 'The Rate of Profit in a Growing Economy', *Economic Journal*, 73(4), 665–74.

——(1966) 'The Outcome of the Pasinetti-Process: A Note', *Economic Journal*, 76(1), 161–5.

——(1978) *The Structure and Reform of Direct Taxation*, London: Institute for Fiscal Studies.

MEEKS, G., and G. WHITTINGTON (1975) 'Giant Companies in the United Kingdom, 1948–69', *Economic Journal*, 85(4), 824–43.

——, —— (1976) *The Financing of Quoted Companies in the United Kingdom*, Royal Commission on the Distribution of Income and Wealth, Background Paper No. 1, London: HMSO.

METZLER, L. A. (1951) 'The Rate of Interest and the Marginal Product of Capital: A Correction', *Journal of Political Economy*, 59(1), 67–78.

MEYER, J. R. and R. R. GLAUBER (1964) *Investment Decisions, Economic Forecasting and Public Policy*, Cambridge, Massachusetts: Harvard University Press.

——and E. KUH (1955) 'Acceleration and Related Theories of Investment: An Empirical Enquiry', *Review of Economics and Statistics*, 37(3), 217–30.

——, —— (1959) *The Investment Decision: An Empirical Study*, Cambridge, Massachusetts: Harvard University Press.

MIESZKOWSKI, P. M. (1969) 'Tax Incidence Theory: The Effects of Taxes on the Distribution of Income', *Journal of Economic Literature*, 7(4), 1103–24.

MILL, J. S. (1848) *Principles of Political Economy*, London: Parker.

MILLER, M. H., and F. MODIGLIANI (1961) 'Dividend Policy, Growth, and the Valuation of Shares', *Journal of Business*, 34(4), 411–33.

——and C. W. UPTON (1974) *Macroeconomics: A Neoclassical Introduction*, Homewood, Illinois: Irwin.

MILLS, O. L. (1921) 'The Spending Tax, *Bulletin of the National Tax Association*, 7(1), 18–20.

MIRRLEES, J. A., and N. H. STERN (eds) (1973) *Models of Economic Growth*, London: Macmillan.

MISHAN, E. J. (1971) *Cost-Benefit Analysis*, London: Allen and Unwin.

MITCHELL, W. C. (1927) *Business Cycles, the Problem and its Setting*, New York: National Bureau of Economic Research.

MIXTER, C. W. (1897) 'A Forerunner of Böhm-Bawerk', *Quarterly Journal of Economics*, 11(2), 161–90.

——(1902) 'Böhm-Bawerk on Rae', *Quarterly Journal of Economics*, 16(3), 385–412.

MODIGLIANI, F. (1975) 'The Life Cycle Hypothesis of Saving Twenty Years Later', in Parkin and Nobay (1975).

——and F. BRUMBERG (1954) 'Utility Analysis and the Consumption Function: An Interpretation of Cross-Section Data', in K. Kurihara (ed.), *Post-Keynesian Economics*, New Brunswick.

——and M. H. MILLER (1958) 'The Cost of Capital, Corporation Finance, and the Theory of Investment', *American Economic Review*, 48(3), 261–97.

——, —— (1959) 'The Cost of Capital, Corporation Finance, and the Theory of Investment: Reply', *American Economic Review*, 49(4), 665–69.

MOORE, B. J. (1974) 'The Pasinetti Paradox Revisited', *Review of Economic Studies*, 41(2), 297–9.

MORISHIMA, M. (1977) 'Pasinetti's *Growth and Income Distribution* Revisited', *Journal of Economic Literature*, 15(1), 56–61.

MOTLEY, B., and S. A. MORLEY (1970) 'The Optimum Lifetime Distribution of Consumption Expenditures: Comment', *American Economic Review*, 60(4), 738–43.

MOYLE, J. (1971) *The Pattern of Ordinary Share Ownership, 1957–1970*, University of Cambridge, Department of Applied Economics, Occasional Paper 31, Cambridge University Press.

MUNNELL, A. H. (1976) 'Private Pensions and Saving: New Evidence, *Journal of Political Economy*, 84(5), 1013–32.

MUSGRAVE, R. A. (1953a) 'General Equilibrium Aspects of Incidence Theory', *American Economic Review*, 43(2), 504–17.

——(1953b) 'On Incidence', *Journal of Political Economy*, 61(4), 306–23.

——and M. B. MUSGRAVE (1973) *Public Finance in Theory and Practice*, New York: McGraw-Hill.

MUTH, J. F. (1961) 'Rational Expectations and the Theory of Price Movements', *Econometrica*, 29(3), 315–35.

NAGEL, E. (1963) 'Assumptions in Economic Theory', *American Economic Review*, 53(2), 211–19.

NELL, E. J. (1967) 'Theories of Growth and Theories of Value', *Economic Development and Cultural Change*, 16(1), 15–26.

NELSON, C. R. (1972) 'The Prediction Performance of the FRB-MIT-PENN Model of the U.S. Economy', *American Economic Review*, 62(5), 902–17.

——(1973) *Applied Time Series Analysis*, San Francisco: Holden-Day.

NERLOVE, M. (1972) 'Lags in Economic Behavior', *Econometrica*, 40(2), 221–51.

NG, Y. K. (1974) 'The Neoclassical and the Neo-Marxist-Keynesian Theories of Income Distribution: A Non-Cambridge Contribution to the Cambridge Controversy in Capital Theory', *Australian Economic Papers*, 13(1), 124–32.

NICHOLS, A. (1969) 'On the Social Rate of Discount: Comment', *American Economic Review*, 59(5), 909–11.

NICKELL, S. J. (1977) 'The Influence of Uncertainty on Investment: Is it Important?', *Economic Journal*, 87(1), 47–70.

——and D. METCALF (1978) 'Monopolistic Industries and Monopoly Profits or, Are Kellogg's Cornflakes Overpriced?', *Economic Journal*, 88(2), 254–68.

NUTI, D. M. (1970) 'Capitalism, Socialism and Steady Growth', *Economic Journal*, 80(1), 32–57.

——(1971) Review of J. Hirshleifer, *Investment, Interest and Capital, Journal of Economic Literature*, 9(1), 77–9.

——(1976) 'Discussion', in Brown, Sato and Zarembka (1976).

PARETO, V. (1896) *Cours d'Economie Politique*, Lausanne: Rouge.

PARKER, R. H., and G. C. HARCOURT (1969) *Readings in the Concept and Measurement of Income*, Cambridge: Cambridge University Press.

PARKIN, M., and A. R. NOBAY (eds) (1975) *Contemporary Issues in Economics*, Manchester: Manchester University Press.

PASINETTI, L. L. (1962) 'Rate of Profit and Income Distribution in Relation to the Rate of Economic Growth', *Review of Economic Studies*, 29(4), 267–79.

——(1966a) 'New Results in an Old Framework', *Review of Economic Studies*, 33(4), 303–6.

——(1966b) 'Changes in the Rate of Profit and Switches of Techniques', *Quarterly Journal of Economics*, 80(4), 503–17.

——(1969) 'Switches of Technique and the "Rate of Return" in Capital Theory', *Economic Journal*, 79(3), 508–31.

——(1970) 'Again on Capital Theory and Solow's "Rate of Return"' *Economic Journal*, 80(2), 428–31.

——(1972) 'Reply to Mr Dougherty', *Economic Journal*, 82(4), 1351–2.

——(1974) *Growth and Income Distribution*, Cambridge: Cambridge University Press.

PATINKIN, D. (1956) *Money, Interest, and Prices*, Evanston, Illinois: Row, Peterson.

——(1965) Second edition of Patinkin (1956), New York: Harper and Row.

PETERSON, A. W. A. (1979) 'Total Factor Productivity in the UK: A Disaggregated Analysis', in K. D. Patterson and K. Schott (eds), *The Measurement of Capital*, London: Macmillan.

PHELPS, E. S. (1962) 'The Accumulation of Risky Capital: A Sequential Utility Analysis', *Econometrica*, 30(4), 729–43.

PHELPS BROWN, E. H. (1972) 'The Underdevelopment of Economics', *Economic Journal*, 82(1), 1–10.

PIGOU, A. C. (1920) *The Economics of Welfare*, London: Macmillan.

——(1935) 'Net Income and Capital Depletion', *Economic Journal*, 45(2), 235–41.

——(1941) 'Maintaining Capital Intact', *Economica*, 8(3), 271–5.

POPPER, K. R. (1934) *Logik der Forschung*, Vienna (translated as *The Logic of Scientific Discovery*, London: Hutchinson, 1959).

PRAIS, S. J. (1959) 'Dividend Policy and Income Appropriation', in Tew and Henderson (1959).

RACETTE, G. A. (1973) 'Earnings Retention, New Capital and the Growth of the Firm: A Comment', *Review of Economics and Statistics*, 55(1), 127–8.

RAE, JOHN (1834) *Statement of Some New Principles on the Subject of Political Economy*, Boston: Hilliard, Gray.

——(1905) *The Sociological Theory of Capital*, (edited by C. W. Mixter), New York: Macmillan.

RAMSEY, D. D. (1969) 'On the Social Rate of Discount: Comment', *American Economic Review*, 59(5), 919–24.

RAMSEY, F. (1928) 'A Mathematical Theory of Saving', *Economic Journal*, 38(4), 543–59.

RAMSEY, J. B. (1970) 'The Marginal Efficiency of Capital, the Internal Rate of Return, and Net Present Value: An Analysis of Investment Criteria', *Journal of Political Economy*, 78(5), 1017–27.

RENTON, G. A. (ed.) (1975) *Modelling the Economy*, London: Heinemann.

REVELL, J. (1975) *Savings Flows in Europe: Personal Saving and Borrowing*, Institute of European Finance, University College of North Wales, London: Financial Times Ltd.

RICARDO, D. (1817) *On the Principles of Political Economy, and Taxation*, London: Murray.

RICHTER, M. K. (1966) 'Invariance Axioms and Economic Indexes', *Econometrica*, 34(4), 739–55.

ROBINSON, J. V. (1942) *An Essay on Marxian Economics*, London: Macmillan.

——(1953) 'The Production Function and the Theory of Capital', *Review of Economic Studies*, 21(2), 81–106.

——(1956) *The Accumulation of Capital*, London: Macmillan.

——(1962) *Economic Philosophy*, London: Watts.

——(1970a) 'Capital Theory up to Date', *Canadian Journal of Economics*, 3(2), 309–17.

——(1970b) 'The Measure of Capital: The End of the Controversy', Second World Congress of the Econometric Society.

——(1972) 'The Second Crisis of Economic Theory', *American Economic Review*, 62(2), 1–10.

——(1973a) 'What has become of the Keynesian Revolution?' in J. V. Robinson (ed.) *After Keynes*, Oxford: Blackwell.

——(1973b) Foreword to Kregel (1973).

——(1975) 'The Unimportance of Reswitching', *Quarterly Journal of Economics*, 89(1), 32–9.

——and J. EATWELL (1973) *An Introduction to Modern Economics*, London: McGraw-Hill.

ROCKLEY, L. E. (1973) *Investment for Profitability*, London: Business Books.

ROY, A. D. (1952) 'Safety First and the Holding of Assets', *Econometrica*, 20(3), 431–49.

RYMES, T. K. (1971) *On Concepts of Capital and Technical Change*, Cambridge: Cambridge University Press.

——(1972) 'The Measurement of Capital and Total Factor Productivity in the Context of the Cambridge Theory of Capital', *Review of Income and Wealth*, 18(1), 79–108.

SAMUELSON, P. A. (1962) 'Parable and Realism in Capital Theory: The Surrogate Production Function', *Review of Economic Studies*, 29(3), 193–206.

——(1964) 'Tax Deductability of Economic Depreciation to Insure Invariant Valuations', *Journal of Political Economy*, 72(6), 604–6.

——(1966) 'A Summing Up', *Quarterly Journal of Economics*, 80(4), 568–83.

——(1967) 'Irving Fisher and the Theory of Capital', in Fellner *et al.* (1967).

——and F. MODIGLIANI (1966a) 'The Pasinetti Paradox in Neoclassical and More General Models', *Review of Economic Studies*, 33(4), 269–301.

——,——(1966b) 'Reply to Pasinetti and Robinson', *Review of Economic Studies*, 33(4), 321–30.

SANDMO, A. (1976) 'Optimal Taxation: An Introduction to the Literature', *Journal of Public Economics*, 6(1, 2), 37–54.

——and J. H. DRÉZE (1971) 'Discount Rates for Public Investment in Closed and Open Economies', *Economica*, 38(4), 395–412.

SCHUMPETER, J. A. (1911) *Theorie der Wirtschaftlichen Entwicklung* (translated as *Theory of Economic Development*, Cambridge, Mass.: Harvard University Press, 1934).

——(1954) *History of Economic Analysis*, London: Allen and Unwin.

SEN, A. K. (1961) 'On Optimising the Rate of Saving', *Economic Journal*, 71(3), 479–96.

——(1967) 'Isolation, Assurance and the Social Rate of Discount', *Quarterly Journal of Economics*, 81(1), 112–24.

——(1974) 'On Some Debates in Capital Theory', *Economica*, 41(3), 328–35.

SENIOR, N. W. (1836) *An Outline of the Science of Political Economy*, London: Clowes.

SHACKLE, G. L. S. (1972) *Epistemics and Economics*, Cambridge: Cambridge University Press.

——(1973) 'Keynes and Today's Establishment in Economic Theory: A View', *Journal of Economic Literature*, 11(2), 516–19.

——(1974) *Keynesian Kaleidics*, Edinburgh: Edinburgh University Press.

SHESHINSKI, E. (1972) 'The Optimal Linear Income Tax', *Review of Economic Studies*, 39(3), 297–302.

SHOVEN, J. B., and J. WHALLEY (1972) 'A General Equilibrium Calculation of the

Effects of Differential Taxation of Income from Capital in the U.S.', *Journal of Public Economics*, 1(3,4), 281–321.

SIDRAUSKI, M. (1967) 'Rational Choice and Patterns of Growth in a Monetary Economy', *American Economic Review*, 57(2), 534–44.

SIMONS, H. C. (1938) *Personal Income Taxation*, Chicago: University of Chicago Press.

SINGH, B., and A. ULLAH (1976) 'The Consumption Function: The Permanent Income versus the Habit Persistence Hypothesis', *Review of Economics and Statistics*, 58(1), 96–103.

SJAASTAD, L. A., and D. L. WISECARVER (1977) 'The Social Cost of Public Finance', *Journal of Political Economy*, 85(3), 513–47.

SLUTSKY, E. (1915) 'Sulla Teoria del Bilancio del Consumatore', *Giornale degli Economisti e Annali de Economia*, 26(2), 1–26.

SMITH, A. (1776) *An Inquiry into the Nature and Causes of the Wealth of Nations*, London: Strahan and Cadell.

SMYTH, D. J. (1964) 'Empirical Evidence on the Acceleration Principle', *Review of Economic Studies*, 31(3), 185–202.

——and G. BRISCOE (1969) 'Investment Plans and Realisations in United Kingdom Manufacturing', *Economica*, 36(3), 277–94.

SOLOW, R. M. (1956) 'The Production Function and the Theory of Capital', *Review of Economic Studies*, 23(2), 101–8.

——(1963a) 'Substitution and Fixed Proportions in the Theory of Capital', *Review of Economic Studies*, 29(3), 207–18.

——(1963b) *Capital Theory and the Rate of Return*, Amsterdam: North-Holland.

——(1967) 'The Interest Rate and Transition between Techniques', in C. H. Feinstein (ed.), *Socialism, Capitalism and Economic Growth*, Cambridge: Cambridge University Press.

SPAVENTA, L. (1973) 'Notes on Problems of Transition between Techniques', in Mirrlees and Stern (1973).

SPIRO, A. (1962) 'Wealth and the Consumption Function', *Journal of Political Economy*, 70(4), 339–54.

SRAFFA, P. (1960) *Production of Commodities by Means of Commodities*, Cambridge: Cambridge University Press.

STIGLITZ, J. E. (1973) 'Taxation, Corporate Financial Policy, and the Cost of Capital', *Journal of Public Economics*, 2(1), 1–34.

——(1974) 'The Cambridge-Cambridge Controversy in the Theory of Capital; A View from New Haven: A Review Article', *Journal of Political Economy*, 82(4), 893–903.

——(1976) 'The Corporation Income Tax', *Journal of Public Economics*, 5(3,4), 303–11.

STONE, J. R. N. (1966) 'The Social Accounts from a Consumer's Point of View', *Review of Income and Wealth*, 12(1), 1–33.

STROTZ, R. H. (1956) 'Myopia and Inconsistency in Dynamic Utility Maximization', *Review of Economic Studies*, 23(3), 165–80.

SUITS, D. B. (1963) 'The Determinants of Consumer Expenditure: A Review of Present Knowledge', in Commission on Money and Credit (1963).

SWAN, T. W. (1956) 'Economic Growth and Capital Accumulation', *Economic Record*, 33(2), 334–61.

TAYLOR, L. D. (1971) 'Saving out of Different Types of Income', *Brookings Papers on Economic Activity*, 2, 383–407.

TEW, B., and R. F. HENDERSON (eds) (1959) *Studies in Company Finance*, Cambridge: Cambridge University Press.

THEIL, H. (1958) *Economic Forecasts and Policy*, Amsterdam: North-Holland.

——(1966) *Applied Economic Forecasting*, Amsterdam: North-Holland.

THÜNEN, J. H. V. (1850) *Der Isolirte Staat* (vol. 2), Rostock: Leopold.

THUROW, L. C. (1969) 'A Disequilibrium Neoclassical Investment Function', *Review of Economics and Statistics*, 51(4), 431–5.

——(1970) 'The Optimum Lifetime Distribution of Consumption Expenditures: Reply', *American Economic Review*, 60(4), 744–5.

TINBERGEN, J. (1935) 'Annual Survey: Suggestions on Quantitative Business Cycle Theory', *Econometrica*, 3(3), 241–308.

——(1960) 'Optimum Savings and Utility Maximization over Time', *Econometrica*, 28(2), 481–9.

——(1975) *Income Distribution*, Amsterdam: North-Holland.

TOBIN, J. (1958) 'Liquidity Preference as Behavior towards Risk', *Review of Economic Studies*, 25(2), 65–86.

——(1960) 'Towards a *General* Kaldorian Theory of Distribution', *Review of Economic Studies*, 27(2), 119–20.

——(1965) 'The Theory of Portfolio Selection', in Hahn and Brechling (1965).

TULLOCK, G. (1964) 'The Social Rate of Discount and the Optimal Rate of Investment: Comment', *Quarterly Journal of Economics*, 78(2), 331–6.

UHR, C. G. (1951) 'Knut Wicksell—A Centennial Evaluation', *American Economic Review*, 41(5), 829–60.

USHER, D. (1965) 'Traditional Capital Theory', *Review of Economic Studies*, 32(2), 169–85.

——(1969) 'On the Social Rate of Discount: Comment', *American Economic Review*, 59(5), 925–9.

VELUPILLAI, K. (1975) 'Irving Fisher on "Switches of Techniques"', *Quarterly Journal of Economics*, 89(4), 679–80.

WALLIS, K. F. (1973) *Topics in Applied Econometrics*, London: Gray-Mills.

WALRAS, M-E. L. (1874) *Eléments d'Economie Politique Pure*, Lausanne: Corbaz

——(1900) Fourth edition of Walras (1874), Lausanne: Rouge.

WATTS, R. (1973) 'The Information Content of Dividends', *Journal of Business*, 46(2), 191–211.

WEBER, W. E. (1970) 'The Effect of Interest Rates on Aggregate Consumption', *American Economic Review*, 60(4), 591–600.

——(1971) 'Interest Rates and the Short-run Consumption Function', *American Economic Review*, 61(3), 421–5.

——(1975) 'Interest Rates, Inflation, and Consumer Expenditures', *American Economic Review*, 65(5), 843–58.

WEINTRAUB, E. R. (1977) 'The Microfoundations of Macroeconomics: A Critical Survey', *Journal of Economic Literature*, 15(1), 1–23.

WESTPHAL, L. E. (1971) 'An Intertemporal Planning Model Featuring Economies of Scale', in H. B. Chenery (ed.), *Studies in Development Planning*, Cambridge, Massachusetts: Harvard University Press.

WHITE, W. H. (1956) 'Interest Inelasticity of Investment Demand—the Case from

Business Attitude Surveys Re-examined', *American Economic Review*, 46(4), 565–87.

WHITEHEAD, C. M. E. (1974) *The U.K. Housing Market*, Farnborough, Hampshire: Saxon House.

WHITTINGTON, G. (1972) 'The Profitability of Retained Earnings', *Review of Economics and Statistics*, 54(2), 152–60.

WICKSELL, J. G. K. (1893) *Uber Wert, Kapital und Rente*, Jena: Fischer (translated as *Value, Capital and Rent*, London: Allen and Unwin, 1954).

——(1901, 1906) *Foreläsningar I Nationalekonomi*, Lund: Berlingska Boktryckeriet (Volume I) and Stockholm. Fritzes Hofbokhandel (Volume 2) (third edition translated as Wicksell (1934, 1935).

——(1934, 1935) *Lectures on Political Economy*, London: Routledge (see previous item).

WICKSTEED, P. H. (1894) *An Essay on the Co-ordination of the Laws of Distribution*, London: Macmillan.

WILLIAMSON, J. (1966) 'Profit, Growth and Sales Maximization', *Economica*, 33(1), 1–16.

WILSON, T., and P. W. S. ANDREWS (eds) (1951) *Oxford Studies in the Price Mechanism* Oxford: Oxford University Press.

WINTER, S. G. (1971) 'Satisficing, Selection, and the Innovating Remnant', *Quarterly Journal of Economics*, 85(2), 237–61.

WOOD, A. J. B. (1975) *A Theory of Profits*, Cambridge: Cambridge University Press.

WORSWICK, G. D. N. (1972) 'Is Progress in Economic Science Possible?' *Economic Journal*, 82(1), 73–86.

WRIGHT, C. (1969a) 'Saving and the Rate of Interest', in A. C. Harberger and M. J. Bailey (eds), *The Taxation of Income from Capital*, Washington: Brookings Institution.

——(1969b) 'Estimating Permanent Income: A Note', *Journal of Political Economy*, 77(5), 845–50.

Index of names

Index of subjects